Film's First Family

Film's First Family

The Untold Story of the Costellos

Terry Chester Shulman

UNIVERSITY PRESS OF KENTUCKY

Paperback edition 2021

Scholarly publisher for the Commonwealth,
serving Bellarmine University, Berea College, Centre
College of Kentucky, Eastern Kentucky University,
The Filson Historical Society, Georgetown College,
Kentucky Historical Society, Kentucky State University,
Morehead State University, Murray State University,
Northern Kentucky University, Transylvania University,
University of Kentucky, University of Louisville,
and Western Kentucky University.

Editorial and Sales Offices: The University Press of Kentucky
663 South Limestone Street, Lexington, Kentucky 40508-4008
www.kentuckypress.com

The Library of Congress has cataloged the hardcover edition as follows:

Names: Shulman, Terry Chester, 1955– author.
Title: Film's first family : the untold story of the Costellos / Terry Chester Shulman.
Description: Lexington, Kentucky : University Press of Kentucky, [2019] |
Includes bibliographical references and index.
Identifiers: LCCN 2019025472 | ISBN 9780813178097 (hardcover) |
ISBN 9780813178110 (pdf) | ISBN 9780813178103 (epub)
Subjects: LCSH: Costello family. | Costello, Maurice, 1887–1950. | Actors—United States—Biography. | Motion picture industry—United States—History—20th century.
Classification: LCC PN2285 .S516 2019 | DDC 791.4302/8092273 [B]—dc23
LC record available at https://lccn.loc.gov/2019025472
ISBN 978-0-8131-5194-6 (pbk. : alk. paper)

This book is printed on acid-free paper meeting
the requirements of the American National Standard
for Permanence in Paper for Printed Library Materials.

Manufactured in the United States of America

Member of the Association
of University Presses

For Hillary

To Deirdre, Dede, and Dore

It’s better to be a has-been than a never-was.

—Maurice Costello

Contents

1

Mise-en-Scène

It was an unlikely face for a screen idol, as would have been obvious in the early years of filmmaking if anyone, just yet, had the faintest idea what a screen idol should look like. The nose was prominent and beak-shaped. The hair was gray in patches, and had receded boldly to expose a wide, balding forehead—like that of a favorite uncle, perhaps, or the family doctor, or a politician. Not a movie star, certainly, at least not as the term would one day be understood.

But to the growing throngs of female movie patrons in the summer of 1910, when he smiled there was no face in America as easy to look at. Because film actors were not credited as yet, his admirers had to address their fan letters—filmdom's first—to "the man with the dimples," or to "the dimpled darling," until he was known simply as "Dimples."[1] The seeds of screen idolatry had been sown; the first great movie star was born.

He had almost arrived too late. The facial accoutrements that became his stock-in-trade were being rapidly consumed by a pair of deeply etched wrinkles, one on each cheek. Maurice Costello was thirty years old when he started making movies, but onscreen he looks fifty. A decade of hard living as a traveling performer had worn on him physically—the "one-a-days," playing a different theater each night; squalid boarding houses where, depending on the season, the show trade baked or froze on lumpy, vermin-infested mattresses.[2] And when it became too much, the bottle brought easy oblivion to an actor returning to grimy quarters after the evening's performance.

Traveling the country's variety circuits at the turn of the century took a personal toll on him as well. According to Maurice's granddaughter, he could be a mean drunk in those days. As a child, Deirdre Le Blanc knew him as a kindly old man living in penniless retirement at the Motion

Picture Country Home in Woodland Hills, California—it wasn't until years later that she learned he drank, and that he occasionally became violent when drinking.[3] She heard the story of an inebriated Maurice slapping her grandmother Mae during an argument, while their young daughters, Dolores and Helene, looked on. "The fight continued," Deirdre said, "until everyone realized that my mother was on the floor crawling around in circles and barking like a dog."[4] The diversion succeeded—Maurice's attention was drawn elsewhere and the crisis passed.

As he tired of life on the road, Maurice began looking for more sedentary ways to make a living as a performer. By the middle of the aught years, he could not have failed to notice the nascent film industry making its presence known wherever he went.[5] By then, the traditional saloon style of variety entertainment—bawdy, old-school vaudevillians playing to cigar-chomping tradesmen and their mistresses—had gone the way of the gas lamp and the brougham.[6]

Manhattan's theater district, now under the control of a confederation of trusts aptly named the Syndicate, had moved uptown to the vicinity of Broadway and Forty-Second Street.[7] This left a score of abandoned theaters in Chelsea and Union Square to the schemes of small-time operators hoping to profit from the exhibition of moving pictures.[8] For a fraction of the cost of a stage production that required actors, stagehands, and musicians, the movie theater owner had only to acquire the latest version of Edison's Projecting Kinetoscope and he was in business.[9] The new medium wasn't a play or a sketch or a number—but thousands of photographic images printed sequentially onto a strip of nitrate (thanks to yet another Edison patent, the hand-cranked Kinetograph camera) and projected in rapid succession onto a white backdrop. The exhibition of movies had vastly improved since Edison's first projector, the Vitascope, was unveiled at Koster and Bial's Music Hall in April 1896.[10] A decade later, assuming the projectionist operated his machine at the proper speed, the fledgling moviegoer might experience something thrillingly close to live action.[11] An evening at the theater was fleeting—but now any living moment could be pulled from the ether and sequestered on a piece of film, for reanimation at a later date. To live again, as it were, for audiences yet unborn. It was a brush with immortality human beings would have never imagined possible.

By mid-1908, most of the "polite" variety theaters in New York had incorporated movies into the twelve-hour marathons they called "continuous vaudeville."[12] When F. F. Proctor's venerable Twenty-Third Street Theater did away with live performances altogether, other operators followed suit. A year later, thirteen former playhouses were showing moving pictures exclusively. "Where will it end?" groaned the *New York Dramatic Mirror*.[13] Meanwhile, the trusts tightened their grip on the theater business, blacklisting actors and independent theater operators who refused to give up their autonomy. Powerbrokers Charles Frohman of the Syndicate and Edward F. Albee of the Vaudeville Managers Association ruled in their separate fiefdoms. Palatial new playhouses, built to attract affluent audiences to the theater and less affluent audiences to the vaudeville stage, generated record profits for the trusts.

While opportunity knocked, Maurice moved his family from Pittsburgh into the epicenter of America's frantic new age of cultural innovation. From its headquarters in the Bronx, Edison Studios fought hard to maintain its grip on the burgeoning film industry.[14] The cost of protecting its multiple patents and copyrights, while fending off countersuits from competitors, had crippled the company, as each new challenge to Edison's hegemony was met with an equal and opposite challenge.[15] By 1903, the film business was caught up in a legal quagmire entirely of its own making. To satisfy the public's insatiable demand for new photoplays, the studios resorted to copying, or "duping," foreign films, as legal gridlock brought the production of American films to a standstill. When French filmmaker Georges Méliès heard of the practice, he and his brother Gaston opened an office in America so they too could join the fray. "We are prepared and determined energetically to pursue all counterfeiters and pirates," Gaston declared upon arriving in New York. "We will not speak twice; we will act!"[16]

Eventually the studios increased their output of moving pictures, but filmmakers still had to share their audience with omnipresent vaudeville. "When I started there were more than 5,000 vaudeville theaters in the country," George Burns recalled. "Anything could be the basis of an act. Mind reading, mental telepathy, and hypnotism were popular. Posing acts pretended to be statues—maybe they did nothing, but they did it beautifully. One performer ate paper, wood, flowers, light bulbs and matches while another man bit railroad spikes in half. There was even 'The Wrestling Cheese,' a slab of cheese that could not be lifted from the stage, and a Chinese act that put chopsticks through their noses."[17]

Before the advent of the first movie theaters, called nickelodeons, New York film producers had to compete with vaudeville for lucrative exhibition deals brokered by variety moguls Edward Albee and B. F. Keith. It was an unhappy alliance between two cutthroat industries, both at odds and in league with each other.[18]

Somehow the rank-and-file stage actor had to make a living in this oppressive climate. Fortunately, stage work was still plentiful in the age of the theater stock company—the term referring to a troupe of actors bound to a single proprietor, or theater, or both.[19] It fell to stock companies and traveling shows around the country to bring live entertainment to the hinterlands—provincial cities like Des Moines, Knoxville, Omaha, and the bane of every performer's existence, Peoria. By 1905, more than 450 stock and traveling repertoire companies dotted America's theatrical landscape.[20] By the end of the decade their numbers had fallen substantially, but, added to hundreds of smaller acts, musical troupes, opera companies, minstrel shows, and traveling circuses, they paint a picture of a turn-of-the-century America inundated with live entertainment.

The opportunity for steady work with a stock company was a godsend for actors, but financial security came at a terrible price. Actor-managers typically kept top billing for themselves, or for a known headliner, dooming the rest of the cast to perpetual supporting status. With nowhere to go but sideways, most stock players spent their careers in obscurity, hopping from one company to the next. Maurice had appeared with many of the stage's better-known stock companies, but he was never a star. Film magazines later touted him as an ex–leading man, though he was just another struggling performer consigned to the nether regions of stagecraft. He had been a singer, a musician, a comedian, a tragedian, a monologist—but for all the miles traveled and the years spent far from home, by the middle of the aught years Maurice had come to the deadest of dead ends.[21] If movies hadn't come along, he would have spent the remainder of his career in stock, before aging out of a genre that was, itself, aging out.

So it was for the majority of theater folk in the early twentieth century. Like Maurice, they had mouths to feed and families to support. Acting was, and remains, the unsteadiest of professions, but the coming of movies and monopoly brought additional uncertainties to the lives of actors.[22] Most knew that it would end someday and that, if they were lucky, they would have enough money socked away to open a tearoom or a billiard parlor. But in front of an audience, all of that was forgotten. "We were in love with show business, with the excitement of getting onstage," George Burns said. "Nothing else mattered. The only politics any of us cared about was why the Orpheum Circuit had booked 'Flora D'Aliza's Educated Roosters' instead of 'Camilla's Pigeons.'"[23]

But something else did matter to Maurice. With the future in mind, he swallowed his pride and stooped to a level that even the lowliest vaudeville stooge would have considered beneath his dignity. Years before his stage colleagues, Maurice saw moving pictures not just for the working-class novelties they still were, but for the world-changing phenomenon they would shortly become.[24]

2

Pittsburgh and North

On July 21, 1877, three decades before the first nickelodeons opened for business there, the city of Pittsburgh stood at the fiery crossroads of the industrial age. Every road, rail, and waterway led to the source of the country's then most indispensable commodity: mass-produced steel forged by the Bessemer process turned the city into a belching cauldron of molten iron and slag. Blast furnace fires blackened the sky by day, painting them a deep, glowing red at night. One visitor called it "the blackest, dirtiest, grimiest city in the United States." To another it was "hell with the lid taken off."[1]

That morning, the city's freight yards erupted as twenty thousand strikers rioted when the Pennsylvania Railroad announced that it had cut its workers' already meager wages by 10 percent. The reduction came on the heels of an earlier cut, and, as one man, workers up and down the East Coast went berserk. In Pittsburgh, local militia units barricaded themselves inside a roundhouse to escape the mob, which tried to smoke them out by firing an oil train and running it into the side of a building. The suffocating militiamen somehow lasted the night and, in the morning, broke out of their fortress and opened fire on the rioters. More than twenty men were killed in two days of urban violence, which left hundreds of burned-out railroad cars and buildings smoldering in its wake. When order was restored, 104 locomotives and over a thousand freight and passenger cars had been destroyed by fire. The damage was the worst ever wreaked on an American city by its own inhabitants.[2]

While the city was burning up, it was also filling up. The population of Pittsburgh had more than tripled since the Civil War.[3] By 1877 it was teeming with working-class immigrants of myriad ethnicities, languishing in tenements as squalid as any of those in lower Manhattan. The effluvia of 145,000 residents was more than the city's antiquated sewer systems could effectively drain out. Raw sewage flowed into open culverts and collected there, rotting under the streets until a hard-enough rain came along to wash it into the Monongahela River. "The shore . . . at the foot of the wharf," the Sanitary Committee reported, "is in an abominable state, being covered with night-soil, brick bats, old tin wear, iron hoops, hoop-skirts, etc."[4]

Raw sewage drained into underground cesspools known as "privy wells," essentially earth-covered pits dug into the ground.[5] Their runoff sank into the ground to create fields of spongy, fetid soil. Of the city's five thousand wells, more than a third that year were discovered to be full or leaking. Sewer gases vented freely into the already fouled urban air through street-level openings called "drops." "On account of the intolerable stench," the report continued, "business is no doubt seriously hindered . . . saying nothing of the pernicious effect of this poison on the health of those compelled to live there." But no by-product of filth-ridden Pittsburgh was more pernicious than diphtheria. In 1877, the health department reported nine hundred cases, nearly half of which had proved fatal. Smallpox was the city's second deadliest disease, killing 289 residents; whooping cough was third. A more daunting statistic shows that a third of the year's 3,408 deaths were the result of contagious diseases and that over half of those deaths claimed children under the age of five.[6] Half that number again were infants under a year old. By the turn of the century, Pittsburgh had the highest rate of typhoid deaths of any city in the developed world. Between 1898 and 1909 it averaged 130 deaths for every 100,000 residents. In New York, the figure was 18; in London, 11.[7]

Maurice George Costello was born into this shuddering universe on February 22, 1877, into a life just as turbulent on the inside of his parents' Penn Avenue house as it was on the outside. When Maurice was five months old, his immigrant father, Thomas, suffocated to death from "inhalation of gas," as the coroner's report stated, while repairing a blast furnace at Andrew Carnegie's Union Iron Mill.[8] Thomas Costello died on a Sunday—the one day of the week that the majority of the mills were closed. While family, friends, and neighbors got ready for church, the Irish laborer headed off to work and to his death. He was twenty-five years old.

With her husband's passing, Ellen Fitzgerald Costello found herself with no means of support, no prospects, and an infant son to care for. The riots had occurred just two weeks earlier, and Pittsburgh's Irish neighborhoods were still under police control. Militiamen roamed the streets, making random arrests. The day after Thomas's death, the uprising's alleged ringleaders were tried and convicted in local courtrooms, which further demoralized the city's working population. Jobs and wages evaporated with the interruption of commerce caused by the riots, pushing already impoverished families to the brink of starvation.

There are no records of Ellen's struggles, of how the twenty-four-year-old immigrant coped with the loss of her husband while at the same time bearing the communal burden of fear and desperation. But she did cope. Federal census records show that by 1880, Ellen and her three-year-old son had moved thirteen blocks west to No. 58 Twenty-First Street.[9] To earn a living, she had chosen one of the few respectable alternatives to domestic work available to a penniless Catholic widow: she rented a larger house and started taking in boarders.[10] The census lists each of them by name, age, and nationality. There were seven lodgers in all (that number could change from week to week); all of them men, ranging in age from twenty-two to thirty-five. All were from Ireland and were employed as day laborers in the mills. Ellen's twenty-three-year-old brother John, a glass blower, had joined the household, presumably to help out financially and watch over his sister as she tended her small dormitory of Irish working men.

The census lists a son: Moris, age three. His name was written as it was pronounced to the census taker: in Britain, the accent falls on the first syllable, not the second one as it does in France and America. By then, the child's prospects had brightened considerably thanks to the small but steady income Ellen's boardinghouse was bringing in. Worker unrest was alive and well, but order had been restored with the arrival of federal troops a month after the riots occurred. Eventually the railroads did away with the hated wage cuts, but it was too little, too late to stop the rise of local labor unions, which occurred in great part due to the riots.[11]

Ellen and her three-year-old son were holding their own in one of Pittsburgh's poorest neighborhoods. At least the fatherless boy was surrounded by Irishmen very much like his father—indeed, Maurice's home life couldn't have been more ethnically Irish if he were growing up in Ireland. Ellen, her brother, and her boarders were Irish immigrants. Along the same stretch of Twenty-First Street stood two more boardinghouses, each filled to capacity with Irish laborers.[12]

Unlike the stalwart Scots-Irish, who came to America by the tens of thousands in the eighteenth century, the Catholic "famine Irish" would never be thought of as dour or humorless.[13] The young Maurice, who later took to the stage as a performer of Irish songs and dialects, came from a culture so beaten down that the pursuit of amusement was as much an act of survival as an evening's entertainment. Not surprisingly, the Irish working classes were enthralled by any sport in which their countrymen excelled. Race walking, known as pedestrianism, had more to do with stamina than actual racing and was therefore well suited to the sturdy Irish-American temperament. To keep the contestant officially at a walk, the walker's feet couldn't lose contact with the ground. In March 1877, the Irish-born Daniel O'Leary, known as "the Plucky Pedestrian," beat seventeen English competitors to win his first major tournament by walking 520 miles—roughly the distance from London to Killarney—in 139 hours. At Madison Square Garden, he beat the New Yorker John Hughes before a capacity crowd, 403 miles to 310. His countrymen rejoiced at O'Leary's victory. Tests of strength and stamina were all the rage in the 1870s, as the age of the endurance sport came into its own.[14] Swimming, skating, bicycling, boxing, walking, and sculling contests—each was designed to drive the contestants to the limits of their physical capacities.

It was in the time of the walking races that Irish New Yorkers began flocking to theaters in the wake of a cultural phenomenon that was, for once, all their own. In 1879, vaudevillians Edward Harrigan and Tony Hart wrote, produced, and starred in a new play that featured an endearingly ethnic story line and an array of "jaunty songs."[15] The duo didn't realize it, but they had invented the American musical. *The Mulligan Guard Ball* pushed Irish-Americans into the theatrical limelight, where they remained the dominant force for the next four decades. It took the anti-pleasure crusades of the Catholic Church to curb their parishioners' enthusiasm for vaudeville, thus allowing Jewish performers to step into the breach.[16]

At the core of Harrigan and Hart's jovial farce was a belated sense of cultural affirmation. As the fictional Mulligan family swaggered through the urban mainstream, their lives intertwined (sometimes affably, sometimes caustically) with their German and African American neighbors, whom the playwrights depicted with wildly exaggerated accents and mannerisms:

> LOCHMULLER: Do you suppose a German would fight mit a nigger?

SIM: Say, look here—do you see dis razor—I'm Sim Primrose, Captain of de Skidmore Guard. Every man of them is N. G., a nice gemman. Now I want you to apologize or I'll draw dis across your jugular.

DAN [Mulligan]: A man has no right to insult a colored man to his face.

SIM: Take it back.

LOCHMULLER: I mean dat a colored man could whip any German in de world.

SIM: Well dat settles it. [*Getting lather and brush and going to Dan*] Now I'll take de grass off Ireland.

While Harrigan and Hart pandered to every imaginable ethnic stereotype, *The Mulligan Guard Ball* changed not only the way Irish-Americans were seen by others but also the way they saw themselves.[17] Unlike their Presbyterian forerunners, who after a century of assimilation looked askance at their immigrant countrymen, the Catholic Irish were thrilled to see themselves no longer being portrayed as drunken, disagreeable outsiders, but as fully vested Americans.

The social changes wrought by the fictitious Mulligans only gradually trickled down, or rather drifted sideways, west from lower Manhattan to the city of Maurice's birth. As Pittsburgh struggled with its own ethnic upheavals after the Civil War, its better-heeled factions looked ahead to the day when the working classes would abandon their "haunts of vice" in favor of more uplifting entertainments. This was more easily hoped for than accomplished. The Pittsburgh Theater, once the city's grandest auditorium, by the late 1860s was off-limits to polite society.[18] The downtown playhouse where Junius Brutus Booth and Edwin Forrest appeared before the war was now the exclusive domain of local rowdies—working-class toughs who drank openly during performances and behaved disruptively throughout. The place was oppressively filthy and it stank. Between shows, the auditorium was attended to "in the most remarkable manner," noted one observer. "[The charwoman] would slush the floor of the parquet and afterward sweep the entire wash into the orchestra, from where it would run into the trap cellar below the stage and become absorbed by Mother Earth. . . . On the floor of the back aisle . . . were two or three hot air registers, which gave forth a pungent odor, that, in addition to the stray gas, stale sizing from the stage, and the exhalations of the audience, made quite an impressive odor that can never be forgot."[19]

When the theater was demolished in 1870, it left the city with a set of high-minded goals for its cultural betterment, but little else. The Mercantile Library Hall opened the following year as a haven for elite playgoers; but, with few aristocrats in a city teeming with working people, it survived only a short time. It took another twenty years for the spending power of the working classes, thanks to a booming economy, to incentivize the city's first modern playhouses. To keep the rowdies at bay, the Duquesne Theater offered its patrons only respectable, family-oriented entertainment. Adding matinee performances to the playbill brought women to the theaters en masse, bringing to an end the stage's time-honored tradition of male sovereignty. At a Pittsburgh variety house in the late 1860s, travel essayist James Parton found "not a single woman present. The place was packed with brawny men and noisy boys, all washed, all well-disposed, though half mad with joyous excitement."[20] With ladies present, male patrons had to mind their manners. In the 1890s, the first rules governing audience deportment were distributed to Pittsburghers in newsletter form. Newly prohibited was foot stomping, spitting, drinking, and "moving chairs around during a performance." In the 1840s Elizabeth Clarendon, actor-manager of the Pittsburgh Theater, climbed off the stage during a performance to horsewhip a male audience member who refused to stop catcalling.[21] The edicts forbade any sort of loud, loutish behavior when the curtain was up. The practice of entering or leaving the auditorium during a performance, the bane of every actor's existence, also was forbidden. "The patrons of this establishment," a theater owner proudly proclaimed, "are of a class that knows better, and of whom a better style of behavior ought reasonably to be expected."[22]

As Maurice Costello exited his teens, poverty pushed him squarely in the direction of stagecraft. Higher education would have been unthinkable to the impoverished son of a widowed, immigrant mother in the 1890s—much less the prospect of studying for a period of years, only to come out even poorer than before. For the Irish laborers Maurice grew up with, it was enough, after a back-breaking shift at the mills, to have a dry place to sleep, and, better still on a wintry night, a warm one.

For diversion, working folk looked to variety (renamed vaudeville in the 1850s to sound more respectable) for its panoply of amusements.

Despite all previous attempts to appeal to a more exclusive audience, vaudeville remained the people's theater.[23] It gave working-class audiences something they wouldn't have had access to otherwise: an evening's escape from the dreary sameness of everyday life, into the kaleidoscopic, ever-changing world of continuous, live entertainment. And for just a few cents it was among the city's most affordable pastimes.

It drew Maurice in as effortlessly as it would any young man looking for a way out of working-class Pittsburgh. He knew what the future held for him otherwise. At the age of eleven, he left public school to work as a "devil" in a downtown print shop. The term came about when a group of young printer's assistants were observed to have so "bedaubed themselves" with ink, that "the workmen do jocosely call them *devils*."[24] Besides refilling the vats, melting down metal type for reuse, and other hazardous jobs, the devil was saddled with tasks unrelated to printing—chores that older, better-paid workers considered beneath them. Mark Twain began his newspaper career as a devil for the Hannibal *Courier* at age thirteen. Besides his regular duties, he had to milk the owner's cow, cut and haul wood, and keep the office's stove burning in the winter.[25]

"I was a hardboiled kid," Maurice said forty years later. "I was fired when I refused to return the salary of the 'boss' which I had won at poker. Then I became a messenger boy, a clerk, and office boy, and held other jobs for brief periods, while nursing a desire to go on the stage."[26] With nothing to lose, he might as well do what he had dreamt of doing and ply a trade that paid its workers something that all the steel money in Pittsburgh couldn't buy them: the adoration of strangers and the ineffable sound of applause. "My life wasn't all roses," he said. "I began the business of life at an early age. . . . I started as a printer's devil at small wages and no chances for advancement whatsoever. Fortunately, though, I developed a desire to do theatricals—the amateur ones."

There was no time like the present for an aspiring performer to trot out a jaunty song, à la the Mulligans, for a raw, receptive Pittsburgh audience. "My first stage work was in vaudeville where I appeared as an Irish comedian and sang a song back in 1894, which many old timers will remember and which ran like this:"

Oh, the Mick who threw the brick
Will never throw another;
For calling me an A. P. A.

He now lies under cover,
And o'er his head
These lines are read—
You can see them if you rubber—
"Here lies the Mick
That threw the brick—
But he'll never throw another."

In 1894, the year of Maurice's stage debut, the theater was wide open for any boisterous young man with a modicum of theatrical talent—especially one steeped in Irish culture. Others like him were already running the show—literally, as aspiring Irish-American singers, dancers, comedians, playwrights, and composers took vaudeville by storm. The Irish stage came into its own thanks in large part to *The Mulligan Guard Ball,* which Harrigan and Hart later expanded into a series of popular spin-offs. They had laid the groundwork—their successors took it from there.

As the floodgates opened, Irish-Americans poured into show business. James O'Neill, father of playwright Eugene, caused a sensation with his stage adaptation of Dumas's *The Count of Monte Cristo.*[27] He would perform the role more than six thousand times during the play's unprecedented twenty-nine-year run. George M. Cohan also made his Broadway debut in the nineties, in tandem with a noisy downtown street that became a mecca for sheet music publishers.[28] When songwriter Monroe H. Rosenfeld heard piano players banging out songs near the intersection of Broadway and Twenty-Eighth Street, he likened the sound to that made by beating on tin pans, and the metaphor stuck: the term "Tin Pan Alley" was coined. The street would turn out hundreds of Irish-themed songs over the next several decades.

The stage's newly acquired Irishness wasn't lost on Pittsburgh, with its large immigrant population. By the end of the decade, O'Neill had played Monte Cristo to enthusiastic audiences at the Duquesne Theater.[29] *The Mulligan Guard Ball* passed through town in December 1898, with Harrigan himself leading the cast.[30] "Some vaudeville people of cleverness," a reviewer noted, also took the stage that night. Dan Fenton did his "dancing lady from Cork." A man called Murphy performed a comedy singing act. "One of the cast, whose cognomen is unplaceable on the printed program, played one of the funniest Irish women on the stage and carried nine-tenths of the comedy." The last act featured "a marvelous exhibition of bag punching" topped off with a three-round boxing match.[31]

Into this latest incarnation of the theater business, Maurice insinuated himself with ever-heightening degrees of self-confidence. "When I was twenty I had my first professional engagement with the Davis Stock Company," he said, leaving the previous five years of his life an unfortunate blur, from the time he began working odd jobs as a teenager to his first professional engagement as a performer.[32] The name "Davis" might otherwise pass by unnoticed if the man it belonged to wasn't Harry Davis, whose gift to civilization was nothing short of life changing. Several years after he hired Maurice Costello, who became the first screen idol, he opened the first official nickelodeon in 1905, and the movie theater was born. Davis had established himself a decade earlier as Pittsburgh's leading impresario—if it sang, danced, or drew a crowd, from the Irish community especially, he had booked it and brought it to town.

Davis scored his first entrepreneurial success in the late 1880s with the presentation of a walking race, for which he provided the venue and also sold tickets.[33] The event netted him nine hundred dollars, which he used to buy out the lease of O'Brian's Dime Museum, a throwback to the age of P. T. Barnum. Soon after, he reopened it as the more exotic sounding Eden Musée. Calling themselves museums, rather than the variety houses they were, gave them an air of respectability—enough for an unchaperoned woman to attend one of the Musée's evening performances and emerge with her reputation intact. Throwing in a sideshow oddity or two gave the "museum" designation its scintilla of credibility, and at ten cents it was relatively affordable.[34] Davis's venture gave its patrons the obligatory freak show, along with a "cabinet of curios" that contained an Indian arrowhead and some Confederate money. To pull business in off the street, a "monster snake" named Old Rube was placed on display in the lobby. Inside, the "Theatorium" featured a half-hour variety bill led by a minstrel-style master of ceremonies called the Lecturer, who appeared between acts to introduce the next performance.

By 1891, Davis was earning twenty thousand dollars a year from the Musée. Soon he had enough money to open a pair of playhouses and form a resident stock company for each.[35] The Casino Comic Opera Company occupied the fanciful structure that once housed the country's first artificial skating rink. On Sundays, the company turned the stage over to "Professor Eugene Smith's Unrivaled Orchestra" and his weekly "sacred concerts."

Perhaps as a throwback to its days as an ice rink, the Casino offered its patrons a rudimentary version of twentieth-century air conditioning. "This Theater is cooled by patent devices," the program stated, "including an ice machine, [with] the capacity of 150 tons. Four large blowers keep up a constant supply of air that has been reduced to [a] temperature of 65 degrees."

After reopening the Casino, Davis formed a second troupe, called the Harry Davis Musical and Travesty Company, to perform at the newly renovated Avenue Theater in the heart of Pittsburgh's burgeoning entertainment district.[36] A chronicler of the Davis era wrote that the great showman "presented his company surrounded by the vaudeville acts. It was the inception in Pittsburgh of what was then known as continuous vaudeville, and the custom was to introduce along about the middle of the bill a short play of one or two acts."[37]

It was with the Music and Travesty Company, during the winter season of 1897, that Maurice made his professional debut. Previously he had worked as a stagehand, but never as a paid performer. His daughter later claimed that he was part of the original Broadway production of David Belasco's 1895 Civil War melodrama, *The Heart of Maryland.* She didn't say in what capacity, but as he was not yet a paid actor, it had to have been behind the scenes. The hero in the play was the great stage idol Maurice Barrymore, father of Maurice Costello's future son-in-law—so if the younger Maurice was part of that production, the two Maurices could have known each other decades before the merging of their families was ever dreamt of.[38]

By the time Maurice joined the Davis Company, the Avenue was the most innovative theatrical venue in Pittsburgh. Decades before live broadcasting, Harry Davis gave the city's baseball-hungry public possibly the earliest known version of play-by-play coverage. "While the Pittsburgh Club is away," his advertisement read, "the games played by them will be reproduced on the stage of the Avenue Theater. . . . Identically the same in every detail as they are played on the field. The diamond is there, perfect and complete, and dummy figures play the game precisely like the players themselves, their movements being controlled according to the detailed description of the game sent direct from the grounds where the club is playing, by wire to the stage."[39]

And now there were movies. While Maurice was launching his stage career, the medium that would someday make him a star swept through

Pittsburgh with all the force of an invasion, which in a very real sense it was. On September 7, 1896, the Avenue and Bijou theaters added to their Monday lineups the exhibition of two different inventions performing the exact same task.[40] The year before, the Lumière brothers had been the first commercially successful filmmakers to project a moving image onto a screen for a paying audience.[41] Fortunately for Edison, his projector was the first to gain a foothold in the American film market. So in the same city, on the same night, while the Bijou presented Edison's Kinetograph, the Avenue demonstrated the Lumières' Cinematograph.[42] The latter came at the end of a long vaudeville program, featuring a string of novelty acts that included "The Matchless Lucifers, Grotesque Athletic Comedians" and "Maud Beall Price, The Double-Voiced Vocalist." With titles ranging from the monumental (*Empress of Russia at the Crowning of the Czar*) to the mundane (*Watering the Lawn* and *The Lumière Family at Breakfast*), each film lasted less than a minute.[43] Introducing the program was Davis's leading man, local Shakespearean actor Beaumont Smith, who spoke of "the marvelous scientific advantages of the new Cinematograph."

Given Maurice's later enthusiasm for movies when other stage actors were still laughing at them, it's hard to believe that he wouldn't have attended at least one of the presentations that night. Could a nineteen-year-old aspiring actor, who knew the Pittsburgh theater scene inside and out, have possibly missed it?

Whether or not the seed was planted then or some other time, Maurice had a long, brutal climb ahead of him. It took him years of traveling the circuits—playing in tent shows, in gaudy saloons masquerading as playhouses, or seedy auditoriums calling themselves opera houses—to solidify his reputation as the jack-of-all-trades performer he would become. In the meantime, film itself needed time to evolve. Taking his inspiration from Méliès and other innovators, filmmaker Edwin S. Porter was among the first to chain together successive dramatic scenes to create a cohesive narrative.[44] While Maurice was cutting his teeth in variety, the pictorial aspects of movies were giving way to the first "story films"—for which the most verbal of professions would reduce itself, not counting the audible flutter of a movie projector, to absolute silence.

Maurice Costello's first professional notices, if they can be called that, came at the tail end of a Pittsburgh critic's ecstatic farewell to the 1900 theater season.[45] The Davis players had moved into the Grand Theater, another Davis property, so the Avenue could be used exclusively for vaudeville. On June 4, the company completed its winter run with the George Sims and Cecil Raleigh comedy *The Grey Mare,* featuring "clever little" Marion Ballou in the starring role.[46] The diminutive actress eventually ended up in Hollywood with several memorable films to her credit, among them *Little Women,* with Katharine Hepburn. When the curtain fell on opening night, wrote a reviewer, "a file of ushers went down the aisle laden with flowers, and when Miss Ballou had them all piled on her arms she was almost hidden." The play's twelve supporting actors received high praise—except for Maurice, whose performance as Stubbs the Butler was deemed "acceptable."[47]

The fact that he had been acting professionally for three years and was still playing bit parts for the Davis Company is telling. Clearly, Maurice had failed to impress. At the end of the season either he was let go or he left of his own accord. Fortunately, there was no shortage of job opportunities for stage performers at the turn of the century, thanks to intense public demand for new plays, and new faces to appear in them. Under pressure to mount brand-new, full-scale productions every week, theater operators unwittingly created a subculture of transitory performers who moved from one troupe to another, from one town to the next. The deluge of performers barnstorming the country was a source of both fascination and trepidation to small town residents. Landlords and creditors hated them for their fly-by-night ways; parents feared for their stage-struck children—daughters especially, as Maurice would discover soon after striking out on his own. First he would go east to get his professional bearings, then wherever the road would take him. Only, by the time he landed his first out-of-town engagement, the place he most wanted to be was the place he was leaving behind.[48]

3

Mae

She could have run away, as any proper young woman of the period undoubtedly would have, if she hadn't loved him so much. The playwright Gus McHugh introduced the winsome pair in the spring of 1902, and they were instantly smitten. Now the besotted actor had a life-altering decision to make: he could leave the woman he loved alone and unattached for the next six months, or tell her how long he planned to be away and hope she would marry him anyway.[1]

He went with the second choice. On June 6, 1902, Maurice Costello married Maria Josephina Altschuh at New York's Holy Church of the Innocents, known as "the actor's church," on West Thirty-Seventh Street. After the ceremony the bride and groom kissed each other good-bye and went their separate ways—she to her mother and stepfather's house in Brooklyn, he to join the cast of *Judged Guilty,* a vaudeville playlet, in faraway Buffalo. There hadn't even been time to consummate the marriage. "They heard from each other rarely," their daughter wrote forty years later. "For the first, and one of the few times in his life, Maurice . . . husbanded his money. He lived circumspectly on the road, worked and studied hard, became as much a model of temperance and sobriety as an Irish actor with Spanish forbearers could be."[2]

For Maria, known from the day she was born as Mae, nothing had changed. She kept her marriage a secret, as she knew her "very English" stepfather would not have approved. Vincent Tresham, a hatter by trade, was a devout Catholic "as only British can be Catholics, and in politics, dress, social outlook" was a staunch conservative. Mae's mother, the former Katie Callendar, was the English daughter of John Callendar, a 33rd Degree Mason said to have taken his degree with Prince Albert in attendance. She married Tresham shortly after the death of her first husband, Lewis Altschuh, an Alsatian immigrant dimly remembered for his hatred of the German soldiers who had destroyed his vineyard and driven him to America.[3] Tresham provided amply for Mae after her father's death, but if he expected obedience in return, he would be sadly disappointed.

Mae introduced Maurice to her stepfather at the start of their courtship, which Tresham could only hope was a passing fancy.[4] During their meeting, the tradesman lit into the man he referred to as "that actor," whose occupation he considered both immoral and indecent. Maurice wanted nothing more to do with Tresham after that, but there would have to be one final encounter. When *Judged Guilty* finished its run, Maurice returned to New York to retrieve the nineteen-year-old wife he barely knew, and to share with his in-laws the belated news of their marriage. Other wounds needed healing besides. "My Dear Sweetheart and Husband," Mae's letter began. "Yours of yesterday received and I am surprised at you sending me that clipping you did, as I thought I was *always* patient and also sympathetic. . . . For goodness sake don't be discouraged there is [no] fellow in this house that wants me I am married and they all know that."[5] The newlyweds quarreled again in early 1903, with Mae writing afterward, by way of apology: "My dear Hubby, Will you please forgive me. I love you. I am sorry to have had you spent a day like this. I did not mean one thing I said I only wanted to find out what you thought."[6]

Mae wasn't sure when Maurice was coming to fetch her, until one Sunday morning a violent pull on the bell cord sent her scurrying to the edge of the stairs. Tresham ushered into the entryway a man whose stage-trained voice she recognized instantly. "Sir, with your kind permission," the caller said, "I should like to speak with my wife." As her stepfather stammered out his reply, Mae hurried back to her room and started packing. A stormy scene erupted, the two men arguing with voices raised until the cause of their dispute appeared at the bottom of the stairs, suitcases in hand. "Now that you're a married man," grumbled Tresham in defeat, "maybe you'll settle down to a decent livelihood and give up this acting business." Gathering his wife and her belongings, Maurice responded: "Sir, your daughter is married to an actor. Good day."[7]

Tresham wasn't the only one who had disparaged Maurice's choice of careers. His mother, echoing the Catholic Church's medieval disdain for actors, had raged against her son's decision to go on the stage. A Costello cousin begged him to attend mass on Sundays, worrying that he was not with "clean company."[8] Scolded another relative: "That dangerous calling you are at, affrights me. You cannot see as it is nor its dangers which are many and frightful. Give my best regards to your mother. She is anxious about you, too. All who see your dangers could not be otherwise. Do not forget your prayers nor other religious duties at any cost."[9]

The best he could offer his bride of six months, in lieu of a proper honeymoon, was a whirlwind tour of railroad cafés and musty hotels, starting in Philadelphia a day or so after leaving the Treshams.[10] Yanked from her staid Brooklyn family and flung overnight into the riotous world of stagecraft, Mae would learn to survive—sometimes alongside her husband, sometimes in spite of him. Nothing could have prepared her for the life she had married into. Going from tradesman's daughter to the wife of an itinerant performer was the start of a lifelong struggle to cope with the humbling realities of show business—beginning with the realization that the man she married was more traveling salesman than stage actor, hawking his theatrical wares from one town to the next. He might be called upon at a moment's notice to conjure up whatever stage business might play to a jaded, fickle audience that, by the turn of the century, had seen every kind of traveling show.

This wasn't the life of an up-and-coming stage star, Mae discovered—it was eking out a living as an unbilled member of a "repertoire" company. Unlike stock and vaudeville troupes, these were traveling shows exclusively, offering patrons an array of amusements that ran the gamut of plays, variety, and operatic performances and that featured actors, singers, dancers, and comedians of every stripe.[11] Very often they played in tents, giving "tent rep," as it was known, a sideshow, circus-like aspect.[12] "When the show arrived," a patron recalled, "there was the tent to be put up, the stage to be assembled. It was a board affair, 30 feet across and 20 feet deep; standing three feet from the floor of the tent."

"There were no drop curtains. What little scenery there was, consisted of flat pieces carried in a trunk, which could be assembled quickly. As for the tent itself, it could house a thousand people at an admission price of ten and twenty cents, with reserve seats selling at a dime each. At 7:30 the band marched to the town circle and played a half-hour concert; then it marched off to the tent, followed by the townsfolk in their Sunday finery, noisy children, and an army of dogs. At least half of the band members changed hastily into other costumes, and the show went on amid the awed murmurs of the audience and the uncertain light of the gasoline lamps hung from the tent poles."[13]

During his stint with the Fisher-Walters company in the summer of 1900, Maurice played the villain in every drama, sang tenor solos after the first act, and did a low-country Irish routine in the second.[14] In Palestine, Ohio, when Maurice was asked to sit in for a missing trombonist in the company's marching band, he gamely agreed, though he had never before played the trombone. To prepare for the evening's performance he returned to his lodgings and started practicing. A short while later, the police showed up and arrested him. To the charge of "annoying persons by playing a trombone," Maurice pleaded not guilty. "I don't see how I can decide this case without hearing the prisoner play," the magistrate grumbled. The defendant was ordered to retrieve his instrument and return to the proceedings posthaste. When court reconvened, Maurice played a rendition of what sounded to one listener like "Climbing that Golden Stair," a minstrel song whose plaintive lyric pined for the Jubilee year when every slave would be set free. "That's plenty," the judge interrupted after less than a minute. "It's pretty bad music, but I'll only fine you one dollar and charge you to keep the peace while you remain in town."[15] After that, Maurice confined his practicing to the woods.

"Cold, dingy hotel rooms," wrote Helene of her mother's honeymoon on the repertoire circuit. "Hot stuffy ones. . . . Towns and theaters in such rapid succession that she recalled them later like pickets in a fence—all alike and close together."[16] A month into their tour, the company stepped off the train in Buffalo with barely enough time to settle in before the evening's performance. Mae wasn't feeling well and made a doctor's appointment for the following day. Maurice and fellow trouper Frank Charleston arrived at the playhouse to find themselves in a predicament as old as the theater itself: the tour's manager had absconded with the receipts and stranded the company. The troupe's assets were seized by the jilted theater owner, as was customary, leaving the performers with just their suitcases and whatever money they had in their pockets. Maurice had been paid earlier in vouchers that now were worthless.

That afternoon the Costellos met in their hotel room for an exchange of dire announcements. "My dear, we will not be opening tonight," Maurice told Mae gravely. "The manager seems to have absconded. The properties are in the hands of the creditors."

"I'm afraid we'll have to do something dear," she replied, "because we're going to have a baby."[17] Although she had been skimming money from Maurice's pay packets for emergencies (as she continued to do throughout their married life), that was now spent and there was nothing left to fall back on.

It was a situation unique to the theatrical profession, but one that a pair of actors on the brink of destitution were especially well suited to handle. Without telling Mae, who they knew wouldn't approve, Frank and Maurice hatched a plan. With their last two dollars they bought a pair of St. Anthony statuettes to use as samples—then, donning identical priest costumes they found in a property trunk, the counterfeit clerics entered the city's Irish section and began knocking on doors. As Maurice told the story, they offered the little statues for sale at two dollars apiece, explaining in their well-practiced brogues that they were immigrants working their way through seminary. A payment of half would suffice as a down payment, the remainder to be paid upon receipt. "Shure, man, an' ye'll niver know the blessin' ye've purchased this night," Maurice truthfully told his victims, before strolling off to the next house.[18]

The scam worked brilliantly, as no one would have dared question the veracity of a pair of Catholic divinity students. By midnight Maurice had not only enough money to pay his hotel bill, but enough left over to put Mae on the next train to Pittsburgh.[19] Having burned her bridges at the Treshams, she would have to go live with Maurice's mother and stepfather until more suitable accommodations could be found. With Mae safely aboard, the pair headed south to finish out the season with Mrs. Boyle's stock company in Nashville. It took all the money Maurice had left in the world to bridge the seven-hundred-mile gap between Buffalo and his next crucial source of income.

Mae learned as soon as they started living together that her new husband drank. She quickly became acquainted with what their oldest daughter later called his "angry temperament," which meant that under the influence he might fly off the handle for any reason, or for no reason. Tolerating his behavior was easy in the beginning. Contemporary descriptions credit Maurice with, if not wit, then the requisite charm and vivacity of a born entertainer. He was fashionably handsome, in the manner of the perennial presidential candidate William Jennings Bryan, with his large head, curly hair, and expansive brow.[20] Regardless of financial circumstances, Maurice was always immaculately groomed and stylishly attired.

He was an adequate provider in the early years of their marriage, given the unpredictable nature of his profession. Like actors then and now, Maurice struggled between engagements to make ends meet. Yet he was able to keep food on the table and a roof over Mae's head, even if, in the beginning, it meant she had to live with his parents for a time. Studio publicists and fan magazine writers later referred to him as a former Broadway star, but that was mythmaking.[21] Maurice achieved little in the way of name recognition during his years as a stage actor, and likely would have been forgotten entirely if movies hadn't come along. Until then he kept at it, if not with the goal of leaving his mark on the theater, then to keep his family's head above water.

In early 1903, Mae arrived in Pittsburgh hoping to find a safe and sedentary place to await the birth of her first child. Sadly, the Tresham's handsome brick house at 181 Skillman Avenue, with its middle-class comforts, would have been an ideal place for the lying-in—quite the opposite of the squalid tenement in which Mae unhappily found herself.

Five years after the death of Thomas Costello, Maurice's mother had married William Coinness, a Lithuanian immigrant employed as a day laborer in the steel mills. He could neither read nor write. They had two children of their own, Maurice's half sisters Nellie and Mary, who were in their teens when Mae first appeared on their Forbes Avenue doorstep.[22] Ellen was still taking in boarders, though the skein of nationalities pouring into Pittsburgh had changed entirely since Maurice had grown up in a house full of Irishmen. In the 1880s, Ellen's lodgers had been surnamed Fitzgerald, Sullivan, Donald, King, and Broderick. Twenty years later they were named Serkis, Auzulewitz, Latviz, Matz, Kerman, and Quader.[23] Eastern Europeans poured into Pittsburgh by the thousands during the Gilded Age, inundating its slums with Hungarian, German, Slavic, Polish, Russian, and Ukrainian immigrants.

According to the 1900 federal census, the Coinness family (including Maurice, who was about to leave the Davis company), their seven Ukrainian boarders, and a five-member German family and *their* boarder—were all living together under the same roof.[24] As always, Ellen's boarders were day laborers, most under the age of thirty. Very likely they were employed at the Pennsylvania Tube Mill complex on the banks of the Monongahela River, several blocks to the south.

The Coinnesses' stretch of Forbes Avenue was now a patchwork of wayward ethnicities. As the "famine Irish" pulled themselves out of poverty and into better-paying jobs, new sources of cheap labor were needed to fill their positions. They crowded into the same weather-beaten tenements that, after decades of neglect, were even more dilapidated than when the Irish lived in them. According to the census, there were two Irish families left on the Coinnesses' block in 1900, as the majority of their neighbors now hailed from the continent.[25]

Into this sea of humanity trudged the middle-class granddaughter of the 33rd Degree Mason John Callendar, now the pregnant wife of a penniless actor stuck on a train somewhere between Nashville and Buffalo. Having returned to the bottom-rung status her forebearers had worked long and hard to pull themselves up from, Mae had no choice now but to make do until a better situation could be found.

4

East to Eden

Unlike its better-known namesakes—one to the east in lower Manhattan, the other across the Atlantic Ocean—Pittsburgh's Soho was never considered fashionable. At the start of the twentieth century, it was barely habitable. The English aristocrat James Tustin, whose country estate covered its hillsides in the early 1800s, named his acreage after London's Soho, which a century later it could not have resembled less.[1]

Dolores Costello was born there, in the city's filth-ridden Fourteenth Ward, on September 17, 1903. That year, Pittsburgh had the highest infant mortality rate in the nation. This distinction was mostly due to the city's water supply: untreated river water into which the city's raw sewage was dumped.[2] Because indoor plumbing was all but nonexistent, working-class residents had to pump their water from backyard hydrants—typically a single water source per every nine families.

Backyards contained what were known as "privy vaults"—large urban outhouses bunched together in twos and threes, or stacked one on top of the other to resemble small buildings. None were connected to sewer lines, so when it rained, wrote an aghast chronicler, they "drained down the side of a hill through an open conduit into a neighbor's backyard. . . . One was found emptying at the curb of a busy street in a thickly populated section. . . . Thence the sewage found its way to the nearest street corner and at last into its proper receptacle, the public sewer."[3]

Rock Street, described as a "hillside battery of disease," paralleled Forbes Avenue two blocks east of the Coinness residence. Thirteen unsewered privy vaults served the street's roughly one hundred residents. As many as nine families had to make do with a single privy. "A long, open sewer drain carrying sewage from both alley and street" ran the length of the street; "during rain or when its sluggish way [was] otherwise forced to capacity," it overflowed into cellars and basement kitchens.

Some residents had no privies at all: "Cleanliness is out of the question when water has to be carried not only from a hydrant in the courtyard but up three flights of stairs as well, and carried not once but twice, for in these cases there is rarely any provision for the disposal of waste water, which in turn must be thrown out or carried downstairs and emptied into the yard drain."[4]

The result was a vicious circle of filth and contagion, to which Soho's youngest residents—newborns like Dolores, especially—were particularly vulnerable. Mothers used the untreated river water to stretch their children's supply of milk; the resultant typhoid, dysentery, and other waterborne bacterial infections were responsible for 36 percent of Pittsburgh's infant deaths at the turn of the century.[5]

The Coinnesses' tenement wasn't the district's most overcrowded dwelling by any means. Soho's worst slum property housed some twenty families.[6] Five families lived in a single dwelling on Rock Street. Doubtless this was of small consolation to Mae, coming off a string of rude awakenings that had somehow landed her in the grimiest section of the dirtiest city in America.

Maurice was on the road with the Boyle Company when Dolores was born, and wouldn't get to see his infant daughter for the first time until the spring of 1904. By then he had reached the next level of theatrical achievement—going from variety performer to stage actor. As noted in the Elmira *Gazette* on April 23, 1903: "There is a strong romantic tinge to the story of "Saucy Jack Barry," which will be given at the Lyceum tonight with the author, Myles Murphy, in the title role. It is a tale of the American Revolutionary period, with the scene laid in Ireland. . . . The company surrounding Mr. Murphy is a very strong one and among the names are those of Walter Huston . . . and Maurice Costello."[7]

Walter Huston was an aspiring stage actor with distant Irish roots, who survived the repertoire to find much better prospects in years to come. In the 1942 film *Yankee Doodle Dandy,* Huston performs a song-and-dance routine straight out of the Harrigan era that he and Maurice cut their professional teeth on.

The company's frantic schedule was all too typical of the one-a-days. From Elmira they caught a train to Wilkes-Barre, a hundred miles south, to play *Saucy Jack Barry* the following night. Then they were off again, backtracking two hundred miles to Oswego, New York, to arrive in time for the evening performance. Ironically, although Mae and Dolores were within visiting range, Maurice was too busy traveling to visit them.

Maurice's transition from repertoire to stock took two years to complete. On May 3, 1905, he ended his first full season on the legitimate stage with a performance of *The Silver King* at Manhattan's Yorkville Theater. The tent-show player now calling himself a legitimate stage actor had worked all through the winter and into the spring without any lapses in pay, playing a dozen parts in as many plays. Maurice's disappearance in mid-1904 corresponded with the time it took him to move Mae and little Dolores from the slums of Pittsburgh to better, safer lodgings in uptown Manhattan. They rented an apartment on 136th Street, just as the great African American migration to Harlem began.[8] Soon Mae was complaining that she and Dolores were the only white residents in the building.

Maurice had moved to the center of the theatrical universe, poised for limitless growth on the most fertile ground that had ever existed for a performer. The Brooklyn stage, then considered an adjunct to Broadway, drew New Yorkers of every station to its playhouses, many of which had resident stock companies of their own. The hands-down favorite owed its spectacular success to its three gifted proprietresses: Cecil, Edna May, and Mary Gibbs Spooner, who built a following so large that even the trusts had to defer to them.[9] With sisters Cecil and Edna May as lead actresses, and their mother Mary acting as chaperone and business manager, the Spooner Stock Company thrived as an all-female enterprise in a business dominated by men.[10] To keep them from crossing the East River and gaining an independent foothold on Broadway, theater moguls B. F. Keith and F. F. Proctor fired the Fifth Avenue Theater's resident company and turned the historic playhouse over to the Spooners.

Maurice helped kick off the 1904–1905 season on September 12 in the Spooner production of *Winchester,* a five-act Civil War drama that featured a climactic on-stage battle scene.[11] In the last act, the Southern heroine (played by Edna May) taps into a telegraph line to stop her Northern lover from getting the order that will take him away from her. Not to be overlooked, Cecil performed a "new specialty" of her own between acts.

With ticket sales soaring, the Spooners leased a second playhouse, the Amphion, so the sisters could perform separately when they weren't playing together at the Bijou, the company's main stage. To say that Cecil and Edna May had a rare gift for stagecraft would be a colossal understatement. Besides acting, they danced, sang, choreographed, composed music, and wrote their own plays—all to the seemingly endless delight of playgoers and critics alike. "Your theater-loving Brooklynite," gushed Fenholm Wolf of the *New York Morning Telegraph,* using the same giddy language nearly every critic reserved for the Spooners, "at the mere mention of [their] name, will toss his hat in the air and indulge in the most frenzied exhibitions of delirious delight."[12]

The theaters were packed to the lobby doors on October 10, when the women opened two shows on the same night. Cecil played a dual role in *A Night at the Circus* at the Bijou, in which Maurice played a secondary character, while Edna May starred in Paul Kester's *When Knighthood Was in Flower* at the Amphion. As Mary Tudor, she "received a perpetual ovation from the time the curtain rose until it was rung down at 11:15." Cecil appeared at the Amphion a week earlier as the "vivacious, spirited, warm-hearted" heroine in *That Girl from Texas,* a comedy written just for her. The supporting cast, wrote a critic, "demonstrated their fitness for the work demanded of them." Maurice was praised, finally, for having "done effective work" in the role of the Count de Chambra.[13] Given his character's Spanish-sounding name, clearly another milestone had been reached: he was no longer playing Irish characters exclusively.

In their newest employee the sisters had an actor whose versatility equaled their own. But, like everyone Maurice had worked for thus far, they wouldn't know what they had lost until long after he was gone. He quit the Spooners in March 1905 to play a number of secondary parts with the American Stock Company, before finishing the season at the Yorkville Theater in *The Silver King.*[14]

After a month-long break, he headed off to do summer stock for the Blaker Company of Wildwood, New Jersey. As the season's headliner, he had to learn two new roles from scratch every week. Starting July 3, Maurice played Terry Desmond in *The Man from America* from Monday to Wednesday, then Dr. Glynn in *The Widow* from Thursday to Saturday. He had Sundays off, no doubt to study his lines for the upcoming week. For his services, the Blaker Company paid him $20 (about $600 in today's currency) twice a month.[15]

Soon after Maurice's return to New York, Mae became pregnant. Just as Dolores's birth had forced him to make the jump from repertoire to stock, the prospect of another mouth to feed provided the incentive for his next great leap forward. Exactly when the first great movie star first appeared on a movie screen is a mystery well worth unraveling. It's often been claimed that Maurice made his screen debut with the Edison Company in 1905, and there would be no reason to doubt that assertion if Maurice himself hadn't said otherwise. In 1915, he told a movie magazine that he was a stage actor until "six years ago, when I began playing for the Vitagraph Company as an extra."[16] This puts the start of his movie career in 1909, and not with Edison, but the Wizard's chief competitor. *Photoplay* reported that as the year when Maurice "went to Vitagraph, being a member of the first motion picture stock company ever formed."[17]

Muddying the waters even further, Maurice told an interviewer in the 1930s that he "continued on the stage until 1905, when seeing a future for motion pictures, I joined the old Vitagraph Company at $30 a week."[18] In yet another interview he claimed he was working in the theater until 1906, before he joined Vitagraph. So, which date and place are correct? As 1905 was his busiest year as a stage actor, there's no way he could have quit the theater to make movies. Maurice's own handwritten business ledgers show that after his stint with the Blacker troupe, he signed up with the Gilmore Stock Company for a series of out-of-town engagements that kept him busy well into 1906.[19]

But what of his supposed beginnings with Edison? Writing in the 1920s, film historian Terry Ramsaye stated that "Maurice Costello, of the Spooner Stock Company, came from the haughty dignity of the legitimate to play a part in Edison pictures, back there in those beginnings so obscure, that even the subjects have been forgotten."[20] He went on to mention J. Searle Dawley (the director of Edison's 1910 *Frankenstein,* probably the first horror film), who worked for the Spooners before joining Edison. "Through Dawley and his dramatic connections," he added, "a number of well-remembered names came into motion pictures." With Dawley funneling ex-Spooner players into the Edison Company, which offered steady work and also paid well, how could Maurice *not* have been one of those "well-remembered" names?" *Variety* claimed that he "started with Edison in 1905," as did many others.[21] In *A Pictorial History of the Silent Screen,* Daniel Blum wrote that "Maurice Costello, a juvenile from the Spooner Stock Company in Brooklyn joined Edison."[22]

So how indeed could so many credible sources be so incredibly wrong? The reportage of contemporary newspapers, supported by film historians both early and late, mostly concludes that by the end of 1905, Maurice Costello had quit the stage and was busily making movies for the Edison Company. But newer, better evidence shows otherwise. According to Maurice's business ledgers, he was employed by five different stock companies in 1905, and played some thirty roles.[23] Even if he had had the energy to add moviemaking to his workload that year, how would he have found the time? Maurice's characteristic memory lapses are more than made up for by the efficiency of his bookkeeping. He accounted for everything he did professionally—every role he played, every dollar he earned, the dates and places of his performances, who he worked for, and how long he worked for them. And not once is Edison or the movie business mentioned in any of them. If Maurice, compulsive bookkeeper that he was, worked in films before 1907, there would be hard evidence of it in his ledgers.[24]

Not that he wasn't considering other options. The more he struggled to meet the needs of his growing family, the greater Mae's impatience with him became. In mid-1906, while Maurice was on tour with the Maude Fealy Company, she gave him a stern ultimatum:

> My Dear Hubby,
>
> Your letter of the 17th inst. received, can't understand why Miss Fealy has the say to cut your salary $10. And if you stand for it I'll have something to say. I was never used to very much but I think I deserve a little more than this. And getting this cutting down will not do. [It] was the same in Nashville and in Spooners. I'll not stand it any longer. You will have to choose between your profession or me. Now Maurice I'm not angry when I say this so don't think it's temper for it's not. You were engaged for the season not for four weeks, and another thing you said you would be here in January. I'll not put up with this life, the attention I ought to get is given others, I will not stay alone and have a game like this. Make up your mind what you are going to do, and I'll come to some agreement. I done this so you could get on your feet. You can get that much money in melodrama. Answer just as soon as you can and oblige your loving wife.
>
> Mae[25]

Maurice had worked too hard and come too far to throw away his stage career just yet. It took him a full year after the birth of his second child to decide to give moving pictures a try. And when he did, it was with the studio that, by the middle of 1907, was the most successful moving-picture company in America.

Helen Adrienne Costello (the "e" wasn't added to her first name until she arrived in Hollywood) was born on June 21, 1906, after a long, hazardous ordeal that should have occurred in a hospital. "[Maurice] came home from the theater to find Mother in advanced labor," Helene wrote in an outline for a memoir that was never published, "with the doctor and nurse in attendance. He took care of the three-year-old Dolores while the labor dragged on and on—almost sixteen hours, the last four of which he spent in almost continuous prayer." When the crisis came, the nurse fainted and Maurice took her place.

> It was a breech birth, and Maurice himself had to help the doctor deliver the poor, ugly, little lifeless thing. . . . The baby was literally tossed aside while the doctor and Maurice struggled to revive the flicker of life in the mother. Not until she was safe did the doctor pick up the baby, intending to send it quietly to the mortuary to spare her the grief of seeing it. Maurice was kneeling at his wife's bed . . . when he heard the doctor's electrifying cry: "It's alive! Get my case, and warm water, and warm blankets!"
>
> It lived, but it was not the boy Dad wanted, and because of the prolonged birth struggle, there could never be another baby. It was [a] girl, and they named it Helene. I am truly the last of the Costellos. I came into the world backwards, bringing pain and tragedy and disappointment. In the years since then, when I have seemed to do everything backwards, I have wished many times that I never had survived the long ordeal of my birth. Yet it was the same animal vitality that carried me through, that also helped later in other tragedies, other crises. I learned early in life to fight—and fight—and keep on fighting. Dolores was a lovely hot-house flower who never had an "awkward age," and whom the world was always delighted to serve. Me—well, I had all the characteristics of a promising shanty Irish welterweight.[26]

For the first family to become famous in movies, the players were assembled. Maurice was poised for rebirth as the first great screen actor. In the next few years he would set himself apart from every other film performer, bridging the gap between the prehistory of motion picture acting and the dawn of its modern age.

5

Chewing the Scenery

Appropriately enough, the Vitagraph Company began life as the by-product of a failed partnership between a cartoonist and a magician. In the spring of 1894, when the variety act known as the Celebrated Reader, Smith and Blackton Combination opened in Haverstraw, New York, there were just two people in the audience—an elderly man and a little girl. "Although the response is not quite what we had hoped for," the magician shouted from the stage, "it makes no difference. . . . The show will go on!"

"The sooner the better lad," replied the old man, "I'm the janitor here and we're waiting to close the house."[1]

On December 7, the Combination appeared at Parshall's Hall in Manhattan for a church benefit, with the twenty-one-year-old English caricaturist James Stuart Blackton presenting a "comic travesty introducing one of his funny faces, cartoons in black and white, artistic landscape sand marine painting." Blackton's partner and fellow Englishman, Albert E. Smith, followed as the Komical Konjurer, presenting "original novelties, including his celebrated cabinet mystery." For the finale, the pair produced a series of "kinetoscopic paintings"—probably magic lantern slides that, when projected on a screen, gave the illusion of movement.[2]

After the short-lived act disbanded, probably due to a lack of bookings, Blackton found employment with the *New York Evening World* as a sketch artist, while Smith took a job as a bookbinder.[3] In April 1896, the pair reunited for a benefit performance in Asbury Park, New Jersey, that would have a profound effect on the future of film both as an art form and as a business. The event was sponsored by the *World Sick Baby Fund*, which offered financial aid to the infants of impoverished New Yorkers, and featured Smith performing "a series of skillful experiments in prestidigitation," with Blackton doing his "lightning sketches." The resulting publicity led to an invitation from the Edison Manufacturing Company to make a series of groundbreaking films.

Blackton described his meeting with Edison, which he said took place while he was still sketching for the *World*. "I went into this room and Mr. Edison was back in a corner busily engaged. His back was to me. I said 'Good morning, Mr. Edison,' but he paid no attention to me. I said a little louder 'Good morning, Mr. Edison!' Still he took no notice."[4] After getting the Wizard's attention, Blackton explained that he had been sent to do a sketch of him:

> He said "You will have to speak louder, I am stone deaf." He beckoned me around to his right ear and by means of sort of bellowing, I made him understand. He said, "Alright, you have a good strong voice and I can hear you young man. Sit down." And then he began to interview me. . . . He asked me, "What is that you have got under your arm?" I told him it was my sketch book. He asked me if I could draw, and said that was the one thing he wished he could do. . . . He asked me if I could make a sketch of him. He was very pleased with it, and said it was very good.

Blackton's version of the story has been called apocryphal, but part of it has the ring of truth.[5] The Wizard's deafness was public knowledge, but few would have known, as Blackton did, that Edison favored his right ear unless they had spent time with him. They must have worked together in some capacity, as a film was made of Blackton sketching Edison. How much of it took place in the Wizard's presence or the cartoonist's imagination is beside the point—the moment that Edison's camera started cranking and Blackton started sketching, both the craft and the business of filmmaking would never be the same. Three months after the first projected movies were shown to an American audience, the Edison-Blackton film was shown to local acclaim at Proctor's Pleasure Palace on East Fifty-Eighth Street. With that, the flagging careers of the vaudeville cartoonist and his crony Smith took on new life in an explosive and revelatory way. As a stage act, the caricaturist's lightning sketches were just a flash in the pan, but when projected on a screen they became the star attraction.

Having entirely familiarized themselves with Edison's novelty, Blackton and Smith incorporated it into a larger scheme of their own design. In early 1897, they scraped together the hundred dollars they needed to purchase the latest version of the Kinetoscope, and went into business.[6] Because few theaters owned their own projectors as yet, Smith easily found work showing movies in vaudeville houses, which were adding photoplays to their live shows as fast as they could get them. Meanwhile, Blackton the showman couldn't sit idly by while Smith operated the projector. During the run of *Black Diamond Express,* a popular film that consisted of a train barreling toward the audience, Blackton added sound effects by beating loudly on a piece of sheet metal and an assortment of pots and pans.[7]

The mechanically inclined Smith set to work retrofitting Edison's Kinetoscope to function both as a projector and a moving-picture camera. Fashioning new parts out of brass, Smith added a movable frame to keep the film from popping out of the sprocket holes—a persistent problem in early film exhibition.[8] According to Smith, they bought a second Edison projector and adapted it "to take, print or exhibit moving pictures."[9]

Trading as the Edison Vitagraph Company, the partners set up shop in a large brick building in lower Manhattan. It had a skylight and an accessible roof for indoor and outdoor moviemaking. In May 1898, the company filmed *The Burglar on the Roof* high above Nassau Street, with Smith operating the camera and Blackton playing the burglar. "We hadn't reckoned on outside interferences," Smith wrote in his autobiography, *Two Reels and a Crank.* "As it happened, Mrs. Olson, the janitor's wife, was sweeping the iron staircase leading to the roof. Observing that the door at the top was open, she trudged up to close it, broom in hand, and came upon our open-air melodrama just at the moment when the policeman was grappling with the intruder. One look was enough for this brave woman. She flew into the battle with broom upraised, screaming and raining blows down on the heads of the startled actors."[10]

"An elaborate argument," wrote film historian William Basil Courtney in 1925, "could be based on the premise that the only important contribution of the Spanish-American War to the history of the United States lay . . . in the impetus it gave to the works of Smith and Blackton in placing the foundation blocks for the motion picture industry."[11]

Indeed, the war gave the fledgling film company something far more interesting to photograph than speeding trains and doodling sketch artists. It brought social impact to moviemaking, giving Edison's working-class gimmick a larger sense of purpose. With the advent of the documentary film, the public could watch important events unfold wherever a camera could be set up, through the virtual reality of the moving picture. Smith later claimed, albeit falsely, that he and Blackton were on hand to film Theodore Roosevelt's historic charge up San Juan Hill—but what of other battles the public was clamoring to see? In lieu of actual footage, the partners pooled their talents to create what may have been the first coherent series of movie special effects.[12]

With nationalistic fervor at a fever pitch, the partners were determined to show battle scenes to a paying audience even if they had to fake them. As Smith recalled:

> At this time street vendors in New York were selling sturdy photographs of ships of the American and Spanish fleets. We bought a set of each and we cut out the battleships. On a table, topside down, we placed one of artist Blackton's large canvas-covered frames and filled it with water an inch deep. In order to stand the cutouts in the water, we nailed them to lengths of wood about an inch square. In this way a little "shelf" was provided behind each ship, and on this shelf we placed pinches of gunpowder—three pinches per ship—not too many, we felt, for a major sea engagement of this sort.[13]

It wasn't enough for the filmmakers simply to document events. Having imprisoned the real world on a strip of nitrate, they would now try to bypass it entirely. "Blackton, concealed behind the side of the table," Smith wrote, "farthermost from the camera, touched off the mounds of gunpowder with his wire taper—and the battle was on. Mrs. Blackton, smoking and coughing, delivered a fine haze."[14] As the camera cranked, Smith's wife blew cigarette smoke over the lens, as the little charges popped and the ships pitched over and sank.

Whether it tricked audiences into thinking it was real scarcely mattered—the cartoonist's imagination and the magician's sleight of hand had joined forces to invent, among other filmic innovations, the movie miniature.

More than a decade passed between Smith and Blackton's initial encounter with Edison's Kinetoscope and the emergence of Vitagraph Studios as the most successful movie studio in America.[15] They added a third partner—William Rock, called "Pop," known for his business expertise and his connections to film exhibitors.[16] Flamboyant, profane, and famously tightfisted, Pop Rock parsed the company's finances with Scrooge-like efficiency. When Rock was asked why he turned off the exit signs at a Vitagraph-owned theater, he said he didn't think they were necessary.[17]

By mid-1910, all three of the first American film stars to be known by name were making movies—two of them for the Vitagraph Company. Florence Lawrence was identified in March as part of a publicity stunt.[18] Florence Turner, known as "the Vitagraph Girl," was named shortly after that. Then came the ex–stock company player Maurice Costello, who, unlike the Florences, was about to experience the as yet unimaginable phenomenon of superstardom. Theater actors had to insinuate themselves into the public consciousness incrementally, one performance at a time—but not so the picture actor, whose moving image flashed across hundreds of screens at the same time, gathering hordes of new fans with every appearance.

But it was an odd kind of celebrity if audiences had no idea who they were looking at. Before 1910, the identities of film players were a carefully guarded secret.[19] It has been claimed that filmmakers refused to identify their actors for fear that, if they were known by name, they would ask for more money. But the studios had nothing to fear compared to the actors who worked for them. Before movies gained widespread respectability in the 1910s, screen players had good reason to conceal their identities—working in movies was considered to be the actor's equivalent of prostitution. "No actor with any pride . . . worked in pictures," Helene wrote. "A man took a job like that in the same spirit that he hocked his mother's watch."[20] Terry Ramsaye wrote that the Edison Studios location in the Bronx was "far enough away from Broadway that abashed actors need not fear they would be discovered in the artistic felony of working in pictures."[21] For stage actors who aspired to become the next Ethel Barrymore or John Drew, or variety performers like W. C. Fields who yearned to play the Orpheum Circuit (he did for the first time in 1900), to act in movies was unthinkable.[22]

For others, pride wasn't the issue. Florence Lawrence was headed for oblivion as a stage actress before she decided to give movies a try.[23] Florence Turner, Albert E. Smith recalled, "stumbled into motion pictures one day when we happened to be filming a scene near Sheepshead Bay close to the Turner home."[24] For Maurice, the alchemic decision to work in movies took just the right combination of courage, curiosity, and pragmatism. Financial necessity had forced him back on the road again in 1906, likely dashing whatever hopes he still had of ever leaving it—until movies came along. Unlike the Florences, Maurice had everything to lose by leaving the theater; surely, he would not have, had he not seen potential in movies that others didn't, and envisioned the future of popular entertainment in a way that others couldn't.

Maurice formally entered the film business in the summer of 1907, though his decision to quit the stage had occurred several months earlier. He kept no more travel ledgers after 1906. There were no more angry letters from Mae after that; no more weekly bulletins arrived to demand that he improve their lot or risk losing her. Clearly, a change was in the offing. In a letter dated December 11, 1906, Mae is uncharacteristically loving—even amorous. "Well dear in regards to you coming home," she wrote, "I'll be delighted and hope I'll not be disappointing. You say if I want you or not, well you know I want you why you dear old wanderer I love you better than life. Just wait till I see you. I'll eat you all up. How I hope I won't be disappointed. Leave on the first train try and let me know when to expect you."[25]

Florence Turner, the first actor to sign a contract with a movie studio, made her screen debut in 1907, in a slapstick comedy called *How to Cure the Common Cold.* "We began at ten in the morning," she said, "and finished in time for lunch."[26] To play opposite the Vitagraph Girl, the company hired a veteran actor from the Brooklyn stage, though it would be another three years until someone west of Bayside knew that his name was Maurice Costello. Helene corroborated the year of her father's induction into the dubious profession of motion picture acting: "In the spring of 1907, Maurice found himself between engagements. Some of his colleagues on stage were taking clandestine jobs in the 'motion pictures,' as the foolhardy and preposterous invention already was called. And a good man could make as much as five dollars a day."[27]

Long before he ever thought of taking a leadership role at Vitagraph, Maurice's attraction to the movie business was purely financial. From the earliest days of their marriage, hardly a week went by when Mae wasn't dunning him for money. Engagements came and went for stage actors—lay-offs and dry spells came with the territory. But even when he had steady work, the supporting roles he was hired to play barely kept the Costellos above subsistence level. Mae complained that she and "the Babes" couldn't survive on his weekly remittances. The more her concerns went unaddressed, the more combative her letters became: "As I have told you often enough there is $50 due me tonight until I receive some money from you don't expect to hear from me again, as I think this is a dirty rotten trick. If you had a house maid looking after your Babes you'd have to pay her, I know this is about all I am in your estimation. So cough up some money or your young ones will go hungry I'm afraid."[28]

In the months before Maurice entered the movie business, the Costellos were a family in crisis. Mae fumed over her husband's ongoing struggle to keep their heads above water. While he was on the road in the winter of 1906, Mae vented her frustrations, at the same time fending off his accusations of infidelity:

> My Dear Hubby:
>
> Three letters and a postal received a short time ago, well its just time you thought of writing. I had just made up my mind not to write until I heard from you. Can't understand why you do not receive my mail. I wrote you just as soon as I got your money orders for the $5 and the $25 dollars and if you did not get them it is not my fault. You surely don't expect me to get down on my knees and beg you to send me money. You ask me to write you a loving letter, I don't think you can expect any more than you give. If I didn't love you I wouldn't be here alone tonight. You don't seem to have much confidence in me when you tell me to be careful when I went to the Dr.s office. I think he has too many single girls to be bothered with a married one.

Then came her usual no-nonsense demand for cash:

> I want my $25 no matter how many nights you lay off or how many sleepers you have. I will write you again tomorrow as I want to get this off with love from the Babes and myself. I am as ever your loving wife
>
> Mae
>
> P. S. my rent is due on the 1st of December[29]

Something had to give, and it finally did when the Vitagraph Company came to the Costellos' rescue, offering Maurice the princely sum of thirty dollars a week (the most he ever made on the stage was about twenty) to work at the studio's bustling compound at the corner of Fourteenth Street and Locust Avenue in Flatbush.[30] Given the rampaging popularity of moving pictures, Maurice had every reason to think he would soon be earning a great deal more.

There are several versions of how it happened. According to *Motion Picture Magazine,* Vitagraph actor/director Van Dyke Brooke spotted Maurice in Times Square and chased him all over town before cajoling him into signing a contract.[31] Helene gave her mother the credit for talking him into giving movies a try: "Mae had heard about fabulous earnings to be had for a job that required no tedious rehearsals, no traveling, no wearisome night hours. They had been her previous complaint against the stage; it was a night job. Cameras could turn only when there was sunlight to illuminate the setting. She proposed that Maurice investigate this source of income, to tide them over until the next engagement."[32]

Maurice's version of the story, with its wealth of additional detail, is likely the most accurate. The way was paved, he said, thanks to a chance meeting with a friend, who introduced him to Van Dyke Brooke: "I knew Van, too, knew he was directing the new-fangled 'attractions' called moving pictures. I'd seen a few of them in nickelodeons. Funny old things like magic lantern slides with the jitters. People laughed at them, but, I remember, I didn't laugh."[33]

> Brooks [*sic*] said to me, "look, Cos, will you work in a motion picture?" I said, "My God, Van, not in those galloping tintypes!" I didn't laugh at them as others had, true. But we were proud in those days. Moreover, it was well known that theater managers threatened to blacklist actors who worked in movies. But Van said, "Come, now, you're young, you have a family, this is off season in the theater. Isn't five dollars a day coming in better than five dollars a day going out?" I thought it over. I thought, maybe no one will know! . . . And that's how I went into pictures. . . . Van said, "If it rains, we can't work, of course, but you'll receive fifty cents just for coming over." And that's what I did receive for my first day at the studio—fifty cents! In those days you got $2.50 if you just put your make up on and it rained and you couldn't work. And if the handle of the camera so much as turned, you got your $5.00. I never used make-up until I became an extra [much

> later in his career]. But I often made a pass with that powder puff, just to get the $5.00.

Even if Mae had tipped the scales in filmdom's favor, it was Maurice who had to throw away a decade-long stage career for the chance to churn out half-reelers at a local movie factory. By 1907, Vitagraph was producing two pictures a week, each lasting about seven minutes.[34] All the most cherished elements of stagecraft—playwriting, staging, and the craft of acting itself—were scattered to the winds by a medium that, so far, had little use for them. As the shock of the transition wore off, Maurice found himself in the right place at just the right time, not only to better *his* lot but also to give the nascent craft of screen acting its first serious course of instruction.

6

A Lusty, Growing Thing

As he started work for the Vitagraph Company in the summer of 1907, Maurice took a hard look at the way Smith, Blackton, and Rock were making movies and saw ample room for improvement—especially where actors and acting were concerned. Emboldened by the level field he was now playing on, Maurice instantly set about redefining what the screen actor should be and do. It shocked him that actors, even those in the lowly film business, had to perform tasks that had nothing to do with acting, in accordance with Vitagraph's long-standing employment policy. When she wasn't charming moviegoers on screen, Florence Turner, known only as "the Vitagraph Girl," was put to work as the studio's financial officer. "I had to attend to all the business affairs of the concern," she recalled. "I was a sort of handywoman! I paid the staff and artistes, I kept the books, and was clerk, cashier, accountant."[1]

When Florence Lawrence left Vitagraph to join the Biograph Company in 1908, it was partly because they didn't make their actors sew costumes and paint backdrops. William Shea, one of Vitagraph's first actors, said that if "any special 'prop' or scene was wanted, the actors were called upon to make it. Frequently, when a picture was to be filmed, actors in costumes came from all directions, with hammers, some with saws, others with paint brushes."[2] In Vitagraph's *Romeo and Juliet,* the actor playing Romeo, Paul Panzer, had to build his own balcony.

On his first day at work, Maurice was given a hammer and told to join a group of actors busily engaged in building a set. There are several versions of what happened next, all of which have Maurice taking umbrage at what he was being told to do and spouting off accordingly. Despite its embellishments, Helene's account captures the precise moment of the screen actor's birth:

> Maurice surveyed this ignoble scene with flaring nostrils. In cold disdain he rejected the claw hammer offered him by one of the Vitagraph partners. "I," he said, with a roar of choleric indignation, "am an actor, not a carpenter. I will not drive nails!" J. Stuart Blackton laid the hammer away quietly. In his long career as a director and producer he met many crises of temperament, but none with deeper effects on the industry. The other actors saw Maurice get away with it. Blackton recognized the hand of fate. All tools were laid aside, and J. Stuart Blackton hired carpenters—at slightly more than he paid his actors.[3]

Flora Finch, the female half of the movies' first great comedy team, told a similar story—which was, in turn, similar to the one Maurice himself told a Hollywood reporter thirty years after the fact: "In those early days, the actors were supposed to double as scenery movers, prop-men, furniture makers, and odd-job men. I was making 30 dollars a week as an actor—a star. They asked me to join in the chores, and I put my foot down. Said I'd be glad to carry a tray, or anything they wanted, to earn my pay, but if I was earning it as an actor, why, then I'd act and they could give the other jobs to other men."[4]

Actress Edith Storey, who started working for Vitagraph Studios at the age of thirteen, confirmed that Maurice Costello was indeed "the first actor we had who refused to wield a hammer. He insisted that he was an actor, not a carpenter, and soon others followed suit and the profession gained new dignity."[5] Albert E. Smith wrote of the event as a separate encounter between himself and the company's brash new employee. Though the changes Maurice wrought were implemented more slowly than Helene's account suggested, by the end of their meeting, the job description of "screen actor" was effectively set in stone:

> Our actors doubled in brass by helping to build and paint sets—usually those in which they were to appear. For tacking canvas on background frames or sewing costumes, they received twenty dollars a week. For acting, they received five dollars a day. Maurice Costello destroyed this dual policy. He had come to us from the legitimate stage. When we disclosed the terms he replied: "I am an actor. An actor does not build sets."

> There was no haughtiness in his manner, and when he became a reigning favorite, an early day Clark Gable, he wore his success with modesty, charm and intelligence.[6]

What D. W. Griffith did for film direction, then, Maurice did for screen acting: that is, he raised the bar to a higher standard that quickly became the norm. And he did it a year before Griffith, who didn't come to work for Biograph until 1908.[7] By then, Maurice had elevated the position of jack-of-all-trades to the premier status of resident actor.

As Maurice watched his Vitagraph colleagues go to work in front of a camera, he was struck by the disparities between film and stage technique. "The acting looked terribly swift, jerky and unconvincing when it was focused upon the screen," he said. "The first time I saw myself on the films I could have torn my hair out. I kept wondering if I had looked like that through the years that I had been playing in stock. I asked my friends and my family. They were reassuring but the pictures weren't."[8] It was a conspiracy of speed—movement-obsessed filmmakers pushed their actors to give them more action; exhibitors sped up their projectors to fit in more movies.[9] Audiences grew accustomed to the feverish pace of motion pictures—comedies especially, as speed lent a cartoonish aspect that could coax a laugh out of even the most mediocre gag.

At Vitagraph, the high cost of film stock forced its directors to cram as much action as they could onto a strip of celluloid in the shortest possible time. Dolores Costello remembered that as "a little tot" she asked a director why he timed his scenes with a stopwatch. The film itself, he explained, "was more valuable than the actors, and they would rush the actors through the scene to save the film . . . and that was the reason for the quick action. It was not the film in itself . . . it was deliberately to save footage. So dad said 'we will bring in the New York theaters' natural acting, and they just were wild. They thought he was completely mad, but he finally got his own way."[10]

Watching himself on the screen for the first time, Maurice wondered why picture actors shouldn't move like real people moved in real life. "I finally figured out that slow movement of the actors would help in giving the correct effects," he told a reporter in 1914. "When the picture was shown on trial the manager sent for me. I went, thinking I was to have a reprimand for having introduced the novelty. That would have been the way of a theatrical manager. That's where I discovered the first advantage of the motion pictures. The Vitagraph Company made me their first leading man."[11]

Shouldn't these accomplishments—groundbreaking changes that Maurice brought about single-handedly—enshrine him among the movies' first great innovators? Given that his screen colleagues weren't sure from one day to the next what their job would entail—and that Maurice had destroyed this "dual policy"—surely a distinction can be drawn between Maurice and other actors of the period. Then, on the heels of his signature accomplishment, came the creation and implementation of what he called his "new style of slow acting." Others gave him credit for this as well. James Baubie of the *Pittsburgh Press* wrote that Maurice "brought about the slower action of the players, which helped make the pictures natural and not simply a free-for-all race and an exhibition of automatons."[12] Likewise, *Photoplay* called him the "pioneer of the slow-motion style of acting."[13]

The fact that he was well remembered for changing the way screen actors act is crucial when evaluating his legacy. Tireless self-promoter that he was, even Maurice might have shied away from the title "Father of Screen Acting." But if he wasn't, who was? Though he was not the first movie star, technically (Florence Lawrence was the first to be publicly identified), he was the first star, actually. In 1924, *Photoplay* dubbed him "the first recognized star in motion pictures."[14] Gladys Hall, whose career as a fan magazine writer spanned forty years, called him "the First Star, the greatest of the stars of thirty years ago, the Clark Gable of the dear, dead days beyond recall."[15] In 1938, a California society page editor referred to Maurice Costello as "the original movie star of 30 years ago."[16] Considering what stardom became, the Florences could more rightly be termed "pre-stars": as their popularity flared and receded, Maurice's grew to epic proportions. In 1912, the *Motion Picture Story Magazine*'s "Most Popular Player" poll gave him four times as many votes as Lawrence and Turner combined. On the night the awards were presented, his fans stormed the gates of Madison Square Garden. As one enamored female voter lamented: "I've seen him getting married so many times that I don't like to vote for a man that has so many wives, but, nevertheless, here's 11 votes for Maurice Costello."[17]

The *New York Press* declared his face "better known to the public than John Drew's. . . . The name of Maurice Costello on the screen is quite as potent as that of the divine Sarah, and it is doubtful, if put to a vote, that the great Frenchwoman would be preferred as a choice between the two."[18] Whether or not that was true, that he was being compared to Bernhardt is significant. To be mentioned in the same breath as the era's greatest international star, was to have achieved something no other screen actor had even come close to.

The Florences were content to let the studios launch their careers, but Maurice refused to wait for the company wheels to start turning on his behalf; he handed out postcards with his name and face on them at local events and appeared frequently at the studio's "Vitagraph Nights." "I can't say I knew how great it would be, how big," he said in a rare moment of modesty, "but I can say that I sensed a lusty, growing thing. If I hadn't, I wouldn't have given up the stage."[19] Long before he was a star, Maurice was attending local movie functions, trying to make his presence known.

In 1941, he told Gladys Hall that he was the very first actor to demand and receive screen credit—not just for himself but also for his fellow actors. "I was also responsible for having the players' names put on the screen. Finally, after my fifth picture, I delivered an ultimatum: I said, 'unless my name goes on the screen with my next release . . . I am going back to my first love, the theater.'"[20] Whether he was exaggerating to make a point or just exaggerating, the *Los Angeles Times* claimed that "movie actors were always nameless until Costello became the first to be billed under his own name." In a publicity memo, Paramount's "Teet" Carle touted him as the screen's first "name" star.[21] Given his own faulty timeline, Maurice couldn't have done what he said he did, at least not when he said he did it. He made his fifth movie several years before the company began putting his or anyone else's name on the screen. But picture actors *were* billed on exterior signs and lobby cards, so maybe his claim wasn't that far off the mark.

Of course, without the Vitagraph Company, Maurice would have spent the rest of his working life as a traveling actor. The company's tireless spirit of innovation, coupled with the partners' dogged determination to sell tickets, had been the secrets of its success.[22] Before Maurice joined the company, Vitagraph had pioneered cartoon and object animation (advanced versions of Blackton's "lightning sketches"), fast-paced comedies, biblical epics, and also classical dramas, with a special emphasis on Shakespeare. In *A Mid-Winter Night's Dream; or Little Joe's Luck*, the studio blended comedy, fantasy, and animation, capped off with a bit of the Bard.

Maurice couldn't forget he was part of a cohesive, hard-working team. By 1907 the studio's output of two films per week was falling well short of demand.[23] Orders were months behind, forcing cast and crew to work frantically and cooperatively to increase supply. As this was his last chance to "make good" (which Mae no doubt kept reminding him), Maurice had to keep pace with the company's shooting schedule.

Probably the earliest of his extant films is Vitagraph's absurdly short, but oddly endearing version of *Midsummer Night's Dream,* filmed in 1909. In its seven-minute rendition of Shakespeare's roughly two-hour play, the company (which now included six-year-old Dolores and three-year-old Helene) is mostly seen frolicking out of doors, showing the same "jerky and unconvincing" movements that Maurice had objected to early on. Not surprisingly, his own performance is comparatively restrained, conforming as he was to his own "slow motion" method.

The Costello's transient status kept them under the official radar until respectability finally caught up with them in the summer of 1910. Census takers paid the family a visit in June, when for the first time they were sedentary enough to merit a listing in the Brooklyn city directory.[24] As Maurice rose into the front ranks of screen actors, his salary kept pace. He moved his wife and daughters into their first real home—the bow-fronted brick row house at 1769 East Fourteenth Street. Until then, they had occupied a succession of transient dwellings rented by the week. Thanks to her father's recently acquired affluence, three-year-old Helene would have a markedly different childhood than her older sister. That she was spared the abject poverty Dolores suffered early on, had much to do with who they became as adults.

At last, Maurice no longer had to travel to stay in show business. What stage actors found especially appealing about working in movies, besides the money, was that "it required no tedious rehearsals, no traveling, no wearisome night hours," as Helene observed. "Cameras could turn only when there was sunlight to illuminate the setting."[25] The prospect of sitting around the dinner table every night had been inconceivable before the start of Maurice's film career. Now, theoretically at least, a normal domestic life could be had.

What Mae could not have envisioned while she was pushing Maurice to give film acting a try, was the cataclysmic effect he would have on untold thousands of American women. How could she have foreseen it?

Superstars like Rudolph Valentino knew what their stardom would entail long before they were stars, but the Costellos wouldn't know what hit them. Years earlier, Mae had asked him sarcastically when she was going to see his name on a marquee—not thinking for a minute it might actually happen.[26] She had meant a *single* marquee, a new theater each day as Maurice traveled from city to city—not hundreds of movie houses across the country showing his name and face to thousands of new filmgoers simultaneously. Maurice would have no idea how to handle his own stardom, much less how to placate the perennially disgruntled Mae, as his exploding career kicked her to the sidelines as no stage wife had been kicked before.

In the fall of 1910, the deluge of fan mail became an open love affair—although the majority of his fans had no idea just who they were in love with. "I was known to the public only as 'Dimples,' sometimes 'Curly,'" Maurice said. "Oh yes, right from the beginning it came in, by the hundreds of letters a week. I did foresee, then, that there was a public, an avid, eager public for moving picture actors."[27] By midyear his signature dimples, combined with studio publicity efforts, had stoked the public's curiosity well past the point of containment. "In those days, all letters written to me aimed at one point: 'Who are you?' they all asked, 'what is your name?'"[28] Because there were no screen credits as yet, and Maurice Costello's name had not appeared in print, outside of Brooklyn he was virtually unknown. Local playgoers-turned-movie fans recognized Maurice from his years in stock, thanks to his earlier attempts at self-promotion. But a torrent of female adoration was about to wash over him in unprecedented fashion.

On October 5, the *New York Dramatic Mirror* became the first publication to put a name to the face—which appears, sans dimples, in a large, grainy photograph at the bottom of the page. Below it read the caption: "Maurice Costello, whose work as a local favorite . . . has brought him late eminence as a leading man in juvenile and heavy characters, has newly distinguished himself as a star and feature in the Vitagraph 'life portrayals' which have made him known in all quarters of the globe. He is a valued member of the regular stock company of the Vitagraph players."[29]

A fully orchestrated campaign to push Maurice into the limelight was under way. A month after his name appeared in print, just the mention of it was enough to fill a Brooklyn auditorium for three sold-out shows. *Motion Picture World,* a Blackton publication, made the most of it:

A VITAGRAPH NIGHT WITH MAURICE COSTELLO
AS THE GUEST AT THE FULTON AUDITORIUM, BROOKLYN

"At the Fulton Auditorium . . . last Tuesday evening," the magazine's *Man about Town* reported on November 26, "about 1600 people attended the three performances and reception at the 'Vitagraph Night' given to Maurice Costello. About three hundred persons were unable to gain admittance. After he had been introduced by the Vitagraph Company's representative, Mr. Costello made a very interesting and witty address in which he thanked all for the cordial response to the announcement of his name and gave them an insight into some of the features of the art of motion picture acting, its difficulties and its inspiration."[30]

The Florences had recently been named—Florence Lawrence in a publicity stunt in March, Florence Turner a few months later. Vitagraph knew the time had come to introduce its first male star to the moviegoing public. Maurice's name and face began popping up in newspapers and magazines, at first in conjunction with its Vitagraph Night gatherings held at local venues. An article in the *Nickelodeon* lauded various aspects of his on- and off-screen behavior, praising the valor and horsemanship he had shown while appearing in a cowboy film on the streets of Flatbush: "He was riding clad in Wild West make-up . . . on his milk white 'Arabian steed' when a runaway [horse] came dashing at frantic speed in his direction. With great skill and coolness he wheeled his horse towards the approaching animal, grabbed it by the halter, and brought it to a standstill."[31]

Two of the earliest film magazines, the *Nickelodeon* and the *Film Index,* ran studio-vetted inserts, to the satisfaction of his information-hungry fans: "Mr. Maurice Costello made a quick trip to his native city, Pittsburg [*sic*], Pa., to visit his mother, whom he had not seen for three years. His reception at his old homestead, he says, reminded him of motion pictures in which he has often portrayed the long absent son or the return of the prodigal."[32]

One can only imagine what his mother, who had denounced his choice of occupations, was making of her son's current success. During their visit did she admonish him for working in a profession that her church considered highly immoral? Two decades later, when the Catholic Church formed the Legion of Decency to renew its attack on show business, it went after the film industry in particular. If Maurice's half sisters Mary and Nellie, twenty-one and twenty-five, respectively, were like thousands of young women in 1910, they were beside themselves with excitement at the news of Maurice's visit.[33]

Several years earlier, the Coinnesses had vacated their Soho tenement, where Maurice lived cheek by jowl with Ellen's seven boarders, and had moved into the brick residence at 2020 Tustin Street, a block to the south.[34] William Coinness had come up in the world, but only as far as the few extra dollars in his pay packet could take him. Ellen no longer had to take in paying guests, at least—for the first time in decades she would not have to share her house with strangers. Though William was given pay raises, he still couldn't afford to move his family to a better neighborhood. For reasons unknown, Maurice didn't help them financially—then or ever. While the Costellos continued to move upward through a series of increasingly affluent neighborhoods, the Coinnesses stayed where they were.

After years of stony silence, Maurice and his wife's stepfather still hadn't settled their differences, though the Treshams and the Costellos lived just a few miles from each other. Maurice seems not to have been on good terms with any of the adult members of his family—even Mae—as what he called his "Great Days" began. Maurice returned home to find his name quickly becoming a household word—not just in Flatbush, but wherever moving pictures were being shown.[35]

7

Great Days

Considering how far they had come, they should have been headed toward a place of redemption and renewal, where Maurice and Mae could have put the struggles of the past behind them and rejoiced that all their hard work was finally paying off. In February 1911, Vitagraph filmed *A Tale of Two Cities* at its sprawling facility in Flatbush—America's first modern movie backlot—with Maurice playing the role of Sidney Carton.

It was the company's most ambitious project to date. Gone were the flimsy backdrops and crude-looking scrims of cinema's early days. Multiple flats gave depth and perspective to the streets of revolutionary Paris, along with a heightened degree of authenticity. For a movie company used to cranking out one-reelers, *A Tale of Two Cities* was a historic departure. It took an unheard-of three weeks to film it, and for an entire week the studio worked on nothing else.[1] With a running time of about fifty minutes, the finished product took up three reels of film. Movies of the period generally ran about a third as long; so, to avoid overtaxing the audience's attention span, Vitagraph chopped the picture into three parts. Also this allowed them to charge three separate admissions.

"The public simply rushed to see it," said G. H. Smith, Albert's brother, because "when it came on the market there was nothing else like it."[2] Seeking to expand its business overseas, the studio shipped hundreds of copies of the film into European markets. By the end of the year, *A Tale of Two Cities* had appeared in more than two hundred theaters in Britain alone. Not only was Maurice's popularity soaring at home, he was an international star as well.

The company's investment in Maurice Costello had paid off exponentially. The partners' shrewd handling of their nascent heartthrob, giving in to his early demands—though they hadn't been entirely sure it was in their best interests to do so—gave them the most popular star the film business had seen up to that time. They let him rise on his own power: from ensemble scenes early on, to featured status as one of the stars of the studio's high-brow "Life Portrayals." Sporting lofty titles such as *Orestes, Electra,* and *St. Elmo,* these were the cream of Vitagraph's crop.[3] Maurice had ridden them to the brink of superstardom; now, *A Tale of Two Cities* would push him over the edge.

"Whatever the script called for I did it," Maurice said in 1941. "We had no stand-ins, no doubles. We were our own stunt men. When I think of the crazy chances I took, the fights under water, the horses I rode, the falls and climbs."[4] Previously he had explained: "In 1910, I broke into the 'big money.' . . . Mrs. Costello and I had been very happy, but now, with stardom, unhappiness crept into our home. I loved my wife and babies but my domestic life went from bad to worse."[5]

In fact, Maurice and Mae were *not* happy before that. Compared to the downturn in their relationship that occurred following the release of *A Tale of Two Cities,* maybe it just seemed like they had been. Before Vitagraph came to the Costello's financial rescue in 1907, their problems were mostly monetary. From then on, the more money they made, the worse their marriage became. According to Albert E. Smith, it started with the bushels of mail Maurice opened "with the help of his two little daughters of future movie fame, Helene, then about five, and Dolores, a few years older. The fan mail of the day was no different, expressions of undying love and desire set forth in soft prose and murmuring poetry. 'Cos' took the letters humorously, but they began to weigh on Mrs. Costello, but in time the poor woman turned to more serious accusations as Cos's popularity led to telephone calls from star-struck adolescents."[6] Maurice carried two fountain pens and a pencil in case he ran out of ink, to keep up with the daily crush of autograph seekers.[7] Once he saw a crowd of men, women, and children race to retrieve his discarded cigar butt.

As soon as he could, Maurice made sure that Mae got her share of the glory. She had not always stood with him, but she had always stood by him. By early 1912, there was little Maurice could have asked for that the company wouldn't have gladly given him. So when he suggested bringing Mae into the fold, they could hardly say no. His daughters were veteran screen actresses by then, having appeared in movies from the time Helene was a toddler and Dolores was six. Whenever young children were needed for a scene, Maurice offered their services for the extra income they brought in. "I shall never forget my first appearance in front of a camera," Dolores said in 1927. "I recall very distinctly that I was dressed in rags. . . . Suddenly very tall men appeared and took our father away. I became white with fright, and ran off the stage crying hysterically."[8]

By age six, Helene (still known as Helen) was a star in her own right, having appeared with "Jean, the Vitagraph Dog," John Bunny and Flora Finch (the movies' first popular comedy team), and the company's newest leading lady, Clara Kimball Young. Helene played opposite her father in *Lulu's Doctor*—she as the precocious Lulu, he as the kindly doctor who repairs her doll's broken leg. Taking the screen name Georgia Maurice, Mae joined the Vitagraph roster in 1911, and the first family of picture actors officially came into being.[9]

With the Costellos thriving in ways that would have seemed unimaginable to them a few years earlier—and with Mae herself appearing in such top-notch fare as *Her Crowning Glory*—how could things have gone so terribly wrong? In her memoirs, Helene referred diplomatically to Maurice's Irish temper, while avoiding any direct mention of his drinking. But he *was* drinking—habitually and to excess. Albert E. Smith blamed Maurice's calamities on Mae's jealousy—failing to acknowledge that it was actually the Vitagraph Company that initiated his decline, with the announcement that the screen's first great lover was, in fact, a husband and father of two. For a woman in Gary, Indiana, hearing the news was "the saddest moment of her young life."[10] Another fan offered a pair of couplets:

Now first, there's Maurice Costello
I guess he's a rattling good fellow;
But Gee! There is no show for me,
He with a wife, and kids two or three![11]

"We know that Maurice drank," said Helene's daughter, Deirdre. "Dolores was never without a derisive mention about his drinking." Her father, the painter and matte artist Lee Le Blanc, knew Maurice well and said that he habitually "drank and cussed."[12]

The second of the two recorded incidents of domestic violence that occurred at the height of Maurice's fame was, by his own admission, alcohol related. Dolores shared the details of the first altercation with Deirdre, who in turn shared it for posterity almost a hundred years later: "Mae and Maurice were arguing. They stood up and confronted each other. According to Dolores, that's when Maurice slapped Mae. Helene jumped to the floor on all fours, crawled manically round in circles, barking like a dog. Immediately the bickering stopped and everyone stared at the little girl on the floor. It took several minutes to get her to stop barking and calmed down."[13]

Fortunately for the Costellos and their careers, the first incident never became public. The second, however, proved too damning even for Mae to sweep under the rug.

As best as it can be measured, Maurice was the most famous actor in the world in the summer of 1912. He was internationally known, thanks to Vitagraph's ever-broadening footprint overseas, which reached as far as the Netherlands. French comedian Max Linder was a bigger star in Europe, but American moviegoers barely knew who he was. He received 1,092 votes (thirty-eight more than Jean the Vitagraph Dog[14]) compared to Maurice's 430,816 in the Popular Player Contest.

In the greatest year of Maurice's stardom, it took two men to drag a single bag of his fan mail through the studio gates. Female fans deluged him with love letters that ranged from the elegiac to the feeble-minded:

Here's to Maurice Costello,
He's my favorite you bet,
And a million million votes
I hope he'll get.[15]

Despite his growing paunch and the rapid graying of his hair, Maurice set the standard for screen idolatry in the early 1910s. Given the dearth of leading men who might otherwise have usurped his position, the first movie fans had to make do with a stellar pair of dimples and a head of thick, curly hair. But looks weren't everything. Fellow Vitagraph player Leo Delaney bore enough of a resemblance to Maurice to play Sidney Carton look-alike Charles Darnay in *A Tale of Two Cities,* yet he received only 6,380 votes in the Popular Player contest.[16] Unlike Delaney, Maurice transcended the limitations of the new medium with the sheer force of his presence and personality. He wasn't the only film actor to accomplish this: leading ladies Florence Turner and Clara Kimball Young could as easily captivate an audience. But as audiences demanded more sophisticated forms of storytelling, Maurice fit his talents to the times he had lucked into, bringing to the developing craft a penchant for innovation unlike that of any other actor. In his decade-long career as a stage performer—from tent shows to repertoire, from vaudeville to stock—he'd played every imaginable part, from walk-ons to lead characters spouting oceans of dialogue, using every trick of the actor's trade. With nothing left to prove to his bosses or to Mae, or to anyone, Maurice put his qualifications to the test and changed the movie business forever.

In the early teens, the studio gave him the opportunity to direct as well as act. Helene claimed that Maurice had directed *A Tale of Two Cities,* but this wasn't the case.[17] It took Vitagraph two more years to give him carte blanche behind the camera. Until then he codirected, mostly alongside his mentor Van Dyke Brooke. But by early 1913, he was one of the screen's first well-known actor-directors, if not *the* first. D.W. Griffith had done both but hadn't become famous as an actor.[18] Vitagraph's Van Dyke Brooke and William V. Ranous also acted and directed, but Maurice's stardom made his directorial accomplishments much better known. By 1915, *Motography* magazine called him "the popular director-star of the company."[19]

No other film showcases Maurice's multiple talents—as codirector, actor, comedian, and screen heartthrob—like *The Picture Idol,* which truly *is* all about him. Clara Kimball Young plays Beth Ward, a starstruck schoolgirl who is having as hard a time focusing on her studies as she is on the attentions of a handsome classmate.[20] She's fallen head over heels for the newly minted phenomenon soon to be known as the movie star—whose photograph she clutches to her bosom each night while lying in bed. Kissing it tenderly, she slips it between her head and the pillow before she falls asleep.

She resolves to meet him at the earliest opportunity. As she passes him on the street, the shot of the effulgent actor—dressed to turn-of-the-century perfection in hat, topcoat, and cane—breezing past the tiny, waifish Young, is an early screen gem. Unaware that she's been following him, he tosses his cigar butt and Beth plucks it off the ground as a souvenir (as had actually happened to Maurice).[21] Underacting to perfection, Maurice plays himself—a larger-than-life movie star—but in his off-hours, after the cameras have stopped grinding. He's so good at it that distinguishing the actor from the actor's impersonation of the actor is virtually impossible.

Seeing the star in person pushes Beth further off the deep end. When she's not following him around town, she's daydreaming about him to the exclusion of everything else. When the actor realizes what's going on, he confers with the girl's parents, as all agree the infatuation must end. In one of the great food scenes of film history, he arrives at Beth's house to have dinner with the family, then does everything possible to disgust her with his uncouth behavior. Young's horrified responses to Maurice's deplorable table manners are both torturous and hilarious. Her revulsion mounts as he shovels food into his mouth, talks incessantly, grabs food from her father's fork, and eats with his knife. When he's finished, the picture idol wipes his mouth on his sleeve with a violent sweep that sends Beth bolting out of the room.[22] Those seated at the table guffaw in triumph, but they're not out of the woods yet. While bidding the family goodnight, the actor reverts to his charming self and Beth falls for him all over again.

It's up to Western drama's ancient preoccupation with men in drag to get the actor out of trouble. He dresses a male colleague (Leo Delaney) in women's clothes, finds four children (two of them Dolores and Helene) to masquerade as his own, and introduces them to Beth as his family. Seeing the hopelessness of the situation, she tears his picture in half.

Compared to *A Tale of Two Cities*, which was considered state-of-the-art in 1911, *The Picture Idol* seems like a whole new medium. The first is essentially a series of animated tableaux, populated by stiff-jointed actors who look as if they were herded into the frame. The second, filmed a year later, is in almost every respect a modern film. The actors move, not for movement's sake, but in the way people naturally move and act. When projected at normal cranking speed, the film isn't jerky or sped up. The pace is fluid and unhurried, thanks to Maurice's slowing of the tempo early on. The action is comedic but never slapstick, funny without seeming contrived or exaggerated. It ranks among the most watchable films of the early silent era.

In *The Picture Idol*, we encounter Maurice at the height of his fame and success, both as seasoned actor and international film star. He brings subtlety and nuance (rarities in film comedy even now) to a film that might otherwise have devolved into the usual displays of face-making one associates with silent comedians. Maurice commands his scenes but never steals them, deferring to his Vitagraph costars at every opportunity. Indeed, he doesn't appear to be acting at all, but simply being. Onscreen he's bold and self-confident, yet affable and easy-going in the manner of such later stars as Clark Gable and Cary Grant, for whom Maurice clearly paved the way.[23] For these reasons especially, long after he had outlived his usefulness to the film business, he was remembered as "the first of the old motion picture stars."[24]

Vitagraph wasn't the first studio to make movies overseas: its archrival, the Kalem Company, brought actors and equipment to Egypt to film *The Fighting Dervishes of the Desert* in early 1912, and there had been others before them.[25] But the sort of marathon expedition Vitagraph's James Young had in mind was, and perhaps still is, unprecedented in the annals of moviemaking.

On December 4, 1912, the Costellos, their two children, and seven of their movie colleagues departed Brooklyn by train to begin a forty-thousand-mile trip around the world. The company took seven days to reach San Francisco, where they boarded the steamship *Tenyo Maru* bound for Hawaii.[26] "It was an experiment for this ambulatory studio," Albert E. Smith recalled, "an attempt to capture the flavor of the Old World in a series of pictures. We provided the troupe with a full portfolio of stories—mostly spy, smuggling and cloak and dagger melodramas. We gave them a director and a writer, then sent them on their way, principally to Japan, China, India, Egypt, Italy, France and England."[27] So that the filmmakers could process their rushes daily, Young devised a portable film laboratory complete with drying drums, tanks, and chemicals that could be hauled with the company's baggage from location to location.[28]

Thanks to Maurice's travel ledger, the company's personnel and its itinerary were painstakingly recorded for posterity. Joining the Costellos were James Young and his wife, Clara Kimball Young; veteran actor William V. Ranous and his wife, Doris Thompson; Albert Smith's older brother and company business manager, W. S. Smith; writer-director Eugene Mullin; and cameraman Harry Keepers. When Albert Smith said he "gave them a writer," he meant Mullin and Young, who each would make story contributions. Except for Keepers, all had to appear in front of the camera.[29]

After a day of sightseeing in Honolulu, the company continued its westward course. On the twenty-fifth, Maurice donned Santa Claus garb to participate in the ship's Christmas festivities. Five days later, almost a month after they had left New York, they arrived in Japan.[30] During the travelers' month-long stay in Yokohama, Maurice directed and starred in *The Wrath of Osaka,* a tragic tale that manages to end happily. They shot local footage for a series of Vitagraph travelogues that showed points of local interest, street scenes, and an encounter with the Yokohama fire department. Eugene Mullin directed Maurice in *Jack's Chrysanthemum,* a cheerier version of Vitagraph's 1910 film *The Love of Chrysanthemum,* which also starred Maurice. In the first film, his character jilts a Japanese girl after his American wife arrives unexpectedly. In the second, instead of being abandoned à la Madame Butterfly, Jack asks Chrysanthemum to return with him to America.

Before they left Yokohama, the company made a side trip to film themselves playing themselves in *The Vitagraphers in Kara Kura.* As Young told reporter Peter Wade, the company's biggest challenge was finding suitable costumes. "The 'flying squadron' were in deep despair," Wade wrote, "a full Japanese costume is a thing of months in the building. But Clara Young's four-foot hairdresser, Toki Arai, had taken a fancy to the pretty Vitagraph lead and she was talkative and knew a society lady who might consent to part with some of her clothes, and the lady knew a high *samurai* who might sell some of his. And thus the problem was solved—society is hard up even in Japan."[31]

After visits to Kobe, Nagasaki, and Shanghai, the company arrived in Hong Kong on a second ship, the *Shinyo Maru,* to begin a two-week stay. "They were met at the waterfront by a zealous Chinese exhibitor, who had been a week in getting ready a luncheon of welcome to them. The luncheon consisted of Chinese luxuries . . . jellied eggs fifty years old, dog meat, sharks' fins, snake meat, bird's nest soup and fried cattle eyes!"[32] In China, they churned out another pair of one-reelers, *The Taming of Betty* and *Love and Botany,* before they left for Burma on a third ship, the *Himalaya.* On February 23, 1913, they checked into the Royal Hotel (which Maurice rated as only "fair") in Rangoon for eleven days of moviemaking and sightseeing. While filming *The Maid of Mandalay,* which featured Clara Kimball Young as a Burmese girl, cast and crew were ejected from the gilded Shwa Dagon temple for forgetting to take off their shoes.[33]

Crossing the Indian Ocean, they landed in Calcutta, which served as a backdrop for two more films: *The Hindoo Charm,* with James Young playing a snake charmer, and *The Spirit of the Orient.* A sixty-hour train trip brought them overland in a tiny railroad car, in which they baked during the day and froze at night. When they ran out of water, the company "sucked oranges with the gluttony of baboons."[34] In Mumbai, they filmed the ending to *On Their Wedding Eve,* directed by Maurice, about a couple who have a lovers' tiff on their wedding night and set off in opposite directions. As fate would have it, they bump into each other on a bridge in Mumbai, settle their differences, and live happily ever after.

Maurice and Mae were courting disaster by bringing their children along. First, they were subjected to the brutal, waterless trip across India. Then, during the filming of *Cupid versus Suffrage* in Cairo, Mae almost lost Helene. "Mrs. Costello, the two girls, and another woman were resting at the hotel," Helene wrote in the third person. "Mae decided to go see the Citadel, a noted tourist attraction. They hired four donkeys with donkey boys and set out. The way led through a native quarter, and several times, Mae had to speak sharply to the boy leading Helene's donkey. He persisted in lagging behind the party. The streets were so narrow that two loaded camels had difficulty in passing, and a little side alley wandered off in all directions."[35]

Mae turned away, and, when she looked back, Helene and the donkey boy were gone. Luckily, she spotted the would-be kidnapper's heel a split second before it disappeared around a corner—otherwise Helene would have vanished into the maze of streets. "Suddenly, as from a distance, [she] heard her mother scream. She looked around and saw she was alone with the donkey-boy, who was trying to belabor the donkey into a trot down a narrow, noisome street." Mae gave chase and ended up stopping the would-be kidnapper by reaching into her blouse, as if to grab a weapon. The donkey boy fled, but was chased down and turned over to the police. "She was not frightened at the time, until it was all over with, but now that her own daughter is that age the memory torments her."[36]

The privations of the trip were beginning to tell on the travelers' dispositions. Tensions mounted after weeks of living and filming together in close quarters. Tempers flared in the intense heat. There were some days when the wives refused to work.[37] Maurice the diarist charted the downward trajectory of his and his wife's relationship: by the time they reached Cairo, they were barely speaking to each other.[38]

The Vitagraphers next left for Italy—Brindisi on the east coast, then Rome. There they joined forces with Cines Studios for twelve days of nonstop moviemaking, filming in some of the city's grandest locations. To Maurice's astonishment, his stardom had preceded him. Adoring Romans mobbed him in the streets. "In Rome his carriage was smothered with garlands and bouquets heaped into it by the throngs," wrote fan-magazine writer Rosalind Shaffer.[39] "In Italy, my god they went mad," Dolores recalled. "In Rome, I can remember as a child . . . he appeared at the theater, they [had their] backs . . . to the buildings throwing gardenias and violets at him."[40] A surviving letter attests to the intensity of the passions he aroused in his Italian female fans—one especially, whose affections Maurice appears to have egged on as their train departed for Venice:

> I well noticed the movement of your finger on the lips before leaving the large hall of the Depot and caught that kiss as a compensation for all my sufferings, and when your arm surrounded my waist, I thought I had reached Paradise. I saw nobody. I only felt your arm that drew me towards you. I was afraid the immense immeasurable joy that pervaded me and made me suffer so, would come forth from all pores—would be visible to everybody. The sight of your adorable wife helped to . . . suppress the cry of joy that came out of my soul. You did not seem to notice the struggle of my poor heart. But when you took my hand and stooped down to me, when I felt your breath passing over my face like a caress, I would have wished to press your beloved head between my hands asking from your eyes another look like the one you threw on me the moment when, at the Cinematograph, I tended you my visiting card. That look told me that you have understood me. But oh my! I would do all this with my thought only. Only in my thought. I could kiss those eyes and confound my soul with yours. The train was about to start and after having sent me kisses together with your wife and your dear little angels you lifted secretly your hand to your mouth and—I felt your lips on mine. Slowly, slowly the train moved off, leaving me behind in a state of despair that I hardly know how to describe.[41]

In Venice, the company filmed *The Lonely Princess* ("an unusually strong, dramatic picture," Wade wrote). They spent their final days on the continent in Paris, before heading home aboard the SS *Amsterdam.* Having "girdled the world" in less than six months, they arrived in New York on June 2.[42] They had made history as the first American movie company to film in multiple overseas locations, many of them in distant lands that had never before seen a movie camera.

8

Smashing Things

Even if the events of November 24, 1913, had never occurred, Maurice's movie-star status would have come under fire from every point of the filmic compass by the end of the year. In early October, after months of advance publicity, the votes were counted and the results of the second-annual Popular Player Contest were in. The news likely staggered him: the screen's most popular actor of 1912 had been demoted to thirteenth place, sandwiched ignominiously between Pathé's Crane Wilbur and the Lubin Company's Ormi Hawley.[1] How had this happened? Shouldn't his trip around the world have only increased his popularity? His stock as actor and director had never been higher—so how had his standing among moviegoers fallen so much lower?

Maurice discovered that unlike the fame of legendary stage actors, movie stardom was fleeting. Theater legends like John Drew and Ethel Barrymore might rule the stage for decades, but not so the film actor. Movie fans were fiercely loyal, as it turned out, but only until the next glittering presence flickered across the screen. Not coincidentally, it was during the time of his plunging popularity that Maurice started to drink more and control his temper less. Three days before Thanksgiving, behavior that had gone on sporadically behind closed doors, probably for years, burst into the open in the most career-damaging way imaginable. On November 25, the day after the incident occurred, the matter of Maurice's violent behavior went irreversibly public.

Knowing a front-page story when it saw one, the *Brooklyn Daily Eagle* pulled no punches: "Actor Costello No Hero to Wife," the headline blared. Even worse was what came after:

> Maurice Costello, 36 years old . . . the leading man of the Vitagraph Company, who is known all over the world by moving

> pictures enthusiasts, was arraigned in the Coney Island Court this morning before Magistrate Geismar, charged with beating his wife, May [*sic*]. On recommendation of the wife, the charge was changed to that of disorderly conduct, and Costello was placed on probation, in charge of Mrs. Mira Hughes. In her affidavit Mrs. Costello stated that her husband . . . came home early yesterday morning and, without cause or justification, beat her about the body with his clenched fists, knocked her down, then kicked her in the forehead.[2]

Maurice and Mae stood side by side in front of the magistrate as the charges were read, casting sorrowful glances at each other. Sobbing in the rear of the courtroom were ten-year-old Dolores and seven-year-old Helene. When Judge Geismar asked the defendant if he had anything to say, he turned to his daughters and wept. Shrugging his shoulders, Maurice replied only that he had been drinking at the time. "Mae then asked the Magistrate to reduce the charge," the *Eagle* reported, "as she did not want her husband to go to jail and lose his position. 'All I want, your honor,' she said, 'is that my husband stop his excessive drinking.' The charge was suspended, and the 'movie man' was placed on probation."[3]

Also in the courtroom that morning was Pop Rock, Vitagraph's now-retired managing partner. Whether he was there for moral support or to assess the damage his star had inflicted on an industry as yet untouched by scandal, can only be surmised. Likely it was for both reasons. Years later, Albert E. Smith claimed that he had always held Maurice in the highest regard, both personally and professionally: "There was no haughtiness in his manner, and when he became a reigning favorite, an early day Clark Gable, he wore his success with modesty, charm, and intelligence."

At least he waited until the probationary period was up before he committed his next violent offense. On Easter Sunday 1914, Maurice and his daughters were motoring through Brooklyn when they arrived at a train crossing. Before the advent of safety gates and flashing lights, railroads hired flagmen to stop traffic in busy, urban areas when a train came through. As the Costellos reached the crossing, either the flagman wasn't doing his job or his warnings went unheeded—because if Maurice hadn't heard the train speeding toward them, he would have driven straight into its path.[4] "Both men admitted the narrow escape caused a war of words," reported the *Eagle*. "According to Costello, the flagman became abusive and finally used a vile epithet." With his daughters present, he "forgot everything else, and slapped the flagman's face with the back of his hand."[5]

The flagman mulled things over for a day or so before he reported the incident to the police. Maurice was again arrested and released on bond. On April 21, he was arraigned in the same courtroom where he had faced Mae's battery charge six months earlier. He was found guilty and placed on probation.[6]

Bruises heal, but film careers did not, as Mae discovered in the wake of the altercation that both hastened and assured her husband's demise. Had she known then what the ramifications of calling the police would be, would she have called them anyway?

Albert E. Smith put the blame on Mae's jealousy more than he did on Maurice's abusive behavior: "The atmosphere of suspicion provoked quarrels, then one day she pressed a charge of wife beating against him. Costello was arrested, and with the arrest went the film career of the most famous idol of the hour."[7] But the fault lay not so much in their quarrels, as it did in Maurice's drinking. After all, he had admitted as much at the trial.

Meanwhile, as Maurice continued to lose altitude in the polls, a new generation of male stars was horning in on his territory. In October 1913, blue-eyed, muscle-bound Francis X. Bushman won fifth prize in that year's Popular Player Contest, continuing his steady rise through the ranks. In second place, thirty-year-old Earle Williams rocketed to fame while Maurice and company were still circling the globe.[8] The lantern-jawed King Baggot came in fiftieth, but he would jump into seventeenth place the following year—three ahead of Maurice.

By 1914, the Vitagraph Company was no longer featuring Maurice as its principal male actor, though he was still one of the company's most visible leading men. Though most of the plum roles were going to other players, he was far from being washed up. By then an established director as well as a key actor, Maurice might have buffeted the changes—most importantly, the industry's ongoing move to the opposite coast—if scandal hadn't derailed him. In February, a female reporter caught up with him on a rainy day in Flatbush, hoping to drum up something newsworthy.[9] Minerva Martin of the *Movie Pictorial* did everything she could to get Maurice to discuss his "troubles," as she called them, but without success. Disarming her affably, he replied: "Didn't you know that an Irishman's troubles never last longer than the telling of them?"[10]

Charming as it was, the retort couldn't have been further from the truth. Maurice's troubles were pervasive and ongoing—not just as an actor, but now as a director. "It was only this morning," he told Martin, "that I came down here in the best of spirits and found insurrection. A lady had gone militant. She wouldn't play the role I had assigned her in the way I wanted it played. The rebellion was the last scene in several acts of similar import. You see, the lady had been playing in the Broadway theater and she hadn't come down to earth. So I had to let her go."[11] Years later, Smith claimed that Maurice wasn't "cut out for the work" of a director, and by then, maybe he wasn't.[12]

Maurice's response to the ongoing collapse of his film career in the spring of 1915 was to buy an expensive piece of residential property at the mouth of the East River. The Bayside, Long Island estate consisted of a turn-of-the-century brick house, a lake, a wooded area, and a private beach.[13] He hired a butler, governesses for the girls, and a chauffeur. He bought a Lozier limousine and a small yacht. He indulged his passion for automobiles by purchasing several of them.

With a showplace to call their own, the Costellos welcomed a stream of notable visitors. "Pearl White breezed in and out," Helene recalled, "a flaming redhead driving a yellow Stutz Bearcat roadster. Diving from the Costello pier, she saved a drowning person. . . . While Jim Corbett and a whole procession of handsome actors frequented the home, [Helene] silently worshipped Wallace Beery from afar."[14] Among the procession was a rising star in two arenas: by 1914, John Barrymore was among the first actors to juggle stage and screen careers with equal dexterity—an accomplishment that one day would transform each of the Costellos' lives in dramatically different ways.[15]

Maurice took the girls out of public school and enrolled Helene at Lady Cliff Academy in Peekskill, New York. Dolores would not be going with her.[16] She had never been apart from her mother and the idea of leaving Mae terrified her. "I was sent to school," Dolores recalled, "but I hated it so violently that my mother was compelled to get a tutor . . . so I would not have to attend."[17] No doubt she would have been better off at boarding school, as it would have spared her the trauma of watching her parents' lives come apart during this troubled period. In a diary he kept a decade later, Maurice bemoaned the state of his marriage, both then and earlier.

"Mrs C began nagging at me," he wrote. "She became unbearable. Called me everything—Here's where she cracked her whip. Claimed she wanted a Divorce when we lived in Bayside, L. I. What a damn liar she is."[18]

In person, as in their letters, each spouse habitually goaded, taunted, and tormented the other. Sandwiched between periods of relative calm, their conflicts might go on for months, die down, and pick up again where they left off. Mae's letters are rife with caustic and deprecating remarks, usually in response to equally provocative comments by Maurice. She decried his suspicious nature and his ongoing failings as a provider. He frequently accused her of being unfaithful. Yet only rarely does Mae mention his drinking, and never as a bone of contention. There isn't a hint of fear or reticence in her letters—she writes what she pleases, with no apparent regard for the consequences. Maybe her husband's violent outbursts were too few and far between to frighten her into submission.

Even little Helene wasn't afraid to stand up to her father when the situation warranted. In 2015, her daughter Deirdre wrote of an encounter between Maurice and her mother, who was then about five years old:

> Maurice had been on a trip. He dropped his trunk and carpet bag in the bedroom, came out and sat down in his chair to read a newspaper. Dolores told me she thought that Mae was in the kitchen fixing dinner; she herself was on the floor playing with her dolls. Immediately, as grandpa sat, Helene, excited to see him jumped in his lap and wanted him to tell her about his adventures. But instead he was irritated.
>
> "For God's sake, Helene, I've just come home from a long, beastly trip and I want to relax a while and read the paper. Get down and play with your toys."
>
> Instead, her sensitivity scorched to the quick, Helene jumped off his lap and tromped down the hallway where she grabbed her father's carpet bag and a toothbrush from one of the drawers in his trunk and headed back to the living room. Plunking down the bag she had dragged in one hand, and brandishing a toothbrush in the other, she stopped in front of her father, scolding, "Here! Go away! Go to hell! And next time, bring ice cream!"[19]

Mae's vigilance was certainly warranted where Maurice's flagging career prospects were concerned. As his popularity dwindled, so did his income, a large part of which came from personal appearances.[20] The Costellos were holding their own in the popularity polls—Maurice lagged behind, but remained in close proximity to 1915's dual contest winners, Earle Williams and Francis X. Bushman.[21] Helene won in the Most Popular Child Actress category, with Dolores coming in eighth. Maurice's star still shined brightly in Europe, at least: England's *Pictures and the Picturegoer* magazine voted him the year's number one male foreign film star.[22] Perhaps British moviegoers were more loyal than their American counterparts.

Then, suddenly, he vanished. The reasons for Maurice's public disappearance in December vary from source to source: Albert E. Smith blamed it on Mae's jealousy and his fallen star's failure to survive his own bad publicity. He claimed that Maurice had become "unsuited" to the job of directing movies. Except the battering incident had occurred two years earlier—so why would the company have waited so long to fire him? And if they were displeased with his work as a director, why would they have made him one of the company's busiest? Several months into his absence, a film magazine reported that "ill health" had caused his departure. But Vitagraph wouldn't have fired Maurice for being sick any more than they would have refused to take him back when he got well. Yet he would never again work for the company as a regular employee.

Could he have quit? Given the enormity of his financial struggles before joining the company, and with Mae on high alert, quitting was the last thing Maurice could have done at such a moment, especially with a Long Island estate to maintain and private schooling for Helene to pay for. Therefore, he had to have been let go, as by then there was a plethora of good reasons for his dismissal.

Los Angeles was open wide for the movie business in 1915. Vitagraph set up its first West Coast offices there in 1911; but it kept its Flatbush headquarters going full blast, though most of its competitors were moving to Hollywood.[23] With limitless room for growth and a dearth of bad weather to hamper its shooting schedules, film's new mecca gave its eastern counterparts a curt ultimatum—go west or perish. With growing competition from afar, the company was already feeling the pinch. Wrote film historian Daniel Blum, "The old guard, Vitagraph, Essanay, and Pathé were the only companies showing signs of surviving the onrush of the powerful and vastly expanding newer companies."[24]

Making things even worse for Maurice, Vitagraph's overseas business evaporated with the coming of the Great War. Economy was in the air, especially where a fading movie star with a drinking problem was concerned. When *Picture Play* magazine ascribed his ongoing absences to "ill health," they were speaking in the press parlance of the times. In newspapers especially, alcoholism fell under the catch-all term "illness." As late as 1935, when John Barrymore suffered a complete physical collapse after months of heavy drinking, the Associated Press told the public he was "ill in a New York hospital with bronchitis and influenza."[25] Friend and fellow veteran alcoholic W. C. Fields spent much of the 1930s drying out in sanitariums for reasons the press well knew, but graciously declined to identify.

According to J. Stuart Blackton's daughter Marion, Maurice had been pushing his luck at Vitagraph for some time: "'Cos,' as he was known to his fellow workers, was the bad boy of the studio, eternally getting into jams, eternally being lectured and threatened with dismissal by the Front Office."[26] The more his popularity waned, the more he drank, and the more he drank the more of a "bad boy" he became. When the partners finally had had enough, they fired him. Whatever the last straw was, it caused a Costello blackout in the press that lasted for the next four months. The darling of the film magazines was officially missing in action. With no news of his activities, his fans could only wonder what had become of him. A rumor began circulating that Maurice had taken a job as a traveling salesman for the American Tobacco Company. The Costellos themselves shared little information about what was going on at the time. Dolores never discussed it, even with her daughter Dede.[27] Helene barely mentioned the period, in part because she was away at boarding school much of the time.

Then, as suddenly as he disappeared, Maurice returned to the screen in April 1916 to star in Vitagraph's *The Crown Prince's Double*, his last featured role with the studio, and then again in August to costar in a sixteen-part serial called *The Crimson Stain Mystery*. The little-known Erbograph Film Company had signed him to play opposite actress Ethel Grandin, hoping that a famous name, faded though it was, might revive the former Universal star's dying career, while bolstering the company's financial prospects. It did neither. The serial's once-great male star, meanwhile, found himself consigned to the annals of film history. The *Picture Play* story, elegiacally titled "Where Are the Stars of Yesterday?" pronounced his epitaph with all the gravity it could muster: "Maurice Costello is another who has faded into oblivion, just a short time after he was the most popular of all screen actors."[28]

On August 6, 1917, Maurice found himself in a Flushing courtroom, having again vented his frustrations on someone unlucky enough to have stumbled into his orbit. This time the plaintiff was Lloyd Mullholland, an army private stationed at nearby Fort Totten. "According to Costello," the *Daily Eagle* reported, "Mullholland was one of a group of soldiers who pass the Costello home frequently and annoy his 15-year-old daughter as she goes to bathe. Yesterday, the actor claims, as his daughter was in his automobile, Mullholland and a number of other soldiers threw kisses at her. Mullholland, he says, became abusive, and [Costello] drew his revolver to scare him away."[29] What Maurice left out was what he might have done to provoke Mullholland. Fortunately for what was left of Maurice's career, the private didn't show up to testify, and the matter was officially dropped.

Possibly the plaintiff had more important things on his mind than Maurice Costello—like the morning's announcement that thousands of Long Island men were approved for the draft and might soon be shipped off to fight what was left of the Great War. But even if Mulholland had come to court, there would have been little to gain or lose on either side. For Maurice, especially, the worst of the damage had been done.

9

Desperation

Helene devoted less than a paragraph in her memoir to the Costellos' decade-long financial decline, and for good reason: there was nothing glamorous or entertaining about her family's slow, excruciating backslide into poverty. It had been a time of "incredible luxury," she wrote, "yet the day was to come when there was neither servants nor food in the $150,000 home, and no more jewelry to pawn. Mother, Dolores and I literally went hungry there, while dad knocked around the United States and Canada, vowing not to come home until every last pawnable asset was gone."[1]

Pawning their assets wasn't the only thing Maurice was doing, apparently, while he was "knocking around" the country. In the late 1970s, a man claiming to be Maurice Costello's biological son contacted Deirdre, who responded graciously. "The 'son' I was in correspondence with," she said, "told me that his mother had an affair with Maurice while he was acting in a play that was in town. But by the time the show left town she was pregnant. When I approached Dolores, she refused to discuss what this man said, telling me it was all nonsense; he was just another nobody after some notoriety. Anyway, I seem to remember that he was from Ohio, and he mentioned in one letter that he was in his sixties or close to sixty. . . . The worst part of all of this is that I can't remember this guy's name."[2]

Give or take nine months, if he was sixty years old in 1978, the dates check out. Nineteen eighteen was the only year Maurice hadn't made a picture since he started working for Vitagraph in 1907, and the family coffers were as empty as they could possibly be. If there ever was a time for a destitute actor to go on an extended search for cash, this was it. As for the man claiming to be Maurice's son, having made his presence known, and finding the family matriarch unreceptive to any further discussions about his parentage, he let the matter drop and was never heard from again.

The ever-tight-lipped Dolores said nothing of those years, except that, unlike Helene, she had to quit school and go to work to support the family.[3] Her qualifications for the kind of employment she was seeking, then and always, were staggeringly obvious. Helene called her sister "probably the most beautiful woman ever to appear on the motion picture screen" and "a lovely hothouse flower."[4] Dolores found work as an artist's model in her late teens, now and then for the famously lecherous illustrator James Montgomery Flagg.[5] It was the first of several entanglements with older, beauty-obsessed men, who saw in Dolores every imaginable possibility. She was already well equipped for the life she was stepping into. She had learned from Mae how to handle controlling, temperamental men like her father, and she knew that without her mother's toughness and resilience, the Costellos would not have survived as a family.

As life hardened Dolores on the inside, it left the outside remarkably unblemished. What emerged from the squalor of her girlhood was a flawless young woman, as perfect a Jazz Age beauty as had yet to be imagined. With her father long out of work, and their Long Island estate denuded of everything salable, it fell to Dolores, later to be joined by Helene, to pick up the pieces of her destitute family and try to put them together again. It was a role that, for better or worse, she would never fully relinquish.

After *The Crimson Stain Mystery,* Maurice found himself at liberty picture-wise, though not by choice. The business was rapidly deserting him—literally, by moving to Hollywood, and by snatching away the public's attention, as successive waves of film stars rose through the ranks of the developing studio system. By 1919, Costello successors Francis X. Bushman and Earle Williams had themselves been supplanted by relative newcomers Douglas Fairbanks and Charlie Chaplin.[6] That year, Albert E. Smith charitably offered Maurice a pair of supporting roles with Alice Joyce, another Vitagraph old-timer, in *The Captain's Captain* and *The Cambric Mask.* He played an archvillain in another film, an escaped convict in another. He played a German spy in *The Man Who Won,* causing a trade magazine to remark: "Maurice Costello sure had a gang of followers in the heyday of his career, and many . . . folks may be willing to spend money just to see an old-time favorite again."[7] Another writer wondered,

"What has become of the old-fashioned girl who used to rave about Maurice Costello?"[8] Indeed the business was changing so rapidly, it had escaped notice that the old-timer's "heyday" was only five years earlier.

Maurice finished out the decade in polar opposition to the way he began it: as a flickering memory to anyone who was old enough to have witnessed the dawn of the film industry but was young enough to have come along for the ride. The start of the 1920s found the Costellos hanging on by a thread—to their Long Island estate, which they would soon have to let go, and to what little hold they had left on show business. Helene's private school education was eventually curtailed, but not before she was old enough to attend plebe dances at nearby West Point. "Mother told me their brass buttons hurt her chest whenever they wanted to dance close," Deirdre said.[9] Maurice continued to get work from Vitagraph: in 1920 he played a gang leader in *The Tower of Jewels.* Meanwhile, Dolores's modeling jobs helped keep the family afloat.

In March 1922, Maurice grudgingly returned to the one-a-days, in a revival of William DeMille's 1905 comedy-drama, *Strongheart.* The Ralph Stuart Company had presented its namesake as the play's lead character soon after the part was written.[10] Trying for a comeback, Stuart took his company on a grueling thirty-two-city tour that wouldn't be finished until May. When Maurice returned to New York he staged a comeback of his own, as his film prospects took a sudden turn for the better. J. Stuart Blackton was happy to promote his ex-star's return to movie acting, so long as he could throw in a plug for Vitagraph: "Perhaps the screen has never reflected any shadow more universally popular than Maurice Costello's, when the Vitagraph Company was swathed in swaddling clothes," read the caption beneath Maurice's haggard-looking photograph in *Motion Picture Magazine*—a Blackton publication.[11]

That fall, Maurice played in a pair of features for the Arrow Film Company, another East Coast holdout. Both were filmed at the Ideal Studios in Palisades, New Jersey.[12] In *None So Blind,* he played an anti-Semitic homewrecker, and in *Man and Wife* he shared the bill with another of his ex-bosses, the former belle of the Brooklyn stage, Edna May Spooner.[13] Third-billed in the cast was rising starlet Norma Shearer, appearing in her next to last picture before she signed with Louis B. Mayer and moved to Hollywood.[14]

In December, Maurice started work at Long Island's Astoria Studios on the first of two productions for Paramount: *Glimpses of the Moon* and

Fog Bound. Two weeks later he headed south to film exterior scenes in Palm Beach. Given the rare opportunity to escape the New York winter, Mae and Helene weren't about to let him go to Florida without them. Dolores came along in a professional capacity, having gotten a small part in *Glimpses of the Moon.* Paramount's publicity department had her alluringly photographed in a bathing suit, standing siren-like on a rock, for publication after the film's release.[15] But when Paramount approached Maurice about signing his daughter to a movie contract, a quarrel ensued and the company withdrew their offer. Dolores never forgave her father for ruining her chances at the studio.[16]

After the family's return to New York in early 1923, a chance encounter with George White changed everything in an instant. His *Scandals* revue had knocked the *Ziegfeld Follies* off its Broadway pedestal, offering racier, faster-paced entertainment better suited to Jazz Age tastes.[17] According to Helene's version of the meeting: "They were walking down Madison Avenue with their mother one day when they met George White, whom they had not seen in years. He said he was starting rehearsal for a new *Scandals* the following week. The two girls, over their mother's objections, asked him for a job. They signed up for $57.50 a week, without a tryout. Dolores, already beautiful, became a show girl. Helene became a dancer and understudy for Winifred Lightner. Half a year, in New York and on the road, with the show."[18]

A full year, in other words. On June 18, *George White's Scandals of 1923* opened at the Globe Theater (now the Lunt-Fontanne) near Forty-Sixth Street and Broadway. It closed after 168 shows and then went on tour. It's unlikely that the Costello sisters signed on with the road company that year (the usual torrent of letters from Mae to Maurice is conspicuously absent), but when next year's show left New York in December 1924, Dolores and Helene went with it. Mae went along too, of course. "We expected to have you here for dinner Christmas," she wrote Maurice from Philadelphia on the twenty-fourth, "but not a word from you, not even a card wishing the girls a merry Christmas and they felt badly over it." And on an even more somber note: "I hope you are taking good care of yourself and remember your promise to go on the water wagon. I hope you will keep your word."[19] Interestingly, this was the only time Mae expressed her concern about his drinking in any of her surviving letters.

Maurice's return to screen acting lasted only as long as the demand for picture actors held out in the last years of the industry's western exodus. He appeared in eight films in 1924: one for Paramount, two for Selznick, two for Vitagraph, and three for lesser-known producers, all of which were gone within the year. Maurice's ex-bosses at Vitagraph were in the process of selling the studio to Warner Bros. (Pop Rock was dead, but the pending sale would leave surviving partners Blackton and Smith extremely well off).[20] The Selznicks—father Lewis and son Myron—had moved to the West Coast, soon to be joined by Lewis's youngest son, David. Paramount continued its operations in Astoria, but in an ever-diminishing capacity until the company left New York for good in 1932.

With the Bayside property now liquidated and his wife and daughters out of town, Maurice braved the winter of 1924–1925 alone and unemployed, with only the Costellos' dog Buster for company. To save money, he vacated the family's rented flat at 10 West Sixty-First Street and checked into the low-rent Pasadena Hotel.[21] On January 3, Mae sent him thirty dollars from Dolores and Helene's first paycheck to pay his rent, and five dollars to keep for himself. When the girls noticed a dog in somebody's window, she told him, they missed Buster so much they cried.[22]

As always, Mae fretted about money: "I hope you will land something soon. For I am worried how to make ends meet. [We] leave for Pittsburgh for a two week engagement."[23] A few days later: "The road stuff is not what it's cracked up to be. Too expensive for my blood, and the girls are disgusted as I told you before. We live some distance from the theater and have to take a cab very often."[24]

In March, the ex-movie star returned again to the vaudeville stage, heading the bill in *Violets,* described as "a little playlet that combines power and pathos in equal measure."[25] Maurice was still on the road when he received a letter from Mae telling him that Dolores had been spotted by a scout for Warner Bros. in Chicago and offered a movie contract. As Dolores later described: "A scout from Warner Brothers sent me a letter with a picture of me on the program. [It said] get in touch with me, and I laughed and put it on the mirror and said 'did anyone else get one of these?' I'd never heard of Warner Brothers as producers. Then the telephone rang and the man said would you take a test, and I said yes. . . . My sister laughed and said 'don't bother, didn't do any good in New York and it won't here.'"[26]

If they could come to an agreement, they would give notice to the *Scandals* company and leave for Hollywood at once. Of course, seventeen-year-old Helene would have to go with them. Naturally, Mae would stay on as the girls' chaperone and business manager.

Maurice objected—strenuously at first, but given his growing impotence in light of recent events, he gave in without a fight. In one of his few surviving letters, posted from his dressing room at the Willard Theater in Richmond Hill, New Jersey, the former head-of-household had to make do in an advisory capacity: "I hope you get a decent figure for her, and be careful when you sign a contract. You should have a lawyer. . . . Now is your chance to show me that real business ability that I've heard so much about. . . . Well I just finished my 1st performance and it went fine, house is packed."[27]

Mae was sure she had seen enough of the movie business to handle the negotiations on her own. By the time Maurice's letter arrived, the terms were already hammered out: Warner Bros. had agreed to pay Dolores $75 a week for three months. If at the end of that time the studio wanted to keep her, her contract would extend for a full year and she would get a pay increase of $25. "Helene, although she wanted to become a comedienne she had to go along," Helene wrote haughtily, "but she refused to take a screen test."[28] As it turned out she wouldn't have to—a studio contract with her name on it had already been drawn up.

On April 5, the Costello women bade farewell to the *Scandals* company in Cleveland and boarded the afternoon train to Los Angeles. "Leaving [them] was terrible, such tears and good wishes," Mae wrote. "Well old dear I hope you will take care of yourself," she added affectionately—then, more typically: "Don't forget to send some money as soon as you can."[29] Mae couldn't help herself: though the studio had guaranteed each of the girls $75 a week (about $1,000 in today's currency), she was still worrying about where their next dollar was coming from.

The single-level divided property at 1242½ North El Centro Avenue was small but affordable at sixty-six dollars a week. It was conveniently located less than a mile from the Warner Bros. studio on Sunset Boulevard, and it had a telephone. Helene and Dolores spent the month of April settling in, with Mae following them literally everywhere they went. They were "introduced around" at the studio—meeting Marie Prevost, Monte Blue, and Irene Rich. "On Sunday, we met Rin Tin Tin the Dog Star and eight of his puppies. Testing for camera. Tomorrow Helen [she hadn't added the "e" yet] plays the part of a flapper for a Mr. Flood and rumor has it that Dolores plays the lead with Rin Tin Tin in his next picture."[30]

The weeks went by, but no better roles were forthcoming. With just three months to "make good," by the middle of May, Dolores was beginning to lose hope. They had been getting "maid parts" and other "unimportant bits," she remembered, "but the real chance was nowhere in sight."[31] Her spirits rose when Warner loaned her to Fox, but she was called back to play yet another maid part. Mae did her best to keep their flagging spirits up, but worried to Maurice that "the girls aren't doing much . . . and they are heartbroken about it. . . . I hope we will be able to stay, for we are beginning to love the place. . . . The sun shines on both sides of the street year round."[32]

When Dolores said their chances were "nowhere in sight," she was exaggerating more than a little. Jack Warner wasn't telling them what they wanted to hear when he assured the despondent women that they would soon have "plenty to do."[33] And they would—starting with Dolores's second loan-out to Fox at the end of May, to appear opposite Edmund Lowe in *Greater Than a Crown.* This time she would not be called back. Among the cast members was veteran screen actor Paul Panzer, who had worked with Maurice in his earliest days at Vitagraph. It was Panzer who had had to build his own balcony for the studio's production of *Romeo and Juliet,* before Maurice's proclamation that actors no longer had to build sets was fully implemented.

That week, Helene got *her* first real part in a Hollywood film, playing the cowgirl Virginia Weatherford in *Ranger of the Big Pines.* The film was a Vitagraph release, though in point of fact, Blackton and Smith's once-mighty company was no more. Warner bought it lock, stock, and real estate, including the Flatbush studio, at the end of April.[34] Helene had been there at the beginning, now she would be there at the end. First, she had to finish playing the hero's sister in *The Man in the Box,* starring Sydney Chaplin. "Yes, the Girls are cast for leads what do you think about that?" wrote an exultant Mae. "I only hope they make good. Helen and I expected to go away on location yesterday, but she didn't finish with the Chaplin picture so we are not going till the first of next week."[35] Her problem was what to do with twenty-one-year-old Dolores while they were gone: "I will put her in a hotel while I am away, for she works very late and couldn't cook her own meals and there is nobody I would care to have stay with her."[36]

On May 31, 1925, Warner Bros. extended the Costello sisters' contracts to their original full-year terms. The probationary period was up—

they were on their way.[37] All that was missing now was Maurice. Mae had been pushing him to "land" something soon—she wanted him to buy a new suit so he could look "prosperous" when he got to Hollywood. If only he could get some work, instead of sending him money to live on every week, she could put it toward his train fare to California.[38] But it was about more than money. Clearly, she missed him. Mae's letters around this time are uncharacteristically chatty, even affectionate. In one, she calls Maurice "old darling," while in another she closes with "love to you and Buster from one who loves you."[39]

If things had stayed as they were, the parents might have gone on as they always had while their daughters rose steadily through the ranks of Hollywood actresses—eventually, like all silent actors, to sink or swim with the coming of sound. But a lion was on the loose in Hollywood, and for the Costellos, from then on there would be no such thing as a world without volatility.

10

The Lion at Warners

The rumblings were everywhere around the lot—he would arrive within the week. The king was en route for his coronation. If John Barrymore wasn't the biggest star in the world in 1925, he was unquestionably the greatest. After a succession of preparatory roles on Broadway, he had changed the English-speaking theater with his groundbreaking production of *Hamlet* in November 1922. Before that, Shakespearean actors, like the Englishman Johnston Forbes-Robertson and Broadway veteran E. H. Sothern, had given heavily mannered performances—voices quavering like opera singers, arms gesturing broadly—reflecting the nineteenth century's taste for the highly embellished.

But the ugliest war in history had changed forever the conviction that beauty and art were one and the same. As the previous generation harked back to its Victorian past, the current one looked ahead to a world visually unencumbered by ornament, as America's sugar-coated veneer sloughed off to reveal the darker places within. The Barrymore Hamlet, a reflection of the postwar generation's growing penchant for introspection, added a distinctly Freudian cast to the doomed Dane's loathing of his murderous stepfather, King Claudius.[1] This new Hamlet was motivated less by old-fashioned revenge than by oedipal jealousy of his mother's sexual betrayal—not just of her dead husband, but also of her son.

"It is with a full and vivid memory of the graciousness, the gentle pathos, the wistful beauty of Forbes-Robertson's *Hamlet,*" wrote Alexander Woollcott in the *New York Herald,* "that we salute John Barrymore's as the most satisfying performance of the role that we have ever seen in the theater."[2] The *Cleveland Plain Dealer* agreed: "Set beside this performance, Forbes-Robertson's prince seems like an elderly statesman, E. H. Sothern's like a Shakespearean scholar speaking lines and Walter Hampden's like a fiery but elocutionary and tricky actor. Barrymore . . . plays Hamlet as simply and naturally as if *Hamlet* was not a sacred legend but a new piece by Somerset Maugham."[3]

This was Shakespeare for a new age. Barrymore's fearless rejection of the theatrical conventions of his youth is understandable given that he was the scion of not one, but two, great nineteenth-century acting families. His father, the Broadway star and occasional playwright Maurice Barrymore, was authentically Victorian. For one thing, he was English, for another, he was a child of the Raj; his father had served in India as a commissioner. And for another, he was the composer of lines that smacked dreamily of Keats:

The air was still and passion fraught the night
Athwart the flags, the ghostly shadows lay
Thy face looked down, so pale in wan moon-light
"Thou are my love, my all" it seemed to say.[4]

Changing his name from Herbert Blyth to Maurice Barrymore, "Barry," as he was nicknamed, came to New York as an aspiring actor, and the handsome young player with the sparkling wit quickly caught on. In 1879, he married actress and comedienne Georgiana Drew; her last name wasn't made up. Georgie's mother, Louisa Lane Drew, had played opposite Junius Brutus Booth and Edwin Forrest in the 1840s. By the time of her daughter's marriage, Louisa ranked among the stage's most accomplished actresses.[5] In the 1890s, her son John Drew was given the title "First Gentleman of the Stage," having mastered the art of Victorian gentility as had no other American actor. Thus the conjoined families, the Drews and the Barrymores, carved out a lasting place for themselves in the annals of the legitimate theater, before passing on their legacies to their three brilliant progeny—by order of appearance, Lionel, Ethel, and John Barrymore.

As Barry's children sought to earn their livings on the stage, each would eventually turn to movie acting for the easy money it brought in between engagements. John made his first screen appearance in 1912, but didn't show up in the popularity polls until after the release of *Dr. Jekyll and Mr. Hyde* in 1920.[6] In the first truly modern horror film—one with a bona-fide monster—he not only starred but also devised the screen's first modern creature effect. His performance grabbed the attention of filmgoers, just as his recent stage triumphs had captivated theater audiences.

"What brought the fans flocking to the box office," his biographer John Kobler observed, "were the same qualities that had attracted them to John's father—the verve, the dash, the physical beauty."[7]

In July 1923, sandwiched between his first and second seasons of *Hamlet,* Barrymore traveled cross-country to appear in his first Hollywood film: Warner Bros. had signed him to star in the screen adaption of the Clyde Fitch play *Beau Brummel.* While making the picture, the forty-one-year-old actor fell in love (if it could be called that) with his dark-eyed, seventeen-year-old costar—the former Lucille Langhanke, newly renamed Mary Astor. "The romance flourished," Mary wrote, "quietly and unobtrusively, under the unseeing eyes of . . . my parents. In the filming of the many romantic, delicate love scenes of *Beau Brummel,* we could stand in each other's arms. . . . We whispered softly, or just stood there, quietly loving the closeness. . . . Between the scenes Jack had the prop man place two camp chairs together just off the set, and we sat side by side."[8]According to Mary, if it hadn't been for the intrusion of her ultra-protective father, Otto Langhanke, a deeper commitment would have been in the offing.

Except that Jack was still married, however unhappily, to his second wife, the struggling poet and occasional dramatist Michael Strange. Given the string of Hollywood scandals that shook the industry to its core in the early twenties—two involving marital infidelity—Jack would have to get a divorce before he and Mary could present themselves as a couple.

Barrymore returned to New York with his romantic prospects unresolved. In late November, *Hamlet* reopened for three weeks of sold-out performances at the Manhattan Opera House, before going on tour.[9] In Washington, DC, President and Mrs. Calvin Coolidge attended the opening-night performance at Poli's Theater on Pennsylvania Avenue, afterward inviting Jack and the play's rotund producer, Arthur Hopkins, to the White House.

"Have you seen many Hamlets, Mr. President?" Jack asked the famously taciturn Coolidge.

"Two," he replied, "You and E. H. Sothern."

"And which performance did you like better?"

"Well, Mr. Sothern's clothes were prettier than yours."[10]

Having defeated an armada of challenges, in February 1925 Barrymore accomplished what no American actor, not even Edwin Booth, had dared to attempt. When no producer in New York would back him, not even his own, Jack put up $25,000 of his own money to produce, direct, and perform his *Hamlet* on Shakespeare's home turf.[11] The skeptical Hopkins predicted umbrage-taking Londoners would "assassinate" him on opening night. In fact, they adored him. The *New York Sun* correspondent counted "eight curtain calls after the first act, almost as many more after the second and so much commotion at the end of the performance."[12]

The critical consensus was nearly as appreciative. James Agate of the *Sunday Times* declared that while Barrymore's Dane brought "fewer tears" than Forbes-Robertson's, it was "nearer to Shakespeare's whole creation than any other I have seen. First a handsome face, intellectual as to the brow. . . . Next an agreeable voice, touching nobility here and there. . . . Add the purest diction, perfect enunciation and unexampled clarity. Now note a slim figure and the general illusion of princeliness and youth. All these are informed—and here is the key—by intellectual capacity of a rare order and analytical power of extreme cogency."[13]

Clearly Agate approved of this new, inward-looking Hamlet. With the help of Margaret Carrington, his drama and voice coach, Jack had done away with the frayed elocutionary styles of his predecessors, to present a more natural approach to Shakespearean language and diction. Wrote *Daily News* critic Hesketh Pearson: "He pronounces 'my' and 'mine' as they should be pronounced, not as 'me' and 'min.' . . . That alone is worth crossing the Atlantic for."[14]

Amazingly, an American actor had taught the English how to play Shakespeare. In two and a half years Jack had remade the classical stage in his own image—a towering achievement by itself—while basking in the reflected glory of the new, raw century.

When Warner approached him again after the release of *Beau Brummel,* by stage actors' standards Jack had done well for himself. The London *Hamlet*'s sold-out run recouped his $25,000 investment and netted an additional $10,000. But that paled in comparison to what Hollywood was now offering: a three-picture deal that would guarantee him $76,250 a picture, plus $7,625 a week more if the studio's shooting schedule went over three weeks. Other amenities included cast and script approval, a bungalow at the Ambassador Hotel, his meals paid for, and a chauffeur.[15] "You can do anything you want in any way," his stage designer Robert Edmund Jones told him. "There is nobody else in that position in the theater today."[16] But Jack wanted nothing more to do with the theater at present. What attracted him to the movie business were the same things that drove his predecessor Maurice Costello to leave the stage eighteen years earlier: the chance to make an easier living as an actor, and the prospect of earning more money.

As Jack sat on top of the entertainment world in the spring of 1925, his future father-in-law was trying to scrape up the money to buy himself a new suit. Film work had dried up as the studios continued their western exodus. Stock and repertoire were dying. Vaudeville suffered, as more and more Americans went to the movies. Maurice tried without success to save the money he needed to bring himself, Buster, and the family's few remaining belongings to Hollywood. "If you are anxious," Mae wrote him, "I will send you the money to do so, but in the meantime, keep an eye open for anything that might come your way."[17]

In the meantime, Maurice had to follow his daughters' adventures from afar. "J. Barrymore in a week or so," Mae wrote on May 20. "They are crazy about him at the studio."[18] A week later: "John Barrymore is expected soon and on his last picture they paid him $10,000 a week and all expenses." (She heard wrong—he had made $25,000 a week.)[19]

It was probably in the early part of June that they encountered each other for the first time—for the first time since Dolores was a child, anyway, when Jack last visited the Costellos' Bayside estate. She gave differing accounts of their meeting. In 1927, Dolores said it happened when Jack passed her on the set and "looked at me rather intently."[20] In an interview for Kevin Brownlow's *Hollywood* television series fifty years later, she said it occurred as she left the studio one afternoon, and that was "the beginning." In the same interview, she recalled that their first face-to-face meeting took place in Jack Warner's office:

> Jack was on the balcony of the old Sunset Boulevard studio, and I stopped to give a veteran change, and my sister [said] "that must be Mr. Barrymore on the balcony." . . . And looking back, you know you feel somebody looking at you, well the next morning up in my dressing room . . . the assistant director came up to the room, said "hurry up, hurry up, JB and JW want to see you," and I said who are they? And he said J. L. Warner and John Barrymore. . . . Jack had a kind of habit of bending in the middle,

> you know being shorter than he was and [having] four inch heels on. . . . He looked at me and said "Miss Costello how tall are you?" And I took my heels off, I put my foot on the ground and I said "I'm this tall Mr. Barrymore."

"Will she do?" Warner asked Jack. Yes, he replied, she would do.

> And in two days I had the part. . . . He came across as I was leaving the set, what we call a dead set, no lights, and he followed me and said "would you like to play that part?" . . . I laughed, and he jumped up—he was sitting on a chair, and he walked off and he hung his head. He thought I was laughing at him because of his grey hair, his temples were grey. I said "did it ever occur to you that I was laughing because it was such a ridiculous question?"[21]

Maurice's reaction to the news that Dolores had been chosen to play the role of Esther opposite Barrymore's Ahab in *The Sea Beast* can be gleaned from Mae's incredulous reply on July 20: "Your letter of the 13th inst. received and sorry you were disappointed with the contents. I was really anxious for you to know that Dolores had such a wonderful opportunity. Playing the lead opposite Barrymore nevertheless has handed many a thrill in Hollywood."[22]

Obviously, Maurice had *not* been handed a thrill. Momentous events he could play no part in were shaping his daughters' lives and careers. Dolores's overnight success in the industry that had beaten him to a pulp only heightened his feelings of jealousy and resentment. But not even Mae could understand why Maurice was unhappy that his daughter was costarring with America's greatest living actor. "Dolores is working very hard," she reassured him. "Mr. Barrymore said she is charming in the part. I only hope Helene lands something soon."[23] A few days later, she did. The most popular child actress of 1915 got her first important adult role in *The Love Toy,* starring the popular stage and screen actor Lowell Sherman. As lovely as she was at the age of nineteen, Helene would never be likened to a "lovely hothouse flower." Slightly heavier than Dolores, with a rounder face and stronger features, her earthier appearance belied a vulnerability that was genuine. Childhood had toughened Dolores while mostly sparing Helene, who leapt into the Hollywood fray (as much as Mae would let her) with all the gin-fueled exuberance a Jazz Age starlet could muster. At her core, each sister was the inverse of the other. Dolores was a fighter not a lover; Helene was a lover, first and foremost. Dolores would have let no one stand in the way of her career (not yet, at least), while Helene would have chucked it all for one great romance. "Helene's first good part was as the princess in *The Love Toy*," Helene wrote. "When the picture was finished, [Lowell] Sherman asked Helene for her picture. She gave him a costume still, inscribed respectfully, as a green girl writing to an established actor. He still had the picture several years later when he became her second husband."[24]

Meanwhile, Dolores had hooked a much bigger fish than Lowell Sherman. Spying her for the first time from Jack Warner's balcony, John Barrymore was wracked by a sudden spasm. As Helene told the story: "He grabbed Warner's arm. 'Quick, man—who is she? There's Esther!'" After he learned who she was, Jack strained for a better look. "My God, I'm getting old!" he groaned, recalling the preteenage Dolores.[25] According to Dolores, Jack turned to Warner and declared: "That's the woman I'm going to marry."[26]

This couldn't happen right away, of course. Not only was Jack still married to Michael Strange, but Mary Astor was still in the picture. Or was she? Their recent rendezvous in Manhattan had given Mary the distinct impression that when they met again in Hollywood, their affair would pick up where it had left off. Perhaps it would have, if just once Mary had stood up to Otto Langhanke. "Jack told me of plans he did not think it wise to tell the family yet," she wrote.

> He was to do *Richard III* in London next season [which he never did] and he wanted me to play Lady Anne. Very carefully a few nights later, he brought up the subject of my doing a play with him in London. Daddy was very cool toward the idea. . . . I think now that this was the critical moment. I think Jack sat there waiting for me to assert myself, to show I had a mind and a will. I could have said, "But this is the opportunity of a lifetime, if I am to really be an actress. . . . I'm going to London, and I'm going to play Lady Anne." But I didn't say anything. The next day at the hotel Jack said to me, "You haven't changed a bit. Nothing has changed."[27]

In Hollywood they saw each other sporadically, as both were on location for much of the summer. On the rare occasions they could be together, Mary sensed that something was wrong: "My uneasiness grew.

There were all the signs and hints that are so dear to the writers of second-rate movie scripts." Visiting Jack's set one afternoon she noticed "another visitor—Dolores Costello. And I saw, with a sick and aching heart, the two camp chairs, placed just off the set, as they had been for *Beau Brummel,* only now Jack and Dolores were sitting in them, talking and laughing. And then I knew."[28]

What Mae had been trying to tell Maurice during the making of *The Sea Beast,* however subtly, was that his daughter's relationship with Jack Barrymore was no longer strictly professional. "Dolores and I have been out on an old whaler for four days," she wrote him in early September. "Mr. Barrymore broke a couple of ribs Tuesday and is laid up. I called him up tonight, he is feeling much better but cannot work."[29]

The story goes that during their first love scene together, Dolores fainted dead away in Jack's arms.[30] This seems unlikely given her tough-as-nails constitution (also the fact that people rarely, if ever, faint when kissing), but three months of feverish proximity to Jack took its toll. By the time *The Sea Beast* was finished, Dolores was as much in love with him as he was with her.

For Jack it was the Langhankes all over again—only this time he chose to persevere. He was better acquainted with Dolores's family, at least; the Barrymores and Costellos had known each other since their earliest days in the movie business. Best of all, the tough but pliable Mae, wary of Jack though she was, encouraged his overtures toward Dolores and even allowed him regular, nightly visits to the family's newly rented house at 1943 North Ivar Avenue.

Though they were born the same year, Mae couldn't resist mothering him. Jack's mother had died of tuberculosis when he was ten, leaving him to the predations of his stepmother, who deflowered him when he was fifteen.[31] Decades later, Jack's psychiatrist placed the start of his drinking to around that time. That same year, his beloved grandmother died in genteel retirement at the age of seventy-seven. Louisa Drew had doted on her "Greengoose," as she affectionately called him, since babyhood and had helped raise him. "Jack never felt safe anywhere after that," his brother Lionel observed.[32]

There had been no maternal presence in Jack's life since then—until Mae. By September he was happily ensconced in the first real home he had known since childhood. Mae cooked for him, washed his dishes, and fussed over him generally. He contentedly called her "mamma." In Mae's nurturing presence, the mantle of great Shakespearean actor fell away to reveal the simpler person underneath. They played cards—a variation of double solitaire called "Russian Bank," and gin rummy.[33] They laughed, smoked incessantly, and talked of the old days of film and theater.

"Mae Costello was one of the grandest persons I've ever known and one of the dearest friends I've ever had," Jack recalled. "Before I married Dolores, Mae and I talked many a night through. We used to put the 'kids' to bed and bicker until dawn about . . . old friends we shared, old tales we enjoyed, old experiences we could relive in the talking. We were gay pals. Once Dolores asked me: 'Are you sure it is I whom you want to marry and not my mother?'"[34]

All this might have gone on indefinitely—Mae's nurturing, Dolores's romantic idyll, Helene's carefree adventures in Hollywood—if not for the return of the prodigal father, whose state of mind couldn't have been more at odds with the peaceful domestic scene he was about to storm into.

11

Alone Time

Maurice brought along on his travels a gray-lined, pocket-sized ledger for use as a personal diary; the initial entry was dated October 23, 1925, the afternoon of his arrival in Hollywood. For the broken-down actor, the small, brown notebook was the only place where he could safely unload his troubles.

Long before he stepped off the train, there had been family discussions pertaining to his newly diminished position in the Costello household, discussions to which he was not privy. It might have surprised Maurice that neither Mae nor Dolores was on hand to greet him at the station. "Arrived in L.A. 2:30 PM. Met by Helene and Louis Warner," he wrote in his diary. "Louis drove me home to 1943 N. Ivar Ave."[1] Warner, son of studio mogul Harry Warner, would one day head the company's music division. He and Helene had recently started seeing each other.

Maurice was given his marching orders almost as soon as he walked in the door. "Helene and I keeping house," he wrote on October 26. "Ok."[2] A few days later he noted suspiciously: "Helene and Lewis returned at 3:15 AM with Mrs. C. and Dolores from Laguna. Rather cool. All to bed about 5 AM. During the day received my Does and Don'ts, as usual."[3] Mae and Dolores were trying to tell him that *they* were now in charge, and if there was going to be hell to pay, from now on it would be his hell, not theirs.

"Got some nagging," he griped in early November, "slamming my family and myself in general."[4] Then the next day: "Up at 7 AM. Got coffee ready & Dolores, then chores. . . . Nothing but nag about This and That. Disgusting, I'll say. . . . Mrs. C gave me to understand that nobody was pressing me to stay here, ordered to stay out of the kitchen, I acting as usual."[5]

Just what "as usual" was, Maurice doesn't say, but a day later he wrote a testament of sorts—a declaration, not of independence, but of abject bewilderment: "Nov 8—Sunday—Up at 10 AM—Have Come to the conclusion that the Hand writing on the wall says they intend to humiliate me. Am treated like anything but a Husband and a Father. I get one slur after another. I'm broke, and believe me they let me know it. Helene is the only one that I can depend on for a kind word. I live in Coersion. Everybody—strangers and all, Treated with utmost respect—but me. She—an Apple with a goodly outside. But Rotten at the Core."[6]

With no idea as yet about why Barrymore was coming over, Maurice made note of his presence for the first time on the eighth: "Jack Barrymore and Bert Dorris. Came in the evening. Everything was O. K. Did dishes at 10:30."[7]

Having to lie low for a couple of weeks while Maurice settled in couldn't have been easy for Jack. With *The Sea Beast* finished, his time with Dolores had been cut in half. He hoped to cast her in *Don Juan,* his second film for Warner Bros., but the studio signed Mary Astor to play the part of Adriana Della Varnese, Jack's chest-heaving love interest. Between takes, Dolores and Jack had to content themselves with occasional moments of semi-privacy, chatting and whispering together in the shadows. "I could not bring myself to admit that it was over," Mary said. "Hopefully I told him of the changes that had been made at home. He said 'well, that's some progress,' and started talking about something else. He was drinking steadily; he often showed up on the set with a hang-over, or he was 'delayed' and came in late, or he didn't come in at all."[8]

The marked increase in Jack's drinking coincided with his return to the Costello fold in early November. There he found his oasis of welcoming femininity on the brink of civil war—Mae and Dolores poised for battle on one side, a fretful, craven Maurice on the other. Helene took a neutral stance: she loved her mother and sister, but refused to stand against her father despite everything he had put them through. She loved him and also pitied him, though not nearly as much as he pitied himself. "Did left over dishes and other chores," he wrote. "Kept to myself all day. . . . Am not feeling so good. Very much worried."[9]

Maurice had good reason to worry. Until he could find work at a studio, he was totally dependent on Mae and Dolores: "When on the way out she asked [Mae?] 'do you want some change?' Didn't like her attitude, she certainly can make a person feel that they are dependent. God forbid that it will last long. Oh! If I only had some work! The slurs are humiliating. Trying to be Husband or Father here is a Greater Joke than the 18th Amendment [indeed, prohibition hadn't stopped drinkers from drinking—including him, presumably]."[10]

Mae and Dolores made clear from the beginning that Maurice would have to earn his keep: "Up at 8:30 a.m. Gave Dolores medicine. Made coffee, Washed dishes. Cleaned around etc. Breakfast. Just one of those days – Sour." The movie star who once kept a chauffeur had now become one: "Brought the car back. Took Mrs. C . . . and Dolores shopping. Back for dinner. Drove down to L. A. and all around. Back about 12 Midnight."[11]

Maurice was the first one up in the morning and the last in bed at night. He ran errands, cleaned the house, did the gardening. What he resented even more than his menial status were the endless "slurs" and "slams." And now he had Barrymore to deal with. Maurice jotted down Jack's comings and goings—offhandedly at first, thinking he was just another friend of the family. No one had told him otherwise. But it didn't take him long to discover the real reason for Jack's visits: he got his first clue when he overheard Dolores tell Mae that the next time Jack came for dinner, she wanted him to wash the dishes so that she could dry.

By early December, all had become clear: "Up at 6 A. M. Got Helene up, finished my work. J. B. here for lunch in make-up. Expect to see him bring his trunk any day now. Went to see preview at Monrovia of the 'Sea Beast,' Myself, Mrs, H & D & Jack &·Lew [Warner]. J. B. always has an excuse to get a drink of water in the kitchen with D. before going home. Mrs. C. tries to cover things up. They must think me a damn fool. But I am *very* wide awake."[12]

He started referring to Mae as "Mrs. Nicotine," shortened later to "Nick." Though Maurice himself was a heavy smoker, for some reason her incessant use of tobacco infuriated him: "Nick was too busy sucking on her cigarettes, I had to do the dishes before I went to bed. While she still sat in the living room smoking cigarettes. A Damn Imposition I call it."[13] Everything about Barrymore now irked him—not just his increasingly obvious courtship of Dolores, but the princely way Jack was being treated around the house. "J. B. was here at night—*hurt* his *foot.* Some service he got. Propped up with pillows etc. One would think He was a Tin Jesus."[14]

If Mae's insults weren't degrading enough, Dolores was beginning to feel her oats as the family's principal financial asset. On December 20 Maurice wrote: "Up 7:30. . . . Washed more dishes. Burned papers. Called them at 9. She smoked cigarettes until 10. Then got up. Dolores nagging.

Called me a G. D. Bum, too much for me. Told her the car was already to go. She could drive herself or do as she damned please. . . . Returned home at 5 P. M. Went to my room and stayed there—spirit almost gone! God Damn Bum. That was the Blow!—and her mother listening in. Too Much—Too Much! 12 O'C. Goodnight."[15]

Years later, Dolores had a sign hanging in her kitchen that read: "May my words be kind, for tomorrow I might have to eat them"; so, perhaps the best that can be said of her abusive behavior toward her father is that it was uncharacteristic. Her daughter recalled rare occasions when Dolores lost her temper and "you wanted to hide in the closet," but said that she never used foul or denigrating language.[16] Apparently, Maurice was the exception. Dolores had spent most of her childhood suffering in silence, while her father's "angry temperament" wreaked havoc on the family. Now the tables were turned, and she could vent her anger with impunity. Why wouldn't she? After decades of poverty, her father hit it big in the movie business only to squander his wealth and success and plunge them all back into poverty again. His squabble with Paramount had cost Dolores her first big break in movies. If Mae hadn't overruled him the second time, he would have ruined his daughters' chances with Warner Brothers.

Now Maurice was threatening the one thing Dolores wanted even more than stardom—and that was Jack. She held her tongue and let Mae do the haranguing in New York, but she would not be silent any longer. "The Day couldn't pass without a few Slams," he wrote, "however I made the best of it. Washed the dishes and went to bed at 1:30 a.m. while her Ladyship Smoked."[17]

Four days after Christmas, a major blowup occurred. In a diary entry titled "A Day to Be Remembered," Maurice wrote despondently:

> At dinner after coming home in answer to a Call for a Job, not caring to discuss it, as it had not been settled upon definitely today. Mrs. asked me about it. And I told her that I did not care to talk about it yet. And she said I had a Son of a Bitch nerve to answer her that way. Whereupon my temperamental daughter *Dolores,* who is backed by Mrs. C. balled [*sic*] me out Disgracefully and in so many words told me that I could not get away with that stuff in this house. (meaning hers) and gave me to Understand in so many words to get out. The Mother Sanctioned.[18]

Once again, just as things were starting to go well for the Costellos professionally—with the girls' screen careers heating up and financial prosperity just around the corner—personally they were tearing themselves apart. Biographers painting with broader strokes have blamed John Barrymore for the family's demise, but Maurice's diaries show that the worst of their problems had nothing to do with Jack: "Driving Nick to shop, etc.," he wrote the day after Christmas. "After dinner she started on me again over Dishes. Called me everything on the calendar. Pimp—Bum, and what not."[19]

His daughter's blossoming romance added insult to injury: "I get Barrymore for breakfast—Dinner & Supper & and last thing at night. It's getting on my nerves."[20] Any day he expected Jack to "bring his trunk." He found Dolores and Jack's pet name for each other at least parenthetically amusing: "J. B. (Winkle! Ha, ha.) was to be here again. So I got out. Some things I *don't* want to *see.* They may incite something, so count me out." He finished with a one-sentence testimonial to the beaten man he had become: "I'm not looking for any trouble." This was entirely true; from now on, Maurice would do the majority of his suffering in silence.[21]

It was an untenable situation that remained tenable just long enough for the Costellos to get through an action-packed 1926—a year of meteoric achievement for one sister, slow and steady progress for the other. It's been claimed that John Barrymore "discovered" Dolores Costello (Dolores, interestingly, was among the first to promulgate that assertion), but she had already starred with Edmund Lowe in Fox's feature film *Greater Than a Crown.* A month before the release of *The Sea Beast,* she was voted a WAMPAS Baby Star—the acronymic title given to promising young actresses by the Western Association of Motion Picture Advertisers. Mary Astor and Joan Crawford were also WAMPAS Babies that year.[22]

What Jack did do for Dolores was to vault her to the front ranks of Hollywood actresses almost overnight. By November she was already one of the screen's most popular female stars. For Helene, the climb would be steeper. J. Stuart Blackton's *Motion Picture Magazine* titled her June photo layout "The Unknown Sister," presenting "the yet-to-be-discovered daughter of Maurice Costello."[23] Without a Barrymore to catapult her to stardom, Helene had to make the best of the B-level fare she was being handed. After *The Love Toy,* a box-office flop, Warner Bros. lent her to Paramount to costar with Raymond Griffith (sporting a profile uncannily similar to Jack's) in *Wet Paint.*[24] Despite Helene's marcelled hair and delightfully vampish appearance, she failed to impress. She was given the part of Mary Astor's maid in *Don Juan.* In *While London Sleeps,* the studio paired her with Rin Tin Tin, the studio's first great star, whom she rescues and who then rescues her in the end.[25]

The film that should have given Helene the career boost she so desperately needed was cursed from the beginning. Ernst Lubitsch was scheduled to direct *The Honeymoon Express,* costarring Helene as the daughter of a philandering alcoholic, but had to bow out due to illness.[26] Then, just after the film was finished, lead actor Willard Louis died of typhoid, which cast a pall over the entire production. The movie debuted to little fanfare and quickly disappeared.

Though none of the six films that Helene appeared in that year did well for the studio, her name and face were appearing regularly on the screen—even more often than her sister, who made five films in 1926. After *The Sea Beast,* Dolores was second-billed in Paramount's *Mannequin,* a rags to riches story starring former Vitagraph star Alice Joyce. Next, she played a shipwrecked orphan imprisoned by a group of desperate characters in *Bride of the Storm.* In *The Little Irish Girl,* she played a "come-on" for a ring of grifters who, in the end, are themselves grifted by the hero's grandmother. One reviewer called it "a jerky, muddled picture," but said that because "Dolores Costello is the heroine, it is just as pleasant, when the plot becomes too complicated, to give up all together and settle down to watching Miss Costello."[27] She starred as a trapeze artist nearly driven to suicide in *The Third Degree,* Warner Brother's final release of 1926. "It is a tribute to the power of her personality" *Motion Picture Magazine* commented, "that her popularity increases in spite of poor pictures."[28]

For a pair of Hollywood starlets newly under contract to the up-and-coming Warner Bros. studio, it was a dream year. Regardless of what critics wrote about the films they were in, Dolores and Helene were unanimously appreciated for their looks and talent. While the warring factions tore into each other at home, they helped each other professionally simply by being Costellos. Writers and publicists rarely praised one family member without mentioning another, Maurice especially. Even Mae got her due in a photo spread that presented mother and daughters in various attitudes of domestic tranquility. The Costello women leaf through a book in their North Ivar living room in one photo; in another they pose woodenly on the front porch. Could Maurice have been hovering nearby, Cinderella-like, yearning to be included? Nowadays when he wasn't cleaning the house or chauffeuring the family around town, he was scribbling in his diary or calling around looking for work. Mae and Dolores had forbidden him to eat with the family when Jack was present. When friends and family members were invited to attend one of Dolores's premieres, Maurice was told to stay home.

In the meantime, Dolores was dropping his name in the press—presumably to get him some work. "My father, Maurice Costello, was in the movies for many years, so I saw much of the studios as a child," she told *Picture Play* in an August interview.[29] Around that time, Maurice got his first part in a Hollywood film, third-billed behind star Jackie Coogan in *Johnny Get Your Hair Cut.* The twelve-year-old child had lost the little-boy cuteness that had so endeared him to moviegoers in Charlie Chaplin's *The Kid.* Like Maurice, he was hanging by a thread to what remained of his film career.

It was the worst of times for any silent star trying to make a comeback. Maurice's earlier attempts had fizzled when his East Coast employers either moved west or went out of business altogether. Now even the biggest stars were struggling to stay afloat with the coming of sound; those who hadn't had a chance to begin with were left to fall silently to the bottom.

12

Trial in Error

John Barrymore's response to everything that happened between himself and the Costello family in 1926, was to disappear. For Christmas he bought presents for Mae, books for Helene, and jewelry for Dolores—then took his yacht, *The Mariner,* on an extended cruise deep into Mexican waters.[1] Several months earlier he had given "Winkie," as he and Dolores were now calling each other, something much better than a bauble—the costarring role in his third film for Warner Bros., *When a Man Loves.* As hard as he could be on the women in his life personally, Jack was unfailingly generous when it came to furthering their careers. His sister Ethel, well into her second decade as a Broadway star, gasped during a screening of the film as her brother "threw" scene after scene to Dolores in appallingly un-Barrymore-like fashion.[2] It had the intended effect: though the film itself was largely panned, critics were fulsome in their praises for Dolores's luminous portrayal of Manon Lescaut.

"I'll probably drink a lot on this voyage," Jack told Henry Hotchner, his business manager, before pulling anchor. "I'm tired of waiting, the silly mix up of it all. Drink has been one of my two great weaknesses. . . . I do not want to hurt the one person I love more than I ever have loved anyone else, for she seems to adore me so trustingly."[3]

He was away for two months. The "silly mix-up" he referred to was simply that he had not yet asked Michael Strange for a divorce. Given Jack's "bad luck" with matrimony, as he put it, the prospect of a third marriage terrified him. But what choice did he have? Keeping his hands off of Dolores, as always, was Mae, whose chaperonage he had been entirely unsuccessful in thwarting. "Why is it that such a lovely girl as Dolores has to have a mother?" he moaned to Hotchner.[4] And the arrival a year earlier of the dyspeptic Maurice had transformed the house that Jack had once hated to leave, into a place he no longer wanted to visit.

Nevertheless, he returned from his sea voyage in February 1927 more in love with Dolores than ever—and more determined than ever to have, and especially, to hold her. The original purpose in acquiring the *Mariner* had been to whisk his beloved out to sea and away from prying eyes.[5] But to Jack's crushing disappointment, Mae refused to let Dolores set foot on the yacht without her. The only way they would ever go sailing alone, Mae assured him, would be as husband and wife. They had set out together the previous summer—Jack, Dolores, her inescapable mother, and Henry Hotchner—into a plunging ocean that at once sent Mae staggering to her cabin. When Hotchner tried to bring her medicine, Jack planted himself squarely in front of her cabin door. "What are you doing here?" his employer asked.

"I thought I'd better give Mrs. Costello this Mothersill's Remedy," Hotchner answered, "I have another box."

"No. You'll give her none of that remedy whatsoever. After all you are *not* a physician. I'll thank you not to practice medicine on this craft." Jack thrust his hand in his pocket and snorted. "Now Hank, go read a book, or look out a porthole. Dolores and I at last can have the after-deck to ourselves."[6]

Jack's dream of being alone with Dolores on a sea voyage faded as Mae's condition grew progressively worse. Finally, Dolores insisted the *Mariner* turn back. "My God," Jack declared, "I shall never again celebrate Mother's Day."

New Year's 1928 found Barrymore ruminating over the prospect of marrying Dolores, and Dolores seriously considering what marriage to Jack might actually entail. She didn't realize it at the time, but she would in effect be marrying her father. Jack and Maurice were only five years apart in age. Both were former stage actors who had abandoned the theater to become movie actors of unprecedented renown. Both were famously handsome. Both were hard drinkers, on whose lives and personalities alcohol had a degenerative effect. Both suffered fits of pathological jealousy, especially when in their cups.

Until the matter of their marriage could be resolved, Jack and Dolores returned to their cloistered evenings on North Ivar, with Mae hovering nearby, Helene dashing in and out, and the deposed head-of-household seething in the shadows. Any diaries Maurice might have kept after 1925 are presumably lost or missing, but during 1927–1928 he filled a pair of pocket ledgers with diary-like entries that have survived. "Beginning another year in this wonderful country," he wrote on January 1. "I hope with better luck."[7]

In February, Maurice found an unexpected ally in his so-far-ineffectual campaign to send Jack packing: "Saw J. L. Warner. Worried about D & J. B. report."[8] The day before, a reporter had called to inquire about the rumors going around that John Barrymore was romantically involved with his daughter. While meeting with Jack Warner, Maurice expressed his concerns that if the press were to learn the rumors were true, it could mean the end of Dolores's movie career. Now the Warners were concerned as well.

By then Maurice was well into planning his escape. In April he bought a new Nash automobile for $1,527. He had been working for almost a year, playing minor parts for low-budget outfits like Sierra Pictures. Producer Joseph Schenck, another Brooklyn transplant, gave him a small part in First National's *Camille,* directed by Fred Niblo and starring Schenck's then-wife Norma Talmadge. Maurice had given Norma her first big break in *A Tale of Two Cities,* but now the roles were reversed: Norma was the star, and Maurice was as hard up for work as a penniless actor could possibly be.[9]

By spring, the Costellos had reached the breaking point. Mae and Dolores were no longer speaking to Maurice, nor he to them. Beside the March 21 date in his ledger, he wrote the single word "Hell."[10] He began staking out the house like a private detective, a practice that better resembled stalking as time went on. What he was snooping around for on the night of April 10 isn't clear, but what he found in Helene's ashtray caught his attention. "Found cigarettes in Helene's car. J. B.'s," he wrote.[11] A soda bottle or a box of matches would have gone undocumented—but unlike a soft drink, in the halcyon days of cigarette smoking, one's choice of brands was as much an expression of individuality as a matter of taste. Maurice knew from the brand alone that Jack was the person sitting with Helene in her car that night.

The irresistible question then becomes, what were they doing there? In her memoir, Helene confessed that she had at least considered the idea of having a romance with Jack. "When a reporter asked her after [his] death," she wrote, 'Helene, what do you think would have happened if Jack had married the other Costello girl? . . . Would you have been more of a mate for him than Dolores?' She replied, 'Not more of a mate, but an evener match maybe.'"[12] It would have been just another clever retort, if not for the cigarettes. They piqued Maurice's interest to the point that he documented their discovery—though it should be remembered that he was a mass of suspicions at the time.

Still, one could conjecture that in early 1927, with Dolores and Jack still a long way from getting married, that Jack and Helene repaired to that time-honored place of semi-privacy where, from the earliest days of the Model T, two people might do something other than talk. Or, perhaps not. On at least one occasion, Helene referred to herself as Jack's "kid sister," but whether or not that was actually true, no one can ever know.

Though Helene couldn't keep up with Dolores professionally, at least she was holding her own. She was voted a WAMPAS Baby Star in 1927, along with a bumper crop of newly minted Hollywood starlets, most of whom would vanish as soon as they were chosen. In *The Fortune Hunter* she was again paired with Sydney Chaplin, in what was described as a "woebegone comedy." Coincidentally, it was in the original stage version that John Barrymore had scored his first great Broadway success. But Chaplin wasn't Jack: his overacting fell flat with audiences, and the film got few laughs.[13]

As usual, critics panned the film but praised Helene. Next, she was third-billed in *Finger Prints* (Myrna Loy was fourth), starring the popular comedienne Louise Fazenda. She flaunted her dancing skills in *Good Time Charley* (called a "Haunting Heart Story of an Old-Time Actor—His Dancing Daughter—and a World of Other Folks!"). In *Husbands for Rent,* Warner Brother's final release of the year, she played opposite Owen Moore.[14]

Helene had a supporting role in *The Heart of Maryland,* one of the four features in which Dolores appeared that year as stand-alone star.[15] In the 1895 stage version, the sight of Mrs. Leslie Carter swinging on a bell clapper, her scarlet tresses sailing in the air, brought audiences to their feet in ovation after ovation. Now it was Dolores's turn to play the Southern heroine who silences the great bell, moments before it can warn of her Northern lover's escape from a Confederate prison. By a strange coincidence, while Helene was costarring in *The Fortune Hunter,* which had made John Barrymore a star, Dolores was starring in *The Heart of Maryland,* which had costarred Jack's father, Maurice Barrymore, as the Northern officer. Stranger still, if the story Helene told in her memoir is true, Maurice Barrymore and Maurice Costello were both part of the original stage production.

Believers in fate might see theirs as converging paths leading to the inexorable union of America's two greatest acting families. But such an occurrence couldn't have seemed more unlikely that spring. The day after Maurice found Jack's cigarettes in Helene's car, the final blowup occurred. "Dolores did her stuff and How! Which wrote finish," Maurice wrote.[16] Years later he told a reporter that it was he, not Dolores, who ended it all: "Things came to a crisis one night. I said to my family, 'I am going to step out of character as a bystander and say something. I want Dolores to stop going with John Barrymore.' Dolores pointed out that she was of age and entitled to do what she pleased. There was nothing left to be said so I left the house."[17]

Barrymore biographer Margot Peters offered a different version of the breakup in her book, *The House of Barrymore*: "The Costello women themselves ignored Maurice until the day he called Jack a blackguard and ordered him out of the house. Then Mae slapped her husband's face and Dolores and Helene wept. Costello slammed the door."[18] A week later, the same day that Maurice started work on *The Shamrock and the Rose* with former Keystone Cop Mack Swain, he moved out of the North Ivar house and into a small apartment on North Hobart Street. For the sake of convenience, the new place was less than a mile from the old one. Maurice had moved out, but he had no intention of staying away. "J. B brought D. home 10:15 p.m.," he wrote while parked outside his former residence on May 10.[19] His earliest forays into spying, which had turned up the cigarettes in Helene's car, became a full-blown obsession within days of his departure. Of particular interest, as always, was the issue of Dolores's virginity—especially because Barrymore was being allowed to come and go as he pleased. Mae had slacked off considerably in her duties as chaperone after Maurice's departure: Jack and Dolores went for nightly, unaccompanied rides in Jack's car and often arrived home well after midnight.

Maurice was gathering information from other sources as well. "Mrs. C and Dolores had hell with J. B. about Dolores' downfall, Guthrie told me," he wrote.[20] Whoever Guthrie was, he told Maurice that mother and daughter were actively pressuring Jack to end his marriage to Michael Strange. Any day, they feared, the best-kept secret in Hollywood would burst into the open. At some point, Jack told Mae that he and Dolores had gone well past the kissing stage. "He also admitted to Mrs. C. that he had been intimate with Dolores," Maurice fumed. "And what a dirty Cur he has been (The world knows what a Rat he Is)."[21]

His suspicions confirmed, Maurice fell into a black depression. "I used to drive into the hills and cry myself to sleep," he said a few years later. "Sometimes I would take my newspaper and read myself to sleep. Sometimes I cried myself out of the idea of murder. I would wake up there in the hills and look at the sunshine and decide this was better than San Quentin, that after all John was not worth murdering."[22]

Toward the end of his diary rant he added, almost as an afterthought: "Guthrie also told me of the Service of the papers and how they cried on the train." Somehow, Maurice had timed the delivery of Mae's divorce summons to the family's departure to attend the New York premiere of *Old San Francisco,* which featured Dolores in the starring role. Warner Bros. spared no expense in re-creating the city's 1906 earthquake, complete with added sound effects thanks to the studio's patented Vitaphone system (essentially a synchronized phonograph record coupled to a film projector). Dolores played the granddaughter of impoverished California aristocrats in the grip of various "political sharks."[23] In a pre–*Charlie Chan* Asian role, Warner Oland costarred as a nefarious landowner who covets the family's *rancho* almost as much as he does Dolores, whom he eventually imprisons in an underground chamber. His timing couldn't have been worse: the San Francisco earthquake crushes him in the last reel, as "all San Francisco quakes, totters, falls and burns. But nary a strand of Dolores' marcelled hair is harmed."[24]

After publicity appearances in Chicago and Columbus, the Costello women would have arrived in Manhattan with greater fanfare, had they shown up on time. "No, I did not get off the train at 125th Street," Dolores told reporters. "We simply overslept." Her snappish response caused one of them to wonder if "she was evading the press because she had something to hide."[25]

The bigger story was something the newspapers wouldn't learn about for another two months. John Yznaga Regan was a "childhood chum" of Helene's when his father was stationed at Fort Totten, a military installation less than a mile from the Costellos' Bayside estate. "He was a college football star when they met in New York," Helene wrote. "They eloped secretly and were married by a justice of the peace at 2:00 a.m. Just as he said, 'I now pronounce you man and wife,' the clock opened and said 'Cuckoo, cuckoo!'"[26] Like her mother and father a quarter century earlier, Helene and her new husband would have to delay their wedding night until their parents were told of the marriage.

Before Jack Regan, the high point of Helene's love life had been her short-lived relationship with Lew Warner (inexplicably it was Dolores, not Helene, who later called him her "first love"), which was quickly smothered under the weight of Mae's overprotectiveness. Mae insisted that Jack and Dolores accompany Helene and Lew whenever they went out. "Any man [she] brought along," Helene wrote, "had life made unbearable by Jack, who was jealous of any man around Dolores. Usually they never came back, so the mother made up the foursome."[27]

The day before she left for New York, Helene told her father over lunch that she and Douglas Fairbanks Jr. were engaged to be married. Though the apparent husband-to-be never owned up to anything besides having "a serious crush" on Helene, it's hard to imagine that she would have told her father they were getting married if Fairbanks hadn't actually proposed.[28] Whatever happened between them, the last thing Helene planned to do on her trip was marry somebody else. To have supplanted the exquisitely handsome Fairbanks Jr.—to the point of sweeping Helene off her feet and into matrimony on the same night—Regan must have made quite an impression. Then again, with Dolores getting all the attention, Helene was especially receptive to the overtures of the "stalwart, handsome young giant."

She waited for the boat trip home through the Panama Canal (clearly, Dolores was in no hurry to return to Jack) to tell her mother and sister about the marriage. To help break the news, Helene enlisted the aid of Democratic committee chairman Ed Flynn, whom she met aboard ship.[29] Whatever their initial reaction, Regan arrived in Hollywood late that summer to find Mae and Dolores in full support of the marriage, and a belated church wedding in the offing. The newlyweds married for a second time on September 29—the same day that Irving Thalberg and Norma Shearer took their vows. "Their wedding night almost cost Helene her life," she wrote in an aside to the publisher she would never find. "She should have had surgical attention first." The revelation that Regan's clumsy assault on her virginity had medical repercussions makes what happened after that all the more understandable:

> The brief marriage that followed was equally tragic. Regan was never a lover. He didn't even have a job, and Helene was making $600 a week. His uncertainty made him miserable. He drank with his own friends and would not even go to the studio with

> her because he would not be her "lap dog." And when they were home alone at night, both just 19, in a world a little too fast for them, they quarreled. He left in January for Washington, got halfway there, and wired her he was coming back. She went on location and left Jack Barrymore to handle him. Regan arrived here broke. Barrymore handled him, very wisely, and loaned him $500 (which Helene paid back) to return to Washington.[30]

In hindsight, Helene could have learned a thing or two from her cannier older sister, who was biding her time as far as marrying Jack was concerned. The fact that he was still married to Michael Strange hadn't stopped him from all but moving into the North Ivar house after Maurice's departure, much to Mae's frustration and dismay. In the meantime, Maurice resumed his nightly surveillance activities, documenting from the front seat of his Nash exactly who went where and with whom. On August 24, he drove by the house to find the lights off and the cars gone. "No wonder," he scribbled. "Family moved to Beverly Hills."[31]

Having gone from rags to riches, then to rags, then to riches again, the Costello women had pampered themselves accordingly. The tiled-roof, Spanish-style house at 1388 Schuyler Road was de rigueur for a Hollywood family of their stature. It was also a signal triumph for a stage mother and her two daughters, who like Cecil, Edna May, and Mary Gibbs Spooner three decades earlier, had fought their way to the top of a profession that was, and still is, notorious for its maltreatment of women. They had let nothing and no one stand in their way—not even Maurice, whose bad temper, exacerbated by alcohol, had cost him their love and respect.

Harder to fathom is the intense cruelty shown to Maurice by his wife and daughter during their last two years together as a family. But it was the Costellos' peculiar failing to have been at their best at the worst of times, and at their worst in the best of times. In the end, it was success that tore them apart, not failure. In her memoir, Helene summed it up with these mournful lines by Kipling:

> Oh the years we waste and the tears we waste
> And the work of our head and hand
> Belong to the woman who did not know
> (And now we know that she never could know)
> And did not understand.[32]

13

Xanadu and Vicinity

Unlike other movie stars, Jack couldn't just buy himself a house in Beverly Hills and move into it. He required a citadel. Perched on a mountaintop a thousand feet above sea level, the three-and-a-half-acre property at No. 6 Tower Road had an expansive view of the Pacific Ocean and the Channel Islands, including Catalina and beyond.[1] At night, the city twinkled beneath it. Better still, the place had limitless potential. To the existing house and grounds Jack would add all manner of architectural folly in the months and years to come: an aviary, a rathskeller, outbuildings for servants and storage, a projection room, a trophy room, and, his favorite addition, a hideaway over the master bedroom reachable only by ladder, where he could repair for cocktails or to read his scripts. Outdoors he installed a skeet range, a kidney-shaped swimming pool, and several artificial ponds.[2]

By early 1928, Jack did not so much live in Beverly Hills as preside over it. In January, he started construction on a second residence he would call the "Marriage House." Whether Dolores would oblige him by living in it remained to be seen. Having recently banished her father, she seemed in no hurry to take up residence with another veteran alcoholic. Jack's boozy fistfight with agent Myron Selznick in February—dubbed "the fight of the century" by the Hollywood press—shocked Dolores and infuriated her mother. "Sober up, you son of a bitch," Mae told Jack, "or leave my poor angel be."[3]

"Sometimes he was drunk," said Camilla Horn, his German-born costar in *Tempest*, the first of three films he made for United Artists. "When we were dancing together in one scene—a beautiful ballroom scene . . . he fell down with me on the floor because he was so drunk."[4] In March, the exasperated Dolores left town with her mother and sister for an extended holiday that eventually took them to Cuba. In Havana, they were reintroduced to the wealthy Del Barrio family: the brothers Earl, Mario, and Arturo—and their formidable mother, Cora, who Mae had attended school with in New York.[5] Arturo, known as "Mussie" (pronounced *Moosie*), fell instantly in love with Helene, and she with him. They promised to see each other again at the earliest opportunity.

The Costello women arrived home just in time to find the Barrymore-Costello romance splashed across the pages of a Hollywood scandal sheet. Mae sent Jack a copy of the exposé, which promised "more of the same" in later installments. Henry Hotchner found him pacing the grounds of his estate, brandishing the column in an agitated state. "I was waiting for a propitious moment to tell Blanche about a divorce," Jack told his manager sharply. "It seems now that moment has arrived."[6]

Actually, the moment had come a year earlier. Unbeknownst to the Costellos, the *Detroit Free Press* ran a full-page story on Jack and Dolores's budding romance, beginning with a lurid headline—"ALL BECAUSE SHE LEARNED TO LOVE BARRYMORE'S HATED KISSES: How Pretty Dolores Costello's Romance with the Famous Actor May Drive Her Parents Apart and Get Jack in New Hot Water."[7]

It took Helene to finally confront Jack on the matter of her sister's increasingly perilous love affair:

> It was a little hard to talk to the amused Barrymore like a Dutch Uncle. The more I talked, the madder I got. The madder I got, the wider his diabolical smile. I told him simply he had to do something to hush the gossip, for mother's sake. He had two alternatives—start to get his divorce so marriage could be at least a possibility, or stay away. Unexpectedly, he patted my shoulder. He hated coercion but he had a terrific sense of humor and he appreciated fair play. It just hadn't occurred to him that people would talk, or that Mother could be hurt. "Put up the family shotgun, sis," he said. "It won't be necessary to bring this up again."[8]

By midsummer 1928, Jack's divorce proceedings were moving along at a comfortable pace. After five years of physical separation, Michael Strange, no paragon of fidelity herself, agreed to give him his freedom. Jack proposed to Dolores, who said yes on the condition that he quit drinking for a period of six months.[9] He went on the wagon, but couldn't stay on it for long. Their wedding plans hit a snag in July, when Jack flew into a jealous rage after Dolores smiled and nodded in response to a male friend's greeting. The incident plunged him into a deep depression that took him weeks, and a return to sobriety, to emerge from.

Earlier in the year, Dolores's speaking voice made its screen debut in *Tenderloin,* costarring Conrad Nagel and featuring an improved Vitaphone sound-on-disc process that, since the release of *The Jazz Singer,* did more than produce incidental music and sound effects. She and Nagel were paired again in *Glorious Betsy,* a costume drama notable for Hal Mohr's dazzling cinematography (especially when Dolores is in frame), also for the liberties Nagel took with his costar during their love scenes, alternately pawing her buttocks and kissing her breasts. No wonder Dolores had unpleasant memories of working with him.[10]

As soon as she returned from Cuba, Dolores literally plunged into the making of *Noah's Ark,* Warner's most epic film to date. The "Idol of Moloch" scene called for her to be blasted with 250,000 gallons of water aimed at her from several directions. "I called it mud, blood and flood," she told an interviewer for the *Hollywood* series. "It was very difficult, it was brutal. . . . It was an enormous set, a huge pool. . . . They had Longhorn steers in there, and human beings, and some dummies."[11]

When Hal Mohr heard what director Michael Curtiz was planning, he instantly quit the picture. "He had the courage to walk off that set when he saw that people were going to be hurt and killed possibly," Dolores said. "It hurt him terribly, hurt his career and . . . the business lost a great cameraman, I lost my great cameraman; he taught his assistant how to light me and that was all."[12] The day the flood sequence was scheduled to begin filming, Dolores arrived at the studio to find that the first shot had gone horribly wrong and that thirty-eight people had been taken to the hospital. "The director had put real people in where there were supposed to have been dummies, in this tank with animals and cows with huge horns. . . . They did not want me to know about it or see it. There was one man left, heavily bandaged. He said 'I'm the least hurt and I'm waiting for an ambulance.' And he *was* hurt. And he said 'I don't know what's happened to the other men. . . . I think someone might have been killed.'" She recalled that "there was great silence on the set that afternoon while we worked—great, great silence."[13]

Actors, she said, were treated "like tools" in those days. Her costar George O'Brien had two toenails ripped off during the flood sequences. When it came time for her scenes, Dolores was fitted with an "Egyptian bra," to which piano wires were attached to keep her from washing away. "When all the water hit it was like a drowning feeling. . . . I was washed into a lot of blankets that people were holding, and went to my dressing room, freezing, saying 'is this the way to earn a living?' . . . So my mother was sitting in the dressing room on the set, the hairdresser and wardrobe woman and nurse were throwing alcohol at me, you know. Mr. Curtiz came in and said 'My sweet, you will have to do this over again.' And I said 'No, no, never, never, never again.'"[14]

"You do have to my sweet, your mother showed," he replied, to which her mother responded, "Mr. Curtiz, I've been sitting in here the whole time, I couldn't bear it." What the Hungarian director was trying to say in his broken English was that her breasts had been visible in the shot. Dolores recalled, "The bra was up on the piano wire and when they threw things over me I didn't know about the bra. All I wanted to do was get away from there, where I could be warm and safe. But I had to do it again. . . . I was there, nude practically. I did it, I repeated the scene. But it was a horrible experience. . . . I was drenched. I was never dry."

In *The Third Degree,* Dolores had a similarly perilous experience: "50 feet in the air on a tightrope, with only a frame made for me to hold on to, in tights. And the men all in overcoats photographing this down on the old Vitagraph lot. . . . I did the dive, it was what was called a Jackson shot in those days. It was matched, and I had to hit a cigarette butt. . . . To do that part of the dive and then to do the part on the tightrope, 50 feet in the air. I had courage."[15]

That Helene had sneaked in through the back door of movie history took nothing away from the grandeur of her accomplishment. That the role of Kitty Lewis in *The Lights of New York* wasn't given to a bigger star, like Dolores perhaps, owed mostly to happenstance. Director Bryan Foy, son of vaudeville star Eddie Foy, had approached Jack Warner in February with the idea of making a short film with a smaller budget that might also do well at the box office. Warner approved the project and left for Europe on a business trip.[16] With his boss out of the country, Foy did what he had wanted to do all along: make the first full-length, all-talking picture. To stay on budget, he managed to finish the film in just seven days.

When Jack Warner returned to find that the short subject he had approved had been expanded to feature length, he summoned Foy into his brother Harry's office. The movie was too long, the brothers agreed—it would have to be cut to the originally planned two reels. Foy knew that time was of the essence: Fox had just released *The Family Picnic*, the first all-talking short film.[17] In desperation, he showed his movie to an exhibitor, who offered to buy it for $5,000 more than the studio had paid to make it. When Harry Warner learned of the offer, he turned the matter over to his brother Albert, who liked the film and agreed to release it.

On July 6, 1928, *The Lights of New York* opened at the Mark Strand Theater in New York.[18] Critics had good reason to hate it; those who saw the coming of sound as the ruination of an art form could rest their case. The acting was stiff (literally, as the actors couldn't move beyond the range of a stationary microphone), the dialogue stilted, the plot nonsensical. But none of that mattered. As was the case in Maurice Costello's time, novelty ruled the picture houses, and moviegoers flocked to see it. The studio went on to recoup its investment sixfold.

In a forgettable role, in an equally forgettable film, Helene became not only the first actress to star in a modern movie—one with spoken dialogue from start to finish—but, with actor Cullen Landis playing second fiddle, the first person to star in one. For all Dolores's glamour and popularity, it was Helene who made history. Not since Maurice Costello's "Great Days" had a screen actor ushered in a whole new era of filmmaking. Al Jolson had talked his way through only a small part of *The Jazz Singer*, which, as far as moviegoers were concerned, was already ancient history.

"Both girls in the big money, the fabulous money that came faster than it could be spent," Helene recalled dreamily. "At the top of the heap, Dolores and Helene were making more than they ever made or ever were to make."[19] This was truer of one sister than the other: for Helene, the success of *The Lights of New York* was too little, too late to save a career that had bounced along, but never quite taken off. The film itself couldn't have been more unflattering to the actors who appeared in it. Foy put so little time into the picture that Helene's flubbed line in the Central Park scene was left in, as were other sequences that, under less frantic circumstances, would have been reshot. Had there been more time to rehearse, Helene's lack of experience speaking in front of a camera wouldn't have been quite so obvious. The movie's thrown-together look caused one reviewer to call it "interesting as an experiment," but "very far from being a finished product."[20] Helene's voice was reportedly criticized, but though pitched a little low, it was not at all unpleasant. Perhaps if she had been given better lines to speak and more time to practice them, the film would have helped her career instead of hindering it.

Warner Bros. starred Helene in one more film, *The Midnight Taxi,* featuring Valentino rival Antonio Moreno as the love interest, before terminating her contract. Years later she claimed the studio fired her because she refused to play second fiddle to Rin Tin Tin. But the real reason was that Helene had failed to gain a larger audience. In the *Exhibitors Herald*'s 1928 ranking of the industry's forty-seven most bankable female stars (Dolores came in fifteenth among the women, John Barrymore twentieth among the men), Helene did not even place, despite her groundbreaking presence in *The Lights of New York.*[21]

For entirely different reasons Dolores was also about to fade out of the movie business. Unlike other silent stars who lost their careers to the coming of sound, her departure was voluntary. With Jack mostly on the wagon and the Marriage House taking shape atop Beverly Crest, Dolores wanted to give her full attention to becoming the wife of John Barrymore and all that would entail. Day-to-day life with Jack, she already knew, would take every bit of her time, energy, and stamina.

Unlike the footloose Helene, who would have been far better suited to stardom, Dolores was never comfortable in the limelight. Three years under contract to Warner Bros. had embittered and exhausted her. Having impersonated all manner of ringleted heroines, she was bored to death with the scripts being handed to her and began to reject them outright. Then, when the studio refused to give her a raise, Dolores went on strike. During the three months she refused to work, it was Mae, not Dolores, who dealt with the studio's representatives. When they threatened to blackball her daughter, Mae promised to take "this to the highest court as a test case," and if they lost, to "take Dolores back to the theater where she belongs." In the end, said Dolores, "Warners came to an agreement and made a contract, but we fought them."[22]

It was *Noah's Ark,* she said, that "just about finished it." When Michael Curtiz jokingly promised to give her "a loving cup" for their tenth film together, Dolores was firm in her reply. "There will be no tenth," she said—and there wasn't.[23]

By the fall of 1928, the professional lives of all three of the Costello women were in decline. Mae had served her daughters ably as de facto agent and business manager from their earliest days with the *Scandals.* With Dolores soon to be married, and Helene the divorcée able to fend for herself, Mae looked forward to easy retirement within the lush confines of Beverly Hills, about as far from the slums of Pittsburgh as one could possibly be.

Ironically, Maurice's film career was taking an upward turn. He had appeared in six films since he set off on his own, mostly third-billed parts for such low-rent distributors as Rayart Pictures. The exception was First National's *The Wagon Show,* which featured Western superstar Ken Maynard and costarred Maurice as Colonel Beldan, the snowy-haired proprietor of a Wild West show. In March, he returned to the one-a-days in a pair of vaudeville sketches, *The Pay-Off* and *The Rat,* which took him as far north as Vancouver and as far south as San Diego. After three months on the road, Maurice returned home for a month before he left again to appear in a sketch called *The Getaway.*[24] He arrived flush with cash, and from the tone of his ledger entries, a far rosier view of the future. Several months earlier, Maurice had rented the bungalow at 322 South Wetherly Street at the foot of Beverly Hills, not just to stay within easy spying distance of his family, but because now he could afford to live in a better neighborhood.

Maurice had gotten his divorce the previous year (Mae had neither responded to nor contested the suit), and when Helene was granted hers in June 1928, each of the Costellos was maritally unencumbered for the first and last time in their collective history. Maurice was now estranged from both of his daughters, the latest rift having occurred over custody of Buster. He had taken the dog with him when he left, presumably without the rest of the family's permission. One afternoon he arrived home to find Buster missing, and only one explanation for where he had gone. "Saw Buster at 1388 Schuyler Road at 11:45 P.M.," he wrote a few days later. "Family has him. Damn crooks."[25]

The stealing, or stealing back, of the Costello's beloved pet was the last straw. Maurice's nightly stakeouts ended for good after that. To his sorrow, Father's Day came and went without a word from Helene. Dolores purposely ground salt into his wounds by leaving his name off the guest list of her planned November wedding.

But on the whole, Maurice was enjoying his new life, though embittered references to the old one abound in his ledgers. "Left Home one year ago today," he wrote on April 17.[26] "Saw Mrs. and Helene, snubbed her good," he gloated a few months later. Maurice had gone on several dates—the first with a woman identified only as "K. H." He went to dinner two or three times with someone named Lois Cornell. In the fall, Maurice met Alice Rinaldo, and they were instantly inseparable—dining together every night, going to the movies, visiting friends. Maurice was happier than he had been in decades. "A perfect day 100%," he wrote after spending it with Alice. She proved to be such a distraction that even the potentially hand-wringing event of Dolores's wedding somehow passed without incident. With Alice in his life, he had even survived his daughter's marriage to John Barrymore—the singular catastrophe he had sacrificed himself on the altar of his family to prevent.

14

Going South

Jack and Dolores were married on November 24, 1928, in haste and secrecy after a tangle of press reports threatened to derail the entire proceeding. Jack's hopes of keeping their wedding a secret went awry from the moment he entered the courthouse to apply for a marriage license. Arriving alone at the clerk's office, he filled out the application in the name of John Blyth Barrymore, using his father's actual last name for his middle name and falsely giving his age as forty-one. No doubt as soon as he left, someone tipped off an Associated Press reporter, who had not heard the gossip and was therefore blindsided: "News of the engagement caused a mild sensation in Hollywood, as none but the closest friends of the couple were aware that anything more than a friendship existed between the two."[1]

Two days after Jack applied for the marriage license, the AP ran a story based on an anonymous tip from a female caller, who claimed that John Barrymore was still married to Michael Strange.[2] A "visibly annoyed" Jack brushed off reporters' questions during a break in the filming of *Eternal Love.* "Well, when are you going to get married?" one asked. "I said that was all I had to say," he replied, stomping off to finish a snow scene. Meanwhile, Dolores told a klatch of reporters that as far as she knew her fiancé was free to marry. When asked for his take on the situation, Maurice was only too happy to stir the pot. "I don't like the look of things now," he groused to a reporter. "It doesn't put anyone in a very good light. I think he ought to clear up the situation."[3]

> I did all I could to stop the marriage. I lost my home, job, and the affection of my children in trying to stop it. Why, John Barrymore is of my generation, not Dolores'. Funny, my divorce was granted on Dolores' birthday, September 17. Everyone says I'm going to

> sue John Barrymore for alienation of my children's affections. My lawyer helped me write them a letter which should answer that. It ended, "I have given my forgiveness and blessing for a long and happy wedlock, Lovingly, Dad." I am something like John Barrymore myself and that is the reason I do not want him for the husband of my baby. Barrymore's contract is typical of the man. No one has anything to say except Barrymore. He has the final word on everything: cameraman, extra girls, electricians. He always will. God help Dolores![4]

Jack put the matter to rest by marrying her the next day in the rose-strewn parlor of Dolores's house on Schuyler Road. The befuddled press wouldn't learn of their nuptials until two hours later. Because Jack had been married twice before, the Catholic couple had to engage a Unitarian minister to perform the ceremony.[5] The groom's friend and biographer Gene Fowler claimed that Jack ended his alcohol fast shortly before the wedding, which might explain the fixed, glassy expression on his face in many of the photographs taken afterward. In one, Dolores gazes up at him stiffly, smiling wanly in a way that seems not quite genuine.

The couple had no choice but to delay the ocean-going extravaganza they had planned for their honeymoon until the completion of their respective pictures. In *Eternal Love,* Jack played a Swiss mountaineer tangled in a doomed love affair; in *Madonna of Avenue A,* Dolores played an innocent young woman whose parent tries unsuccessfully to come between her and her alcohol-soaked boyfriend.[6] Doubtless, it was the easiest part she ever played.

"I have a gift for you," Michael Curtiz told the bride at her reception. "It is the gift of a day for your honeymoon." Instead of having just Saturday and Sunday together, they would have Monday also. As the festivities wound down, Mae wept openly as Jack and "her angel" slipped out through the garage, while a limousine sat in front of the house to decoy the press. After the guests had gone, she spied among the leftovers a bit of handiwork she knew to be Jack's: binding the miniature bride and groom together atop what was left of the wedding cake, was a tiny ball and chain.[7]

Jack would no sooner have taken Dolores on the average honeymoon than he would have bought her the average mansion in Beverly Hills. Douglas Fairbanks and Mary Pickford, the epitome of Hollywood royalty, took the Grand Tour after their marriage, starting in England and ending in Paris six and a half weeks later.[8] Nothing so conventional would have appealed to Jack. With his dream of having Dolores all to himself on the open water still unrealized, nothing short of a mammoth sea adventure with an impossible destination would suffice.

Six hundred miles off the coast of Ecuador, the Galápagos Islands thrust out of the Pacific Ocean to a height of twenty-one hundred feet above sea level. Their distance from the mainland had discouraged human despoliation for centuries, protecting rare species of animals and presenting Charles Darwin with the pristine field laboratory from which he would produce *The Origin of the Species* in 1859. Comparatively rare as a tourist destination even today, in 1928 foreign visitors were practically nonexistent. No commercial airline regularly flew there, and unlike Doug and Mary's honeymoon trip, no luxury liners, railways, or posh hotels waited to pamper traveling movie stars every step of the way. Jack could not have chosen a more remote and potentially hazardous place in which to begin his married life with Dolores. Perhaps as a concession, Jack booked a leisurely cruise aboard a passenger vessel that first took them to Balboa, Panama (then called the Canal Zone), where they would join the *Mariner* and its crew.[9]

Almost as much as the rage-filled diaries of Maurice Costello, the Barrymores' honeymoon diaries bare the souls of legendary film actors as they've rarely been bared before. These enchanting, one-of-a-kind volumes have survived ninety years and innumerable family upheavals to chronicle the adventures of a pair of Jazz Age movie stars at the height of their powers and the peak of their fame. On the day of their departure, Jack presented Dolores a red, pocket-sized journal stamped with the name "Snackett's Diary" in gold letters on the cover, to keep as a personal record of their travels. They would keep a second volume jointly for later presentation to Mae.

The first page of the Snackett's bears the blissful inscription: "Present from my Winkie, December 30, 1928: Dolores C. Barrymore aboard the S. S. Virginia on our own dear honeymoon. We are to meet our own dear yacht, 'The Mariner' at Balboa C.Z.—from there we are going on a fishing trip except to stop at Ecuador—Cocus island and Galapagos. I am thrilled to death. It is such fun spending a vacation of almost 3 months away from everybody with someone you worship."[10]

The next night, while the passengers celebrated New Year's Eve on deck, the newlyweds stole below just before the clock struck midnight:

"Aboard the *Virginia* my darling and I spent a quiet day—Last night we left the people who asked us to join them at five minutes to twelve so that we could spend the New Year together and away from everybody. (I have just kissed Winkie he has the sweetest smile) I was so miserable coming through the canal last year that this more than balances it. I am almost afraid to say how divine everything is—Winkie looks magnificent & he is dear—we didn't get up till lunchtime."[11]

Going through the canal, was she "so miserable" because of Jack's drinking or the news of Helene's elopement—or both? Things had changed drastically since then—Jack had been a loving and sober husband so far. But would it last? The next night, before pulling his wife into bed, Jack pulled her onto the dance floor. "Winkie my darling surprised me tonight—he asked me to dance (a thing he doesn't like doing much) he dances divinely—it was such fun—I am so happy that we are all married up. It's heavenly when you've found someone you love!"[12]

They danced again the following night: "Slept about 12 more hours and feel marvelous. My darling Winkie and I danced again this evening. We had breakfast on our own verandah. I adore my dear husband—we are having a real honeymoon—please God always keep him as sweet and nice as only he can be—We passed the most beautiful coast today, San Salvador."[13]

On the fourth, Dolores wrote: "Winkie and I spent the whole day in our rooms—had lunch on our veranda and read—we didn't go up at all—it was a sweet lazy day—went to bed at 8:30, too hot to sleep—Haven't heard from mother in a couple of days—can't understand it—but know how much she hates spending money on radiograms—I'm afraid this life will spoil me—it's blissful."[14]

On January 5, "My darling and I didn't go on deck until after 4 o'clock. (Stayed with him in the Barber shop until he had his shave—I adore being with him *always*) The Chief engineer Mr. Carstairs & the man who installed the engine showed us the engine rooms—it is a wonderful sight! (just like the *California*)—We watched the 'Masque Ball' for a while this evening—then we came down to our cabin. I adore my egg—I love telling him *everything*."[15]

On January 6, "Went for a swim today in the ship's pool—it was sweet to look up—and find my own dear Winkie watching her [like Helene and Jack, Dolores often referred to herself in the third person]. He had ordered our lunch to be served on their own veranda—It's been an heavenly day—We had the Menkes to dinner with us—We arrive at Balboa tomorrow—

immediately got the stewardess to pack for me—loathe it—*We* get to our own dear boat tomorrow."[16]

In the second diary, Jack addressed his comments directly to Mae.[17] On January 1, "Mama Darling—The sea air is doing your bastard son in law lots of good and Winkie Dink is the belle of the boat—much love, B. S."[18]

On January 2, "Had one of those boat days—doing nothing in particular—Hunnikit wore her red dress and funny red shoes—and looked like the meanest cherry in a Manhattan cocktail—and terribly sweet & absurdly young—we met two nice people, friends of Jack Dempsey's we like better than anyone else on the *boat*!"[19]

On January 3, "Fat Mama—There is only one guy on this boat who dances as well as me. He back heeled his wife as if he didn't know her! And climbed up Winkie as if she was a cliff with daisies on top of it. A fat man out of your past life asked about you. Arunsby. He looks like Karl Schmidt's mother. Winkie is a happy cat I think. Anyway he loves her more than ever."[20]

On January 6, "Have just packed Winnick's two douche pans and given her a bite on the nose—this packing is Hell. But Thank Christ it's over—hope there is a radio[gram] tomorrow at Bulbous Boa from Mama & Helene. Goodnight, Jack"[21]

In Balboa, a district of Panama City, the Barrymores spent a couple of days drawing crowds and being feted by Colonel Mason Mitchell, who had served with Theodore Roosevelt's Rough Riders. On the ninth they joined Otto Matthies, Jack's boat captain, on the *Mariner* to prepare for departure. "We leave today on our own dear boat," Dolores wrote. "Winkie and I went for a drive—stopped at the Church of the Golden Altar—(the altar was built before Morgan destroyed old Panama)—it is very beautiful. Winkie and I said a prayer outside—I only hope both our prayers were for the same thing—I love him so much."[22]

The next morning, the *Mariner* dropped anchor at Isla Afuerita, an island off the Panamanian coast. "Went ashore in the most beautiful Island. It has a lovely beach. We want to buy it & call it Paradise Island," Jack wrote, adding, "This is absolutely the Paradise of the world here—I've never seen anything like it *anywhere.* Winkie is a *grand* fisherman!" On the thirteenth, Dolores wrote ecstatically:

> What a divine day!!—Otto rowed us ashore in the skiff for a bath—I don't believe any two people spent such a honeymoon—

> as soon as he left us—we took off our bathing suits and had a bath in the most heavenly small deep pool in a mountain stream—ending in a waterfall—I have never giggled so much or been so happy—The natives were washing the laundry from the boat at the end of the stream they gave us a dried coconut shell to pour water to rinse ourselves. We later visited them in their huts—Had dinner on deck while the sun was setting.[23]

"You would have died today, seeing Winkie & I bathing in that stream," Jack told his mother-in-law. "The natives here have never seen a blonde and they can't get over Winkie."[24] Dolores astonished Jack and Otto by dropping a curlew with her first shot, which began a killing spree of massive proportions. On January 16, they reached Cocus Island, a deep-water paradise 340 miles from the Costa Rican mainland. Of the day's adventures, Jack wrote contentedly:

> The small egg is sleeping on deck in the moonlight curled up with its head and looks about seven. She had a grand day—we went ashore on the Enchanted Island with long waterfalls all over it falling like white silk ribbons into the sea, about three hundred feet high. It is really glorious—we all have to come here someday. She caught lots of fish but the sharks got the big ones so we are going to stay here another day to get Mama a fish big enough to put in the dining room! She insists on catching it herself!![25]

Having shot an alligator, harpooned a giant ray, and hauled a flailing, seventeen-hundred-pound shark aboard the *Mariner,* the Barrymores took a break from the mayhem on the nineteenth to go ashore. Jack showered in a waterfall and chipped their names into a coconut tree, carving "sweet cat" beside Dolores's. When fishing resumed that afternoon, Dolores caught a twenty-five-pound Wahoo, which Jack hoped to hang on Mae's wall: "We tried to skin Winkie's Wahoo this evening—(that doesn't sound right somehow!!), but the skin was too thin so we are waiting till she gets a bigger one for Mama's Dining Room. Gee—we had a good time today."[26]

They took pity on a large frigate bird that mistook Jack's bait for a meal and got caught in his line. "Otto threw him on [the] boat to rest," wrote Dolores, "as he was almost drowned—stayed for a while, threw up, then flew away."[27]

They reached the Galápagos on January 23, but due to rough seas couldn't drop anchor until late the next day. Meanwhile, Dolores confided, they spent the day "reading, taking pictures, and loving each other." The next morning, the skiff took them ashore to Isabela Island, the largest of the archipelago, where they became so enthralled by the animals they saw, that for a moment they stopped shooting them:

> First thing we saw was a big marine iguana. They are strange things—found a huge Sea Lion asleep, we went very close to him, he looks like Buster. We walked about a mile Inland—came back to boat for lunch and then went fishing, caught my first tuna—50 lbs.—also shark 85 lbs. thought I'd pass out before I got them in—my darling caught tuna—shark got all but his head. We went to another part of Island, climbed over rocks of lava. Looks like a dead world. Found a whole family of Sea Lions—The largest one (the father I presume) scratched his ear with his flipper in the most unconcerned manner.[28]

During their two weeks of island hopping, Dolores wrote of the "Galapagosians" they encountered along the way. On February 3, "Left Seymour Is. [for] Anchorage. 5:45 A M. Arrived Chatham Island 3 P.M.—My darling, Otto & I went ashore—were met by a dizzy Ecuadorian who spoke French—my wink surprised me very much by being very apt at the language. We brought him back to the boat & gave him a drink." She went on, "This is a queer little place—there is a Norwegian family here sending dried fish to Guayaquil—one man is very picturesque—looks like all the Norwegians in the world. There is also an Indian family living at the shore. The woman is strange looking. The young French spoken one informed us that the Governor was at Floriana."[29]

On February 4, "Went fishing early this AM—Winkie & I got one Tuna each, 9 Groupers & Spanish Mackeral. Winkie shot 2 Man of War birds. When we were gone the Governor's Secretary came to the boat twice. The Gov. must be awfully busy in this Galapagosian 'town' to need a secretary. They are sending two horses down tomorrow so that Winkie and I can go to Progress (5 miles) to the Plantation & meet his

Highness Don Cohos Alvarado. . . . Been playing Paderewski in honor of mama this eve."[30]

On February 5, from Chatham Island:

> Winkie & I went ashore at 9 AM to visit the plantation. We were met by Sr. Alvarado (I don't know why I should write about this day—I'm sure I'll never forget it). We started out on Donkeys—halfway we were met by horses which we were transferred to. Then Sr. Cohos made a dashing entrance into the scene, after an hour we reached the ranch, had lunch then started out to see the ranch—we rode over 4 hours. It is a divine place, but after 6 hrs on a horse you can only think of one thing. The first sight of the shore we got was the Norwegian Flag & nothing looked more beautiful to us. We were all in.[31]

If in the beginning Dolores was mostly along for the ride, by the end of the expedition she was an accomplished huntress, whose skill with rifle and rod easily matched that of her husband. Only once, when Jack and Otto went ashore without her, was she not beside them to bang away at seabirds, or pull deep-sea fish out of the water. By the time the Barrymores set off for the Ecuadorian coast on February 6, they had shot hundreds of birds and, with rod, harpoon, and seine, had caught thousands of fish. Save for the few that ended up on the ship's dinner table or hanging in Jack's trophy room, their carcasses were tossed back into the sea. The couple drew the line at killing mammals, apparently, because the many sea lions they encountered went unmolested.

When word reached the mainland that a pair of movie stars were about to descend on the Ecuadorian city of Guayaquil, crowds gathered at the docks to welcome them. They were manageable at first, but by the time Dolores and Jack reached their hotel, the crush of townsfolk trying to catch a glimpse of the famous couple had swelled to mob-like proportions. Decades before celebrity bodyguards and personal assistants, the job of coming between Jack and his Ecuadorian female fans fell to Dolores. "Found it almost impossible to get out of the hotel, huge crowds," she wrote on February 11. "Many girls came to our Room—with presents. After I had told one noisy girl (as I can't speak Spanish I used many gestures) that my darling was asleep, hoping she would desist. She made more noise to make him get up, which he didn't do right away so she walked in the bedroom to see him."[32] In Guayaquil, they were fussed over by prominent Ecuadorians before they traveled to Quito by train for two days of sightseeing and antique buying. After checking into their hotel, Jack and Dolores delighted the manager by stepping out on their balcony to quiet the crowds.

On the seventeenth they returned to Guayaquil to attend a gala presentation of *Beau Brummel* at a local theater. As the guests of honor, they felt obliged to appear, but, for deeply personal reasons, they chose not to sit through the entire movie. Having to watch Jack make endless love to Mary Astor, when Dolores knew he had been romantically involved with her at the time the movie was made, would have been excruciating for her. "We didn't watch the picture, for Winkie is a dear, considerate thing," she wrote.[33] It was a gallant gesture on Jack's part, though it spared him considerable agony also. Still, he could not have found a more thoughtful way to celebrate the last night of their honeymoon journey, before they began the long trip home.

While Jack and Dolores were away on their honeymoon, Mae and Helene traveled again to Cuba—partly for vacation, partly to decide whether or not Mussie Del Barrio would be returning with them to Beverly Hills as Helene's husband. He had proposed when he was in town for Dolores's wedding—now they would have to bridge the physical distance between them before the idea of marriage could be seriously considered. The indomitable Cora had already laid down the law: under no circumstances would she permit her son to leave Cuba and move to the United States. "He was entirely dependent on his mother's wealth, and she wanted him with her," Helene wrote. To make matters worse, Mae had "refused to live with Dolores and Jack, and she refused to leave Dolores *with* Jack and go to Cuba with Helene. Thus Helene knew that marriage with 'Mussie' . . . was impossible."[34]

Why Helene couldn't have left Mae to fend for herself in Beverly Hills, with Dolores and Jack just a few miles away, had everything to do with the state of her mother's health. Helene wrote that "the knowledge came suddenly" after her return from Cuba—that is, the knowledge that Mae had suffered a heart attack. This explains why the newlyweds, having just returned from their honeymoon, were spending their evenings on Schuyler Road instead of at the Marriage House, leaving Mae to wonder if all was well in the Barrymore bedroom. One evening they arrived to find her houseman, Walter Ziegler, blocking the entrance. "Mrs. Barrymore," he said, "your mother asks me to say that it's time you did your own housekeeping."[35]

Mae suffered a second heart attack in late July. On the thirty-first, Jack's cousin Georgiana Mendum sat up with her all evening, while Dolores and Jack attended the party they threw for Ethel Barrymore, who was in town to star in a pair of plays at the Biltmore Theater. Georgie's kindness was something Dolores never forgot.[36] Two nights later, while Dolores and Jack were visiting Ethel on Tower Road, Helene came home from the studio to find her mother in bed and awake.[37] Mae asked for something to warm her feet. Helene brought her a hot water bottle, then lay across the foot of her own bed and fell asleep. "The next thing she knew, only a few moments later, the nurse was calling the doctor to say that Mrs. Costello had died," Helene wrote.[38] Though she was only a few feet away, she would have to learn of her mother's passing secondhand. A simple chest X-ray would have revealed that Mae's heart was enlarged to three times its normal size. Decades of chain-smoking had certainly hastened her death.[39] In eleven days, she would have been forty-seven years old.

Dolores was forever changed by Mae's death. So was Jack, and so too was their marriage. "Only those close to Dolores knew how great her grief was," her secretary Kay Hunter recalled, "or with what tender, unfailing devotion Barrymore attended her."[40] Dolores had lost her best friend and closest confidante, her lifelong champion and advocate. She would have to fight her own battles from now on, and there would be many to come.

A week or two before her mother's death, Dolores discovered she was pregnant. She wondered if the immense weight of her grief might harm her unborn baby. Thereafter she decreed that pregnant women should never attend funerals. "She forbade me to go to my mother-in-law's funeral when I was pregnant," her daughter recalled. "She remembered how stricken she was at my grandmother's when she was pregnant with me."[41]

Mae's death was nearly as devastating for Jack, as it marked the beginning of his storied decline. His better angels had thrived under Mae's steadying influence—without her, his demons would run rampant. "If she had lived," director Arthur Lubin commented, "Jack Barrymore's end would have been very different."[42] Ethel saw a change in him immediately.

When she asked Henry Hotchner why he was drinking so heavily, Jack's manager shrugged. "I don't know," he replied. "Is there always a reason?"[43]

Jack's worsening behavior made his grief-stricken wife even more despondent than she already was. He had a "diabolical side," Dolores told Barrymore biographer Hollis Alpert in 1963. His jealousy was "a terrible thing to behold."[44] When David O. Selznick asked her to dance at a party one evening, the result was a police-style interrogation that lasted until 3:30 a.m. "What did he say to you?" Jack asked her over and over. "*What did he say to you?*"[45]

"What is wrong with you?" Dolores shouted back during one of his tirades. "I want to be your friend. Didn't you ever have a woman who was your friend?" She must have known she was asking the impossible. "Actually, he was terrified," she said. "His insecurity stemmed from his mother's death, and then his grandmother's (not to mention, which she didn't, losing his virginity to his stepmother at the age of 15)."[46]

To Jack's growing annoyance, Dolores had turned to Helene for solace and support in the wake of Mae's passing. "I don't know what to do about [her] sister," he complained to Hotchner over cocktails in his tower hideaway, "but I can always tell when Winkie has been down to see her. As you know, Helene is strongly mental and forthright; she has aggressive convictions about what husbands ought to be and do."[47]

"That doesn't seem unreasonable," his manager replied.

"No, but I told her that of late that it isn't so easy to stop drinking as it used to be. She got quite excited at this. Then she said 'it isn't true; you're just putting on an act when you say that.'"

"Putting on an act!" Jack repeated slowly.

"But is it true?" Hotchner wondered. "I mean true that you find it harder to go on the wagon?"

"Yes," Jack admitted, pouring himself another drink. "What do you think I can do about it?"

"Well, you're getting older, and the habit stronger. But you do have terrific will power, when you care to exercise it. The question is, do you really want to stop drinking?"

"I'm not sure that I do," Jack said, looking Hotchner in the eye. Then, after a long silence: "It helps me not to worry too much about the future."[48]

15

Sherman and the Nut

Helene would not have married anyone if Mae had lived, at least not right away—and if she had it would not have been Lowell Sherman. The forty-three-year-old screen star was almost twice her age. Like Jack, he was twice divorced. Like Mussie, he had a domineering mother, to whom he remained overly attached. And, like Maurice Costello, Sherman had been a New York stage actor before he broke into movies.

By 1930, not only had he survived the silent era with his stardom intact but he was also the first American actor-director since Maurice Costello to build a successful career doing both jobs simultaneously (Lionel Barrymore's stint as a feature-film director came and went relatively quickly). Sherman appeared in six films that year (among them *General Crack*, Jack's first talkie), two of which he directed. Two years later, he directed Mae West in *She Done Him Wrong*, the film that saved Paramount from bankruptcy.[1]

Jack sang his friend Sherman's praises to Helene in true Jack fashion. "He's an old son of a bitch," he said, "but he's an amusing son of a bitch."[2] If Helene needed anything at that moment, it was amusement. After leaving Warner Bros., she appeared in a string of forgettable roles for some of the smallest studios in Hollywood. "When the Schuyler Road home became intolerable," she wrote, "she went to stay with Jack and Dolores, in the weird Tower Road house." Every night she waited up for Ethel to return from the theater to tell her "typically Barrymore stories, full of death and ruin and destruction" until the wee hours. As told by the empress of the American stage, "they could take anybody's mind off of anything."[3]

Alone and adrift, Helene welcomed Sherman's advances. "[His] kindness during this trial did much to make things easier. He began asking her to marry him almost daily." When she finally accepted it was with the understanding that there would be no formal engagement or public announcement. Instrumental in getting her to say yes was Jack, whose motives, as Helene rightly suspected, were not entirely selfless. As far as he was concerned, the sooner Helene married Sherman, the sooner she would have better things to do than conspire with Dolores to keep him from drinking. "Whatever the reason, Jack's recommendation was characteristic," she wrote, "and exactly the kind to influence a straightforward mind like Helene's."[4]

Hoping to brighten up the holidays, Jack took Dolores and Helene, both still in the doldrums, to New York for a lavish vacation and shopping spree. Following behind them on another train were Sherman and his ever-present mother, Julia. On September 17, Jack threw a dinner party for Dolores's birthday at the Brevoort Hotel, which all three Barrymore siblings attended. Lowell Sherman brought along a jeweler sporting a tray of items, including numerous rings and a jewel-encrusted wristwatch. "Mrs. Sherman wanted the wrist-watch," Helene wrote, "so she helped him persuade Helene to take an eight-carat emerald set in platinum with eight baguette diamonds. She wore the ring to the party and showed it off. Irene Barrymore, Lionel's wife, said 'Oh, isn't it lovely!' Dolores just said 'Oh!' That killed comment. Helene said, 'Well, I hope we'll be very happy!'"[5]

A month later the stock market crashed and the jewelry parties ended. Jack lost $100,000; Dolores $86,000. Because Helene was spending money faster than she was making it, she had less invested and lost $3,000. After her return from New York, she moved into the ultra-fashionable Beverly Wilshire Hotel and began giving extravagant dinner parties for family and friends.[6] When the last of her money ran out, she borrowed to stay afloat.

Jack, Dolores, and Helene said their professional good-byes to the 1920s in the Warner Bros.' revue *The Show of Shows*; it featured a cast of hundreds that included Helene's old nemesis, Rin Tin Tin, and Myrna Loy doing a Chinese dance number shot in two-strip Technicolor.[7] Jack did his best to steal the picture with a sputtering rendition of Gloucester's soliloquy from *Henry VI,* while Dolores and Helene song-and-danced their way through "Meet My Sister," a studio-sized production number in which the sisters showed their vaudeville prowess in ways unseen since their days with the *Scandals.* As this would be Helene's last hurrah as a movie star, there could have been no better send-off.

As if the arrival of sound wasn't cataclysmic enough, whatever hope Maurice still had of getting another movie part went the way of the prosperous twenties, which had gone the way of the Great Depression. As the studios slashed production schedules in the deflating economy, any doors that might have remained open to him slammed shut. The crash only accelerated vaudeville's decline, leaving a glut of unemployed stage performers (there were some fifty thousand in variety's heyday) to compete for an ever-shrinking number of spaces on the bill.[8]

At the same time, whatever positive developments there had been in Maurice's life—his relationship with the mysterious "Alice" mostly—evaporated with her sudden disappearance from his ledgers toward the end of 1928. Before the breakup came the usual flurry of intelligence gathering, jotted down on his nightly stakeouts in front of Alice's Carthay Circle apartment: "Lights went on at 3:15 AM," he wrote on December 14. A few days later: "Dark except light in hall. Shades up."[9]

His mistrust of women had entered the compulsive stage, and it was about to get worse. Vivienne Sengler, a twenty-five-year-old struggling piano teacher, claimed that Maurice Costello had asked her to marry him after a performance of *The Getaway* in Stockton, California. Whatever happened that night, it could not have prepared Maurice for the bombshell that took a full year to detonate. On December 11, 1929, Sengler's charge hit the front pages of newspapers from coast to coast. The *Brooklyn Daily Eagle,* having faithfully covered Maurice's transgressions since 1913, ran its headline extra bold: "COSTELLO, FIGHTING $100,000 SUIT, SAYS GIRL PROPOSED." The paper reported that the "one-time idol of Broadway" was facing a $100,000 breach of promise suit. Costello, identified as "the father of Mrs. John Barrymore and Helene Costello, prominent film actresses," denied the existence of any understanding with Sengler and called the suit an attempt to "shake [him] down." He claimed that she had proposed to him and that since then he had not seen her. Sengler claimed that Costello had proposed to her in Stockton on September 16, 1928, and that they had planned to wed in April. But, she said, his attitude toward her had changed and he refused to marry her.[10]

Not surprisingly, Maurice gave a different account:

> The girl's mother, Mrs. Rita Costello Sengler . . . met me in the lobby of the Pantages Theater in San Francisco when I was playing there in the spring of 1928. She traced our lineage and pointed out that some of our supposed relatives are priests in Iowa. When Mrs. Sengler's daughter came to Hollywood about a year ago she

> came to me and asked for advice in marketing some scenarios she had written. I supposed she was some kind of relative and advised her from time to time. I jokingly told her she ought to marry some young fellow and settle down. She said she wanted to marry me. Since then—that conversation took place in my Hollywood home—I have not had anything to do with her, as the proposal startled me.[11]

Maurice was telling the truth—mostly. In fact, he *was* performing at the Pantages on April 20. And in December he was in Hollywood when he said Sengler came to see him about selling her scenarios. But on the date Sengler said he proposed to her in Stockton, September 16, Maurice was home on South Wetherly.[12] Indeed, if Maurice had asked Sengler to marry him, he would have noted the event in his ledger, where he recorded everything of importance—but there is not a single mention of her.

What he neglected to tell the newspapers, was that he and Sengler had been corresponding for several months. In one of his letters, Maurice asked her to save him "all her kisses." As it became increasingly evident from her letters that she was emotionally unbalanced, he gradually stopped answering them. Her admission of incest with her father must have shocked him. "[Your] little mustache 'gets' me! (Just like my daddy wore—he taught me how to kiss like they do in France)," she wrote, "no sheik is complete without one—for 'kissing a man without a mustache, is like eating an egg without salt.' (My Daddy told me that)."[13]

Sengler corroborated Maurice's version of the story with her offhand reference to his suggestion that she find a husband. "So I realize that you were right—I should marry (My doctor has been preaching the same thing to me for the last five years). So from now on—I shall be a 'Yes' girl."[14] In another letter, Sengler told him she had turned down seven marriage proposals and also told him of her recent sexual awakening: "Well—the reason is that they did not inspire me with *Love,* the only thing I value in marriage, and secondly because I lived in a world of darkness and 'innocent' ignorance until a few months ago, when a kind of friend put into my hands a book called 'Sane Sex Life, and Sane Sex Living (The Art of Love)' by Dr. H. W. Long." (The book, which can still be purchased, offers explicit descriptions of sexual practices.)

Sengler often talked about marriage in her letters, just never about marriage to *him.* Subsequent correspondence shows her becoming increasingly unhinged until, on July 30, she wrote a last, frantic plea to her imaginary soulmate:

> My Darling:
>
> Why did you not answer the letter of explanation I wrote to you on May 19? The mental strain of this "mystery" is proving too great for me. I have lost everything—
>
> Maurice, if you respected me at all—you would have filed suit for damages against those damn —— gossip women who ruined my life and happiness. I have suffered so great and I have played my loyal part to the end. Sweetheart, won't you be kind and courteous enough to tell me the one word that will either make or break me—Do you love me still or not?
>
> I cannot live without your sweet soul and personality—Life is nothing but memories of you now—I can think of nothing but you—You were my perfect ideal of manhood and honor.
>
> My own, unless I hear from you within *ten* (10) days, I shall end it all—Dear heart—it's *final* this time. So help me God—*I mean it.* I fear I am losing my mind—My only request is that your dear letters that have been my only joy of my sad life be buried with me—also one of your pictures. That is all I ask—I have been loyal and true to *YOU* to the end! (These Hollywood men are begging me to marry them—it's driving me insane—for I love *you* more dearly every day).
>
> I count the moments—hours and days until I hear from you.
>
> My wonderful Daddy—My Lover—
>
> Farewell
> Always and Forever
> Your loving baby and Sweetheart
> Vivienne[15]

Whatever her real reasons were for the lawsuit, they had nothing to do with money—she knew perfectly well he didn't have any. Among the more obvious examples of his poverty, his living room was bare save for an old easy chair and a divan. Added to her oedipal obsession with a washed-up movie star, clearly it was a last-ditch effort by Sengler—an accomplished pianist, composer, and voice teacher—to become famous. In December 1930, a year after she filed charges against Maurice, Sengler told the press that she was dropping the suit; once again, she made the papers. And again in 1932, when she sued the Hallor family for $100,000, alleging that they had slandered her in front of Maurice, thus ruining their relationship. On May 21, with all the parties in court (including Maurice, who showed up to testify on the Hallors' behalf), Sengler testified that while she was renting a room with the Hallors, family members had made derogatory statements about her that reflected badly on "her moral character." Anna Hallor, the head-of-household, denied the plaintiff's charges and claimed that her ex-boarder was insane.[16] Sengler would barricade herself in her room, Hallor testified, as "protection against 'spirits.'" Two days later the judge dismissed the case, and that was the last anyone heard of Vivienne Sengler.[17]

In an interview Maurice gave in March 1929, while Jack and Dolores were on their honeymoon, he told a reporter just how dire his financial circumstances had become. He had worked a total of five weeks the previous year, and had not worked at all in the current one.[18] If not for the Vine Street Stock Company, which gave him a part in the play *Weak Sister,* he didn't know what he would have done. Gazing northwest from the porch of his bungalow, Maurice pointed obliquely toward the hills: "See the sign which reads 'Hollywoodland'? See that white blur just to the right of the water tower? That's the Costello mansion. My former wife and daughter Helene live there now. Just above it . . . is the home and estate of John Barrymore. . . . Every morning when I leave this little house I pause and look up there. . . . It gives me a heartache. Sometimes I wonder if I can go on. Sometimes Helene comes down to see me. My baby girl! And Barrymore for a son-in-law? Bah."[19]

As usual, Maurice didn't blame himself for his problems. He was incapable of self-criticism—even when writing to himself in his own diaries. He spoke at length for the first time about what he called his "downfall." "I loved my wife and babies," he said, "but my domestic life went from bad to worse. My wife slapped me in public, and in 1914 [actually it was 1913], as many persons may recall, she had me arrested on a wife-beating charge, an accusation that was untrue."[20] But it *was* true—he had admitted as much in court. Maurice came close to telling the truth about his career-ending split with Vitagraph. But he stopped short, as he always did, of admitting that drinking was mostly the cause: "My starring days ended in December 1915, when I had a nervous breakdown and didn't work for a year. . . . Then I returned to Vitagraph for another year, but my star was descending." He finished with an account of his most recent troubles, including the Barrymore affair:

> Dolores made *The Sea Beast* in 1925, just before my arrival in October 1925. . . . Upon my arrival I sensed that I was as welcome to my family as some dreaded disease. I was given to understand that my wife was managing the children. We had never gotten along, as I have said, but I had done my best for the sake of the children. I did not want John Barrymore in the house. He was a married man and my ideas are old-fashioned. I protested, but in vain. Then it was that I played my last role as husband and father. When John and Dolores were married last fall I sent them a note in which I wished them well.[21]

Maurice and Helene had grown closer by then, but not close enough for him to rate a front-row seat at her wedding, much less an invitation to give the bride away. On the afternoon of March 15, 1930, Maurice slipped into the Beverly-Wilshire moments before Jack Barrymore started down the aisle with Helene (wrapped in flowing lace gown, a film magazine noted, and wearing "a little Juliet cap with white blossoms"), to meet the stalwart groom at the altar.[22] Clenching a monocle in his furrowed brow, the balding Sherman looked more like the father of the bride than the husband to be. Maurice needn't have worried about running into Dolores, who was eight months pregnant and wouldn't have dared to be seen in public. She was also furious at Helene for refusing to postpone the wedding until after her baby was born and, therefore, wanted nothing to do with the ceremony.[23] Partway through the service, Helene started to weep—because of her mother's recent death, it was surmised. In a wedding photograph taken after the ceremony, she looks sullen and dazed, as if the reality of having made good on her promise to marry Sherman had just then sunk in.

"It cost me a small fortune, but the loot . . . was terrific," she wrote. Among the 155 wedding guests were Mae Murray, Prince Mdivani (Murray's fourth husband), Edmund Lowe, Ina Claire, and Evelyn Brent, who served as matron of honor. "It was a little like Louis and Antoinette reveling in the Tuilleries—while France starved and rioted outside. As for us, the rioting took place in our own home. We fought from the first.

What was worse, Lowell fought with Julia, who lived with us. Their wrangling almost drove me crazy."[24]

Neither Helene nor Dolores had set foot on a sound stage since *The Show of Shows* in 1929.[25] Helene blamed her new husband, who, she said, forbade her to work in pictures. Dolores was absent for a much different reason: on April 8, 1930, she gave birth to a baby girl, christened Dolores Ethel Mae Barrymore after some initial disagreement between the parents. "My mother wanted to call me Nancy," their daughter explained, "but my father was 21 years older than she was, and could be very intimidating. He wanted to name me after my mother, who adored my Aunt Ethel and wanted to name me after her, but also her mother Mae. Eventually it was shortened to Deda, then to Dede."[26]

One of her earliest memories was her mother's nightly practice of bringing a custard dish full of raisins at bedtime. "One night the raisins took effect in a horrible way," Dede said. "I reached into my Dr. Denton's—those were the pajamas with the little feet and the buttons in the back—pulled out their contents and threw them against the wall. Then I began finger-painting. I thought I was doing something great until my parents walked in and my mother let out a bloodcurdling scream. My father slapped his knees in uproarious laughter." She remembered sitting on the floor with him as he showed her how to put on her socks: "Only he didn't stay to see if I was successful or not. I thought to myself, aren't you going to stay and see if I can manage this? He walked out of the room with that walk of his that was like a gorilla."[27]

As Dolores receded into domesticity, Jack entered the most productive period of his screen career. While other silent stars were fading into the past, his famously beautiful stage voice all but guaranteed his continued success. When it was heard for the first time in the 1930 film *General Crack,* all moviedom waxed ecstatic. To one reviewer, the voice was "infinite in its variety of expression, dramatic and distinct, yet quiet and smooth."[28] His next film, *Svengali,* was the first of the classic sound roles for which he is best remembered. Audiences hadn't seen anything quite like the gaunt, beak-nosed predator of George Du Maurier's nineteenth-century novel. With Hollywood's era of classic monsters in full swing, what might have been another horror film became, in Jack's hands, a nuanced portrait of the many-faceted villain, not all of whose facets were villainous. "Although a sinister figure," Jack observed, "he is a wise, dirty, glutinous Polish Jew, with no conscience and a supreme contempt for all those nice, clean, straight-thinking English Christians."[29] Flashes of the young Jack in his Shakespearean prime (which could still be glimpsed when he was sober) abound, especially toward the end of the film. As his eyes well up with real tears in his final speech to the actress Marion Marsh, it is clear why so many still viewed him as the greatest actor of his generation. "They wouldn't let me do Trilby because we were married," Dolores said of the role that ultimately went to the seventeen-year-old Marsh. "It would ruin the whole thing, Zanuck said. Romance you see. The mystery of it and all that, and we were just two married people. It was ridiculous."[30]

Jack wasn't drinking during the making of *Svengali*; he had been scared sober on a recent voyage aboard his new yacht, the *Infanta.* While sailing off the coast of Guatemala, he suffered a gastric hemorrhage and collapsed in agony. A terrified Dolores disembarked at the nearest port and summoned a local doctor, who ordered her husband to stay in bed for the remainder of the voyage. Jack already felt imprisoned—any hope of rekindling his romance with Dolores had faded in the aftermath of childbirth. "She is perfectly fanatical about that child," he told Hotchner. "She's forgetting me entirely in her new love for the baby."[31] Now his failing health had confined him to quarters. "I am told that if I don't quit drinking, I am sunk," he lamented. By then, both husband and wife knew there would be few chances left for recovery.

Probably the earliest surviving photograph of Maurice Costello, c. 1894. (Courtesy of Dolores Barrymore Bedell)

Dimples in evidence, Maurice flashes his famous smile, c. 1912. (Courtesy of the Denise Barrymore Collection)

Dolores, age nine, by Sarony. (Courtesy of Dolores Barrymore Bedell)

Mae, at right, playing her daughter's nurse in a scene with John Bunny, Flora Finch, and five-year-old Helene, in Vitagraph's *Her Crowning Glory* (1911).

Maurice offers to mend Helene's doll in *Lulu's Doctor* (1912).

Maurice eats with his knife in *The Picture Idol* (1912), as a horrified Clara Kimball Young looks on.

On location while "girdling the world" for the Vitagraph Company. Upper row from left: Mae, James Young, Doris Thompson, and Eugene Mullin. Bottom row: Dolores, Maurice, William V. Ranous, Helene, and Clara Kimball Young, in costume. (Courtesy of the Denise Barrymore Collection)

Dolores, Maurice, and Helene, with Clara Kimball Young sitting in for Mae Costello, during Vitagraph's round the world filmmaking expedition. (Courtesy of the Denise Barrymore Collection)

Mother and daughters feeding the pigeons in Tokyo, January 1913. (Courtesy of Dolores Barrymore Bedell)

Weary but still smiling, Mae rides in a Venetian gondola, May 1913. (Courtesy of the Denise Barrymore Collection)

A photograph from one of Dolores's scrapbooks titled *Down on the Farm*. Helene turns her head away while Mae clutches a chicken. Dolores stands at far left. (Courtesy of the Denise Barrymore Collection)

Snapshot of Dolores at a Long Island beach, c. 1919. (Courtesy of the Denise Barrymore Collection)

The Costello sisters pose in matching swimsuits and bathing caps. (Courtesy of the Denise Barrymore Collection)

The Costello's tree-shaded residence in Bayside, Long Island, where Pearl White and Jim Corbett were frequent guests. (Courtesy of the Denise Barrymore Collection)

The four Costellos with unidentified suitor and Buster in the foreground. (Courtesy of the Denise Barrymore Collection)

Helene and her father brave the surf in Miami Beach, where Maurice and Dolores were appearing in the Paramount film *Glimpses of the Moon.* (Courtesy of the Denise Barrymore Collection)

Nineteen-year-old Dolores (fourth from right) clutches her rag-doll prize after winning a Miami beauty contest. (Courtesy of the Denise Barrymore Collection)

Starlets Dolores and Helene Costello at around the time of their arrival in Hollywood. (Courtesy of the Denise Barrymore Collection)

New homeowners Mae and Dolores pose on the steps of 1388 Schuyler Road, Beverly Hills. (Courtesy of Dolores Barrymore Bedell)

Helene poses seductively at the height of her brief stardom, c. 1927. (From the collections of the Margaret Herrick Library, Academy of Motion Picture Arts and Sciences)

The now-famous Costello sisters sat for Broadway photographer Irving Chidnoff in June 1927, when they came east for the opening of Warner Bros.' *Old San Francisco*. (Courtesy of Hillary Bedell)

Dolores at her loveliest in *Glorious Betsy* (1928), gloriously photographed by her favorite cameraman, Hal Mohr.

Dede gazes reproachfully at her father, John Barrymore, April 1930. (Courtesy of the Denise Barrymore Collection)

Dolores celebrates her birthday at a Hollywood restaurant in the mid-thirties. Her friend, actress Minna Gombell, is at left. (From the collections of the Margaret Herrick Library, Academy of Motion Picture Arts and Sciences)

Johnny goes for a pony ride, as Dolores hovers protectively beside him. (Courtesy of the Denise Barrymore Collection)

Dr. John Vruwink, Dolores's husband to be, plays in the sand with prospective stepchildren Johnny and Dede, summer 1936. (Courtesy of the Denise Barrymore Collection)

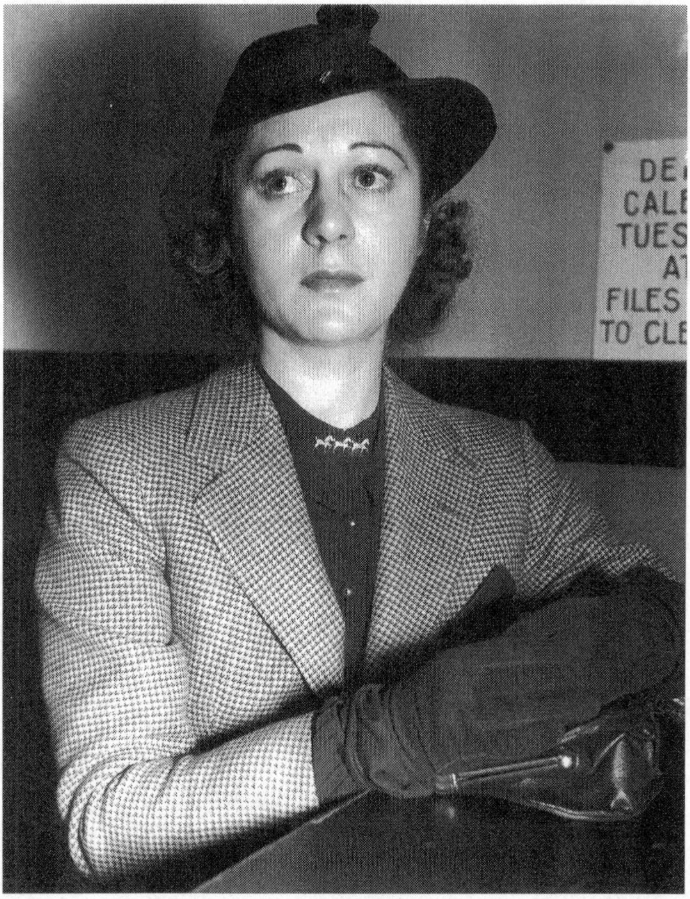

Helene presses her claim against ex-husband Lowell Sherman's estate, November 19, 1935. (From the collections of the Margaret Herrick Library, Academy of Motion Picture Arts and Sciences)

Maurice and Dolores pose with Dede and her kitten outside of the Windsor Boulevard house in 1936. (Courtesy of Hillary Bedell)

Movie extras Maurice and Helene Costello stand between actor Robert Young and director King Vidor during a break in the filming of *H. M. Pulham, Esq.* (From the collections of the Margaret Herrick Library, Academy of Motion Picture Arts and Sciences)

Maurice chats with Diana Barrymore in June 1942, less than a month after her father's death. (Courtesy of the Denise Barrymore Collection)

An emotionally rejuvenated Dolores pushes her live-in grandson Tony around the ranch, accompanied by her former housekeeper, Annie Ziegler. (Courtesy of the Denise Barrymore Collection)

Orson Welles pulls a rabbit out of Joseph Cotten's coat on the set of *The Magnificent Ambersons,* as Dolores looks on. Welles's insistence that the cast watch him perform magic tricks annoyed her.

Maurice and caretakers at the Motion Picture Country Home, where he spent his last years. (Courtesy of the Denise Barrymore Collection)

Maurice enjoys a hug from an admirer at the Motion Picture Home in the late 1940s. (Courtesy of the Denise Barrymore Collection)

16

The Middle of the End

Helene left Lowell Sherman several times over the brief course of their marriage—for the last time on November 11, 1931. His response was to initiate what was arguably the first modern Hollywood divorce, replete with slanderous accusations and petty mudslinging. After Lita Grey Chaplin's 1927 suit against Charlie Chaplin (more of a statutory rape trial than a divorce proceeding) came a succession of "love divorces": Ann Harding and Harry Bannister's split was called the "Kiss Divorce" because they kissed each other good-bye afterward. Miriam Hopkins and Nancy Carroll got a "Mail Order Divorce" from their respective spouses, so named because they happened quickly and with little fanfare. When Monty Banks's ex-wife sent him a bouquet of flowers, theirs was dubbed the "Gardenia Divorce."[1]

Sherman permanently put an end to the love divorce; the fawning suitor of a year and a half earlier unleashed one of the most damaging marital smear campaigns in Hollywood history. He set the tone when he pilfered $100,000 worth of Helene's jewelry and then quickly returned it at the advice of his attorney. In his complaint, the accusations flew. Helene's ungovernable temper, he said, was made worse by her drinking, which was habitual and excessive. Helene denied the accusation and later claimed that she had "been mildly tight" only once during their marriage. She was twenty-two years old at the time, she explained, and "no one is an addict at that age."[2] Actually, she was twenty-three when they got married, and twenty-five by the time the case went to trial in May 1932. Like her father, Helene wasn't above fudging the truth to combat bad publicity.

Sherman's next accusation proved both damning and inescapable: not only was Helene a habitual drinker, she was an avid reader of pornography. Admitted into evidence were fourteen books that Sherman claimed were hers—among them John Cleland's *The Memoirs of Fanny Hill.* Helene said that the books belonged to Sherman—they and two play scripts accounted for the sum total of his library—and that he had pasted her bookplate in them.[3]

On May 10, Sherman testified that his wife kept books of an "erotic and filthy nature" and also that she had called him "a fat old man" and told friends that "he was finished in pictures."[4] Maury Cohen, Sherman's secretary, told the court that he had perused a volume at his employer's residence titled *Forbidden Books by the Old Bibliophile.* "I told him it was a dirty book and I didn't think he should permit his wife to have it." According to the Associated Press, Sherman then told Cohen "that it was his wife's private property and to put the book back where he found it."[5]

The story smacks of perjury from beginning to end. Cohen's claim that he had read Helene's pornography in his employer's presence, and then taken umbrage that Sherman had "allowed" her to read it, is ridiculous enough. Cohen then testified that Sherman had told him to act as censor of Helene's reading material. Cohen was put in charge of an "entire room constructed in the basement of the home," the AP reported, "to keep the liquor left over after the Sherman-Costello wedding. Thousands of dollars' worth of liquor had been purchased in anticipation of that event. And after the ceremony . . . [Cohen] kept his supply up."[6]

It begs the question that was never asked: If Sherman really wanted to keep his wife from drinking, why did he have a basement full of liquor? Cohen said that Helene called Sherman "a lousy performer" and even threatened to kill Sherman's mother. She was fond of throwing highball glasses at her husband, he added, and on one occasion entered his bedroom, pulled back the covers, and gave him a "highball shower."

Charles Beyers, Sherman's business manager, testified that at dinner one evening, Helene turned to him and said, "Don't pay any attention to me, I'm going to get drunk," which she proceeded to do. A cousin of Sherman's told the court that "every time I saw Miss Costello—and I saw her frequently—she was drunk." Finally, Sherman's mother, Julia, took the stand to portray herself as the family "peacemaker," for which her reward was only "blows and abuse."[7]

When court reconvened the next day, Sherman's lawyer, W. I. Gilbert, asked for a recess until 2 o'clock. At noon he disclosed that two of the obscene books, *The Memoirs of Fanny Hill* and another title, had gone missing. "Who stole these books?" Superior Court Judge Thomas Ambrose asked when told of the theft. Gilbert said he had no idea what happened to them. After conferring with his client, the attorney asked the court to dismiss Sherman's half of the case—no doubt due to the missing evidence.[8] The question of what became of the books was never answered.

When it was Helene's turn to testify, instead of delivering the coup de grâce, she pulled her punches and said only that Sherman had "always acted in a very suspicious manner, and this caused me to suffer an inferiority complex. It made me very nervous." Six minutes later she had her divorce, but the damage was done. "The bitterness," she wrote, "the veiled hints of dirt that never went any farther than hints, had ruined her after all. She had been out of pictures for a year, at Lowell's insistence. If anyone took her back now, it would be after a destructive absence and in the face of all these whispers."[9]

She had not asked Sherman for more money, though she certainly could have. Instead, she settled for the $30,000 they had agreed upon a year earlier. "He had lied and lost his nerve at the last minute, and that was all. Whether he was afraid she would prove he had lied, whether he just couldn't face her, or whether his nerve just broke when he couldn't face her . . . she can never know now."[10]

Sherman never got to tell his side of the story. In December 1934, he contracted pneumonia while directing Pioneer Pictures' *Becky Sharp*, starring Miriam Hopkins. The movie was a month into production when he entered Good Samaritan Hospital. He died on the twenty-eighth, three days after Christmas. Had Sherman lived just a little longer, he would have been the first director to make a film shot entirely in modern Technicolor. Rouben Mamoulian quietly took over the picture, scrapped Sherman's scenes, and reshot the movie from scratch.

On February 15, 1932, a week before his fifty-fifth birthday, Maurice Costello walked into a Beverly Hills drugstore and collapsed. He was rushed to California Lutheran Hospital, where he was diagnosed, perhaps wrongly, as having suffered a cerebral hemorrhage. His doctors backed off their original dire assessment the next day, telling the press that his condition was much improved and that, barring any relapse, he would likely pull through. Dolores rushed to Maurice's side after hearing the news and deluged him with "nurses, flowers, specialists and sickroom dainties."[11]

When he was released five days later, Jack and Dolores sent a limousine to take him home.

Ironically, it was Jack who had laid the groundwork for Maurice and Dolores's reconciliation two years earlier. Maurice was sick with the flu when he opened his eyes one afternoon to find his son-in-law standing over his bed. "We've had our differences," Jack told him gently. "Now I am here because you're one of the old theatrical men raised in the same traditions that I was. You're ill and I'm here to help you."[12] Maurice burst into tears. Back in his daughter's good graces, he met his two-year-old granddaughter Dede for the first time. He was finally admitted into the Barrymore's ever-expanding Tower Road estate.

Three and a half months after Maurice's stroke, on June 4, Dolores gave birth to her second child—a son. He was christened John Blyth Barrymore, to honor the man whose name had been Herbert Arthur Chamberlayne Hunter Blyth before he changed it to the more theatrical-sounding Maurice Barrymore. Dolores had proudly given Jack an heir to both his surnames. Between pregnancies, Warner Bros. had coaxed her out of semiretirement to star in *Expensive Women,* a Pre-Code hodgepodge of risqué business, in which Dolores is made love to by a succession of tuxedoed suitors—John Barrymore look-alike Warren William foremost among them.[13] Depression-era audiences had reason to believe the once-silent actress, with her perfect voice and matchless beauty, would take her place among the early doyennes of the sound era. Except that Dolores's place was no longer in front of a camera. Lounging in queenly splendor on the patio of her estate, surrounded by the lushness of its gardens, pools, and ponds, she was asked if she would ever make another picture. "Would you?" she replied.[14]

The question was no longer if, but when, things were going to blow up again. Jack had sworn to Dolores that if she gave him a son, he would quit drinking. The oath wouldn't make it through the afternoon of John Blyth's birth. Spying a klatch of newspaper reporters gathered outside Dolores's hospital room, the inebriated Jack mistook them for kidnappers and ordered his manager to fetch him a revolver "instantly." "I'll stay up all night," he vowed, "and shoot any bastard that comes within a hundred yards of my son." When Hotchner returned with the pistol, Jack ordered him to stand guard. "Don't let a soul come near the place," he instructed, "unless properly dressed in hospital white. I'm going out for a few minutes."[15]

Minutes turned to hours. Dolores called for him repeatedly, but no one knew where he was. Eventually they found him sprawled on the bed in an empty hospital room, fully clothed and fast asleep. Attempts to rouse him were unsuccessful. Dolores's heart sank at this latest dashing of her hopes. Jack had dashed his own hopes as well. "I swore that if God gave me a son, I would never drink again," he told Hotchner. "What happens to a man who makes a sacred oath, then breaks it?"[16]

In mid-June 1932, Jack ducked out of John Blyth's christening party, where imbibing would have been frowned upon, to get himself a drink. Inexplicably, he turned up unannounced at the Hollywood home of Dolores's obstetrician, Dr. John Vruwink, where a family dinner party was in progress. Jack chatted amiably with the guests, among them the doctor's elderly mother, but Vruwink knew what he was really after. "You need a drink," he said, filling a tumbler with whiskey. Jack sipped it and grimaced. The old lady smiled warmly at this apparent rejection of hard liquor.

"Don't you like it?" Vruwink asked.

"Like it?" Jack replied, "I could go down on it."[17]

After Helene's bitter divorce and subsequent humiliation at the hands of her ruthless ex-husband, she set sail for Cuba—for the first time without Mae Costello at her side. Before her departure, a pair of burglars broke into her Beverly Hills home, tied up her Filipino houseboy, and made off with $57,000 worth of her jewelry. Ten days later the insurance company tracked the items to Chicago, and had to pay $10,000 for their return. As soon as they were back in her possession, Helene hocked them for the $7,000 she needed to stay solvent. When she couldn't repay the money, the jewels were put up for auction. In the depths of the Depression, they fetched just $8,000. The $30,000 Helene received from her divorce settlement was already spent, forcing her back on the financial roller coaster she had been on all her life. "Hollywood's coldness, its willingness to let her spend money without giving her a chance to make more," she recalled bitterly, "prompted her to leave it shortly after the jewel robbery episode. If Arturo Del Barrio was in the back of her mind, she was not aware of it." With her resources depleted and Mussie waiting for her with open arms in Cuba, doubtless he was closer to the front of her mind than she was willing to admit. "Mussie's American mother, Cora, called at the Hotel Presidente. 'Helene, let's get it straight—you're not going to break his heart again.' 'I don't intend to, Cora' she replied."[18]

On New Year's Eve 1933, Helene attended a party at the home of Otto Precht, a wealthy German importer-exporter, where members of the Del Barrio family were present. She tried to ignore Mussie, she claimed, but "dancing in the warm moonlight that night, he asked her to marry him again and it all came back."[19] As with Lowell Sherman, there would be terms and conditions. As with Jack Regan, Helene insisted the marriage be kept secret until they could be married a second time, closer to home. They returned in May, after her divorce from Sherman was final, for what was to become Helene's fifth wedding ceremony in as many years. The newlyweds dallied on the West Coast until September, when a popular uprising threatened the military dictatorship of Cuban general Gerardo Machado and Mussie had to return home. As a wedding present, he promised to give Helene her own movie studio if she came back with him to Cuba—a promise he was actually in a position to fulfill. The wealthy Del Barrios had their hands in all manner of financial enterprises, mostly Jai Alai games that brought in $30,000 a week. Mussie had invested heavily in the budding Cuban film industry; with two partners he formed BPP Pictures for the purpose of making films for export to the United States. The fledgling filmmakers were thwarted at every turn by the worsening political crisis that brought the Machado regime to the brink of collapse in August 1933. When massive strikes toppled his government a month later, Cuba found itself on the brink of civil war.

"The motion picture studio that was her wedding present had never been used," Helene wrote. "There were two cameramen, Cubans, sitting around drawing $6 a day. She wired Fox Movietone News in New York and made a deal to sell them newsreel footage. She covered the revolution with her two cameramen, but made very little money at it. Still she did get to see it from third row center." Years later Helene told her daughter Deirdre that there were times when bullets whizzed and bombs fell all around her.[20]

Helene was at home one morning when she got word that the Cuban police were searching houses in the area for contraband items, such as American cigarettes and firearms. Helene barely had time to slip on her girdle and thrust Mussie's .45 caliber revolver "deep into the front" of it, when the police arrived. Seeing that the gun was visible through her negligee, Helene threw on her husband's bathrobe before letting them in. "They were very polite—exceedingly so, after her Alphonse and Gaston performance of 'Won't you sit down?'" But when she tried to sit down, "the gun wouldn't let her." As the police began searching the house, she realized that she hadn't checked to see if the gun was loaded or even if the safety catch was on. After they left, Helene dared not reach into her girdle to retrieve the gun for fear it would go off. Eventually, Mussie's brother Mario showed up with a pair of scissors and gingerly snipped the girdle up the side. The gun fell out, leaving a detailed imprint on Helene's nether parts that remained for several hours.[21] "She was the Pearl White of Cuba," Deirdre said. "Once she was robbed during this huge rainstorm. They tied her to a tree in the pouring rain, then stole all her jewelry from the house."[22] Curiously, this was Helene's second jewelry theft in a just over a year.

Mussie's autocratic mother, Cora, was even more of a drag on Helene's third marriage than Julia Sherman had been on her second. She wielded the power of her purse with singular effectiveness, to keep her son and daughter-in-law living not just near her, but *with* her. Helene knew she would never allow them to have a life of their own. Defying Cora, the couple moved into a finquita, a "little farm" on three acres, but her money didn't go with them: "Things were cheap, but she by no means had inexhaustible funds. Mussie would not work. He had a class obligation not to work. 'You don't understand, I'm a Del Barrio,' he said."[23]

Dolores was mostly mum on the worsening state of her marriage after John Blyth was born. She shared little, publicly or privately, about the effects of Jack's drinking on his health and on their relationship—except to tell Hollis Alpert that when he was drinking he was a different person, and, alternatively, that when he was sober there was "no more sober person."[24] As their marital ups and downs see-sawed through periods of relative sobriety followed by bouts of heavy drinking, the quality of Jack's screen performances rose and fell along the same timeline. That he was sober during the making of *Svengali* in 1931 is evinced by the fullness and clarity of his performance. Not coincidentally, it was also a good year for his marriage. John Blyth was conceived that fall, about the time a reporter overheard Jack and Dolores cooing to each other lovingly on the telephone. A photo taken while Jack was making *The Mad Genius* in April shows Dolores smiling broadly and Jack looking calm and content.[25]

The year 1932 saw a change of studios for Jack—from Warner Bros. to the palace of the moguls Mayer and Thalberg. At MGM, Jack took his rightful place beside the star players of the greatest of the studio stock companies—joining Greta Garbo, Joan Crawford, Wallace Beery, and his brother Lionel in the episodic epic, *Grand Hotel.* Jack's hotly awaited pairing with Garbo would not disappoint: the film was a box-office smash, going on to win the Academy Award for Best Picture. Despite the heart-wrenching beauty and pathos of his scenes with Garbo, the effects of Jack's drinking were beginning to tell. A pervasive stiffness had crept into his screen persona, as though he had lost something vital and real. Later that year, Jack was cast as the fictitious character he was well on his way to becoming—the failed alcoholic actor Larry Renault, in *Dinner at Eight.* "Oh, that is wonderful Jack!" director George Cukor exclaimed after a take. "Why shouldn't I be?" he replied. "This is a combination of Maurice Costello, Lowell Sherman, and me."[26] As brilliant as he is in places, especially in the final scene when Renault realizes he has no way out but suicide—Jack is still a far cry from the actor that Alexander Woolcott once called "so utterly free from all that is of the stage stagey."[27] Indeed, stagey is just what he had become.

Jack was entering the next phase of his decline, both as actor and husband. By the start of 1933, Dolores was as close to her wit's end as she could be without actually reaching it. In a fit of jealousy, Jack installed wrought iron gratings over the windows of the main house, either to keep Dolores's imagined lovers from sneaking in, or those already in from sneaking out. With Helene still in Cuba, Dolores had to handle Jack by herself for the first time. In the old days, Mae would rush to her side at the first inkling of trouble, ripping into Jack with talons bared. Unlike Helene, whose natural response was to run from conflict, Dolores resolved to dig in her heels.[28]

While Dolores was blaming Jack for their marital problems, Jack was blaming Dolores. He complained to Hotchner of her disinterest in him after the children were born, her ongoing attempts to stop him from drinking, and, of no lesser importance, their intellectual disparities. As Helene put it cattily: "Jack was simply bored to death! Dolores was a good woman, but dreadfully conventional, and she was married to a man with a chain-reaction personality who abhorred convention. 'She's beautiful—but my God, I can't just sit around and look at her!' he groaned to me after a spat. Then he added drily, 'Or can I?'"[29]

It was true, Dolores was no match for her husband's wondrously inquisitive mind. Jack was an antiquarian in actor's clothing, an inveterate collector of books, furniture, objets d'art, and historical artifacts. He was an autodidact of epic range, richly conversant on a wide array of subjects. He had cogently discussed nuclear physics with Albert Einstein (as Einstein himself related), British politics with Winston Churchill, and Buddhism with the Indian prophet J. Krishnamurti.

Conversely, Dolores's interests were focused almost exclusively on motherhood. This was mostly, though not entirely, by choice. A hidden clause in her Warner Bros. contract allowed the studio to terminate their agreement if she became pregnant—which, when she did, they did.[30] They had refused Jack's request to let Dolores play opposite him in *Svengali,* thinking that audiences wouldn't accept the mother of John Barrymore's daughter as the virginal Trilby. The studio rehired her in 1931 to star in *Expensive Women,* but when she became pregnant a second time, they released her for good.

The Barrymores rarely entertained by that time, because when they did there was often a row over which of their male guests Jack was certain Dolores was in love with—and vice versa. The only man he would let near her was her gynecologist, and even that became a problem. "Goodnight and *goodbye,* you son of a bitch," he told John Vruwink after a house call. "Don't come back. If I ever find you in this house again I'll break your goddam jaw." When Dolores demanded an explanation, Jack said: "I don't want him around here because he's stuck on you, and I don't want anybody stuck on you touching you, especially the way this guy has to touch you."[31] When he was sober again, Jack readmitted Vruwink to the family compound, where Dolores was now being held a virtual prisoner.

17

Over Her Head

Finally the moment came when Dolores realized she could no longer stand by and let nature take its course: when it struck her that Jack's problems were not just marital, but also medical. According to the story passed down by generations of Barrymore biographers, in October 1933, Jack was called in for a retake after completing his scenes for the movie version of the Elmer Rice play *Counsellor at Law.* In one of the great bravura performances of the early thirties he stars as a fast-talking Jewish lawyer torn between his Lower East Side roots and his wife's high-brow social aspirations. Jack flubbed the first take opposite actor John Qualen, made a face, and tried again. He blew up a second time, then a third. He continued to stumble, always at the same place, until director William Wyler called for a break in the filming to give his flustered star a chance to regroup and study his lines.[1]

The resumption of filming saw no improvement. Hours went by, as Jack struggled helplessly to get through the scene. After the fiftieth take, producer Henry Henigson arrived on the set to witness what Gene Fowler later referred to as "the astounding event." After the fifty-fourth unusable take, Wyler called it a night.[2]

Actor-director Vincent Sherman, probably the last living witness to the making of *Counsellor at Law,* shared additional details of Jack's performance in a memoir written in 1996. Wyler had hired him to reprise the role of Communist agitator Harry Becker that he originated on Broadway. In his book, Sherman supplies both a prologue and an epilogue to the story of what has long been regarded as the beginning of the end of Jack's screen career. According to Sherman, it wasn't—Jack had been going up in his lines well before that:

> Barrymore was in his early fifties at the time but looked older. His jowls hung loosely, and the make-up man had to tape them up

> every morning. He was married to the beautiful Dolores Costello, whose father was Maurice Costello, a famous actor and matinee idol. She had appeared with John in several films at Warner Brothers [actually, only two]. There was talk that their marriage was foundering. . . .
>
> At last the day came when we were to do our big scene. I was sure that it would not require more than a few hours. It took almost four days. Barrymore was having trouble remembering his lines, and the studio was concerned how he would handle his scene with me. It was highly emotional for both of us. . . . The scene began, as in the play, with him lacing into me for making Communist speeches, getting arrested and beaten up by the police, and causing my mother grief. . . . Barrymore had only a few short speeches at the climax, whereas I had long, emotional ones. For some reason he'd dry up and go blank. He was apologetic to Wyler, who was patient, and especially to me, as we had to repeat take after take. They finally put up a blackboard for him at the side of the set with key lines on it in large letters, which he was skillful in using. A sidelong glance or turnaway that seemed natural would allow him to focus on his next line.[3]

After the twentieth take, Sherman asked Wyler if he could take a break.

> He said quietly, "I don't blame you." He ordered the stage doors opened and told me to go into a dressing room and lie down until I felt better. I detected that he was becoming annoyed with Barrymore but was holding back his anger. After a short rest I recovered my energy, and we began again. Seven more takes, twenty-seven in all, and Wyler thought he had what he needed. Subsequently, he became well known for his many takes, but in this case I think he was justified. . . . At the end of each day as I left the studio, I felt genuinely sorry for [Barrymore]. He had been warm and friendly to me all through the shooting, and I could sense that he was deeply troubled. Everyone was afraid that he might start drinking, which often had happened in the past, but so far he remained sober.[4]

Then came the day of the fifty-four takes. John Qualen told Sherman they had started his scene with Jack after lunch, and worked straight through dinner before Wyler gave up, saying they would try it again tomorrow. The next morning, Qualen saw that something was "decidedly wrong" with Jack. "Barrymore came in bleary-eyed, his face swollen, wearing one red sock and one blue. They sent him home and shot other scenes." As Gene Fowler was preparing to write *Good Night, Sweet Prince,* his biographical memoir of Jack, he called Qualen to ask about the fifty-four takes. "When Barrymore went home," Sherman wrote, "he was so upset he called his neighbor, John Gilbert, and went to his house, where he spent most of the night drinking. Barrymore told Gilbert that he was afraid he was losing his mind. I later heard that Barrymore was haunted by the fear of insanity; his father had died in an institution."[5]

Sherman had heard right about Jack's father: Maurice Barrymore died in a Long Island asylum from an advanced case of neurosyphilis that caused him to go slowly, and very publicly, insane. It was also true that by the end of 1933, Jack was afraid he would end up exactly like him.

According to Sherman, except for the all-night bender with Gilbert, Jack was sober during the making of *Counsellor at Law.* He still wasn't drinking in early 1934, when he tackled the role of the egomaniacal theater producer Oscar Jaffe, in Howard Hawks's *Twentieth Century.* The film offers a long, last look at the actor many still believed to be America's greatest, briefly restored to the height of his powers. With unfailing (and unfathomable) lucidity, Jack races through page after page of Hecht and MacArthur's sparkling dialogue at breakneck speed and without a hitch, to give the most brilliant, and funniest, of all his screen performances.

With Jack teetering on the verge of a crack-up but fighting hard to stay on his feet, Dolores picked the best and the worst of times to try to save him from himself. But what other choice did she have? After *Twentieth Century* was finished in February, Jack fell heavily off the wagon. In desperation, Dolores vowed to get him professional help by whatever means necessary. Given his terror of ending up in an asylum, she knew she would never get him to submit to a psychiatric evaluation voluntarily, so she took a different approach.

"Little by little I got the story of the Good Samaritan episode," Helene wrote.

> Dolores lured him to the hospital under the pretense of "seeing a friend." He whipped a doctor, ripped uniforms off two nurses,

> and nearly wrecked the room before they got him into a "restraint." Regardless of what you would like to think, "restraint" in a psycho ward means a strait jacket. I shuddered to think of Jack, hating confinement and coercion of any kind, bound up in one of those things. When I saw Jack, I was heartbroken at the change in him. I was never one of his blind admirers. I knew his faults. Neither was I my sister's doting partisan. Jack carried within his great genius the seeds of his own destruction. Dolores watered it with her wifely tears.[6]

The version shared by Fowler was told to him by Hotchner, who out of respect for the living omitted the worst of the details, and it has been retold almost verbatim by successive biographers.[7] By all accounts, except for Helene's, Jack submitted voluntarily to the psychiatric examination. The truth of her story might therefore be called into question, if everything that happened afterward didn't suddenly make sense. Helene's version gives Jack a motive for his subsequent actions, as well as a demonstrable reason for mistrusting Dolores. So it wasn't alcohol-induced paranoia after all that led him to think she was plotting behind his back—in fact she *was* plotting behind his back. Dolores obliquely admitted as much in 1963, when she told Hollis Alpert that when Jack was in the hospital, he attacked his nurses repeatedly.[8] This only could have happened if he was being held against his will—and the only way they could have held him, was if Dolores had signed the commitment papers. To assist with his care, she occupied the room next to Jack's for the duration of his two-week stay. By the end of the ordeal, she had lost twenty pounds.

The doctors found nothing organically wrong with Jack's mind. His memory loss and violent episodes, they determined, were caused by his drinking. Dolores told Alpert years later that she had stopped just short of formally committing him. It was a decision she regretted: "I sometimes think it was my fault that all that happened afterward happened. I wouldn't put him away. I wouldn't do it."[9]

Daunted but undeterred, Dolores told Hotchner that from now on she would take charge of all matters pertaining to her husband's health. She had had enough of his "pacifying of Jack."[10] After *Twentieth Century,* RKO signed him to star in the courtroom melodrama *Hat, Coat, and Glove,* as the artist-turned-murder suspect Robert Mitchell. During rehearsals his memory lapses worsened, causing delays and disruptions in the production schedule, until it dawned on the producers that if they were going to finish the film, they would have to replace him. Ricardo Cortez quietly took over the role. To Dolores, even more upsetting than the news of Jack's firing, was Hotchner's admission that he had neglected to tell his employer why he was let go, for fear of upsetting him. She viewed this as yet another example of Hotchner's fecklessness. "When it was plain that [Jack] was exhausted from having made nine pictures in two years," Dolores recalled, "when he was fast becoming an almost hopeless alcoholic, Hotchner took him to an osteopath!"[11]

Jack's prim, bespectacled manager had yet to encounter filmdom's "Madonna of the Screen" in full battle mode. As Jack looked on, Dolores lit into Hotchner for having lied about her husband's dismissal. "Tell him the truth!" she shouted. "Jack can take the truth. He doesn't know he was fired!"[12]

"I've been fired?" Jack asked.

Hotchner surrendered. "I turn him over to you, Dolores," he said, and for a short while he did.

"He had been drinking steadily for two years," Dolores told Alpert. "It hardly seemed that he drew a sober breath. Combined with the drinking was his habit of spending and squandering the immense amounts that he earned. And while he was doing this spending I tried to save, cutting down on the expenses it was left to me to handle. It was as though I knew how it would end."[13]

There are differing accounts of how the "trouble" started aboard the Barrymore yacht on the night of August 18, 1934, but the essentials are these: In early summer, Jack, Dolores, their children, and a fleet of nurses left Los Angeles by train to join the *Infanta* and crew in Vancouver. From there the diesel schooner sailed into northern waters, its course set for the faraway seacoast village of Ketchikan, Alaska. The purpose of the trip, as far as Dolores was concerned, was to try once more to put Jack on the road to sobriety. This time she would tolerate no interference from Hotchner, or any other "pacifying forces." She told him "not to try to keep in touch," for fear that at his boss's request he would attempt to foil her twofold plan—which was to remove any alcoholic beverages that Jack had hidden aboard the *Infanta,* then to keep him at sea until he was sufficiently dried out.[14] Dolores had hired a nurse to assist with Jack's care, and a pair of governesses to attend to the children.

The plan fell apart almost immediately. Marooned on the open water without access to liquor, Jack swallowed anything he thought might contain ardent spirits—mouthwash, camphor, ammonia. When that was gone, he gulped down the contents of Dolores's perfume bottles. He asked to go ashore, citing urgent business matters in Vancouver that required his immediate attention. Dolores reluctantly agreed, only to find Hotchner waiting for them on the dock. "Why did you come?" she asked angrily. "Why should he not come?" Jack interjected. "He's my business manager." Jack inquired about a pending film offer from British producer Alexander Korda, but Dolores cut him off. Her husband was in no condition to discuss business, she told Hotchner, and couldn't possibly make a picture at the present time.[15]

The real reason Jack wanted to go ashore became evident soon enough. At a nearby restaurant he asked the waiter for a glass of beer. "Not a drop of it!" Dolores exclaimed. She would leave him, she said, and take the children with her, if she ever caught him drinking again. He ordered a glass of ginger ale instead. When Dolores left to go shopping, the men resumed their conversation. Jack said that he was being kept prisoner aboard the *Infanta*. "I am being given sedatives, especially when in port. Why?" Instead of telling him the truth—that Dolores was only trying to save their marriage—Hotchner thoughtlessly suggested the Barrymores book passage on a commercial liner and go abroad. Could it not have occurred to him that any passenger ship would be stocked to the scuppers with alcoholic beverages? Hotchner's betrayal at this critical moment earned him Dolores's undying enmity. Thenceforth, she referred to people she considered spineless and self-serving as "the Hotchners of the world."[16]

The Barrymore cruise resumed in mid-July. Several weeks later, Hotchner received a disturbing telegram:

> FAMILY LEFT VANCOUVER SATURDAY BY MOTOR TO SEATTLE, THENCE BY TRAIN LOS ANGELES. PROBABLY ARRIVE TONIGHT OR TOMORROW. IF THEY INTERVIEW YOU LISTEN, BUT BE AS NON-COMMITTAL AS POSSIBLE. WILL YOU MEET ME AT LONG BEACH ABOUT EIGHT FRIDAY MORNING? USE YOUR OWN JUDGEMENT ABOUT SEEING THEM AT THE HOUSE, AS IF CASUALLY, NOT MENTIONING THIS WIRE. REASON FOR THEIR LEAVING, IN CASE OF ANY INQUIRY, WISHING AVOID BAD WEATHER ON ACCOUNT OF THE CHILDREN.[17]

Dolores and Jack told different versions of the story, both acknowledging that a violent episode occurred that left Jack's nurse, Margaret Hastings, with a broken nose, and the Barrymores with a pending lawsuit. According to Jack, the nurse was blocking his cabin door when he opened it too quickly and accidentally hit her in the face. His wife offered a similar version, but with one important difference—there was nothing accidental about her husband's actions. The blow sent Hastings pitching into Dolores, who fell heavily on to the deck. He had made a "serious attack" on both of them, she said, and had deliberately punched Hastings in the face. She shared additional details with Helene, who wrote that Jack "mopped up the deck" with both of them, and that after "beating up Dolores" it took the whole crew to subdue him.[18]

They couldn't contain him for long. With Dolores panicking and Hastings bleeding profusely, Jack wrestled free and made his escape. He returned the next morning after an all-night binge to find that Dolores, the children, and their attendants had abandoned ship. "It was the end," Helene wrote. "Jack's own thoughts, as the *Infanta* steamed slowly down the coast, went to his grave with him."[19]

It wasn't the end—not quite. Still refusing to give up on her marriage, Dolores summoned Dr. Samuel Hirschfeld, Jack's physician, for an eleventh-hour consultation. Jack arrived home on the twenty-fourth to find his wife and his doctor on the premises in conversation. Two days later, he held a five-hour meeting with Hotchner in his office over the garage. He was sober, he swore, because "there are times when a man does not *dare* drink. This is one of them." He had to act quickly—he had overheard Dolores and Hirschfeld arranging for his examination by a team of specialists. "This kind of thing once happened to a close friend of mine in the East. My friend was privately examined by physicians. A few days later a petition was signed by his wife. It was presented to court, then signed by a judge. My friend was put into an institution. Finis! He never came out of it."[20]

Whether or not the story was true, his friend's demise bore a striking resemblance to that of his father. Only it wasn't Maurice Barrymore's wife who committed him. With Ethel then a rising star on Broadway, and Lionel crisscrossing the country in a play, the responsibility for signing the papers fell heavily on the shoulders of nineteen-year-old Jack.

"Dolores is no longer in love with me," he went on. "I deeply loved her, as you know. I love my children and this home. Another domestic smash-up is proving too much for me. I think the fateful seven-year period that dogs my marriages is ending once again. This is the third bus accident and it doesn't look as though I can bounce out of it." After a prolonged silence, Jack added: "We must get away without letting Dolores have any idea we are leaving. She would come down on me like a flash if she suspected it. . . . But we've got to act fast. Will she never understand that for a man of my age and temperament, a fixed habit can't be cured by making a prisoner of him and giving him bromides?"[21]

He wouldn't get away without a last, gut-wrenching confrontation with his heartbroken wife. Eighty-seven years later, their daughter Dede remembered "like it was yesterday" her parents' angry voices booming through the house on their last day together as a family:

> I was in the kitchen with my brother John, who was two. He was in his high chair and was unaware of what was going on in my parent's bedroom. They were arguing very loudly. I remember my father's breakfast was sitting there on the table getting cold. They were his favorite sunny-side-up eggs smothered with pepper just the way he liked them. I was so stressed out, I had to do something, so I got up from my chair and walked over to my father's place at the table. I ate his eggs, pepper and all, as this terrible fight was going on just down the hall. My analyst told me that what I did made perfect sense. He said I was trying to put my father inside me because I knew he was going to go.[22]

As a measure of how desperate Jack was to get out of California, he insisted upon flying, despite two previous terrifying experiences on airplanes. All that mattered was to get as far away from Dolores as quickly as possible, beyond any jurisdiction in which she could lock him up. On his way to the Glendale airfield, Jack stopped off at a drugstore and telephoned her, explaining that a radio engagement had come up and that he had had to leave immediately for New York. To throw Dolores off the track, he told her he would be traveling by train. He promised to keep her apprised of his plans and whereabouts. "Good night and good luck," Jack said before hanging up.[23] Neither spouse knew it, but it would be the last time they would speak to each other as husband and wife.

18

Three on Their Own

Rumor had it that to keep Maurice Costello from starving to death, the studios made an unofficial agreement to occasionally throw him some work.[1] Whether or not this was actually the case, Maurice was sporadically employed during the 1930s, but in the most humiliating way imaginable for an ex–movie star—first in bit parts, then as a film extra. It was no longer a matter of professional pride, as he hadn't any left, but of financial survival. In early 1934, as his son-in-law shined as brightly as ever in *Twentieth Century,* Maurice was cast as a "hotel guest" in Paramount's B-level film *Search for Beauty,* starring Buster Crabbe and "30 international beauty contest winners."[2] He appeared as himself in the eleven-minute short *Hollywood on Parade,* chatting with "old-timers" Flora Finch and Florence Turner.[3]

Film magazines had kept the first screen actors' names before the public in occasional "whatever became of" stories, having discovered that down-and-out ex–movie stars made excellent copy. But no matter how hard the press tried to drum up sympathy for them, none of the original Vitagraph stars managed to rebuild their careers. Making them objects of public pity seemed only to have worsened their prospects. Not quite the same was true for the second wave of movie heartthrobs: Earle Williams worked as a secondary player up until his death in 1927. At the age of seventy-one, Francis X. Bushman got a credited speaking part in Billy Wilder's 1954 film, *Sabrina.*[4] In the early fifties, film and television reintroduced such later stars as Lillian Gish and Buster Keaton to a generation who no longer viewed them as has-beens, but as living history. By then it was too late for the original players, who either had been ground down past the point of resuscitation, or had passed away before the world could rediscover them.

By the middle of 1935, with Mae long dead and Jack Barrymore headed east on an extended trip that would eventually take him to India, the

Costellos entered their final incarnation as a family. During Maurice's professional demise in the mid-teens, Mae had served as ballast, doing yeoman work in keeping the family together until the next and last head-of-household took charge. By the early 1920s, Dolores was heir apparent. She had strong-armed her parents into allowing her and Helene to join the *Scandals* company in 1923. In Chicago, she threw a tantrum so violent that it reversed Mae's original decision not to let her sign with Warner Bros.[5] Years later it was Dolores, not Mae, who dispatched Maurice before he could capsize her romance with Jack.

More recently she had engendered, albeit unwittingly, Jack's hurried departure from the Tower Road property. For this, interestingly, she blamed Hotchner. On August 30, 1934, she wired him curtly: "I HOLD YOU PERSONALLY RESPONSIBLE FOR ANYTHING UNTOWARD THAT MAY TRANSPIRE."[6]

Hotchner, who with his wife, Helios, followed Jack east on his journey, handed him the telegram. "Isn't this a clear indication that she thinks me incapable of handling my own affairs?" Jack said, more convinced than ever that Dolores was trying to commit him.[7] At his attorney's suggestion, Jack agreed to a psychiatric evaluation, which to his great relief showed no evidence of "psychosis or any other kind of functional disturbance of the nervous system." Still he did not feel safe. "I want to put a lot of ocean between myself and my worries," he said. "I need a moat for my castle. The Atlantic is just the right size."[8] Hotchner instantly booked passage to England aboard the *Berengaria* and they departed New York on September 8. Just in case Dolores's bloodhounds had followed him onto the ship, Jack bolted his stateroom door until the liner was well out to sea.

Dolores was in limbo for the next several months, suspecting but not knowing where this was all going to end. She tried to communicate with Jack, without success. In November, the first of her letters caught up to him in Madras, India, where he was beginning Ayurvedic treatment for his alcoholism (he would end up in a brothel). Against the advice of his attorneys, Jack decided not to answer it. He waited another four months before composing what he called his "letter of farewell": "This is a rather difficult letter to write to you," it began, "but believe me, I do it after considering everything very deeply. We might as well face the fact like two civilized people that it is quite evident for your own happiness as well as mine that our life together has come to an end. In fact, as you know, our proper relationship as husband and wife really terminated about a year ago."[9] In closing, Jack said he hoped to see the children soon and that in the interim they could come to a speedy settlement of their affairs.

Jack was away for another eight months. When he returned to Los Angeles in the fall of 1935, Dolores and the children had vacated the Tower Road property and the terms of their divorce agreement had been hammered out. Dolores would get sole custody of the children. Though Jack had made only one picture the year before, he agreed to pay her $850 a month (equal to about $15,000 in today's currency) in child support. He would continue to pay the premiums on a $235,000 life insurance policy maintained for Dede and John Blyth. Adding to Dolores's personal wealth, including the Schuyler Road house, Jack signed over $50,000 in Liberty bonds—bringing her net worth, minus the properties, to $165,500. Dolores gave him the Tower Road estate, but not before placing a $50,000 lien on the property in the event he defaulted. She let him keep the *Infanta* without encumbrances.[10]

Jack had been gone for seven months, and still the press didn't know the Barrymores were separated. In April, Dolores lied to a fan magazine writer who inquired about Jack's whereabouts, blurting, "Jack's hunting big game—hunting everything!"[11] A month earlier, Jack told the Associated Press that he and his ex-wife Michael Strange, their daughter Diana, and Michael's husband, Harrison Tweed, were heading off on an Atlantic cruise aboard the *Infanta*. When the reporter asked why the current Mrs. Barrymore wasn't going with them, Jack replied that she was staying home because the "children needed her." All was well with their marriage, he insisted. When a reporter posed the same question to Dolores, she gave a different answer. "I know nothing whatsoever of this trip," she said truthfully. "In fact, this is the first time I have ever heard of it."[12] The next day's headline announced, just as truthfully: "BARRYMORE'S EX-WIFE TO SAIL SEAS WITH HIM: Michael Strange and Her Husband Invited on Cruise While Dolores Costello Stays Home."

Save for his "letter of farewell," Dolores hadn't heard a word from her absent husband since their last telephone conversation the previous August. She had written him a letter stating that as his plans seemed "so indefinite," she would await further news from him before "deciding what to do."[13] That news never arrived. Months passed and the bills were piling up on Tower Road, as Jack had sent her no money to pay them. Emmet Camomile, Jack's property manager, and Dolores were at loggerheads over the running of the estate. Then came the farewell letter, and enough was enough. In April, she rented a large, brick house on Irving Boulevard in the posh Windsor Square section of Hancock Park, and moved herself and the children into it.

The last straw came unexpectedly in the form of a nineteen-year-old Hunter College student named Elaine Jacobs, who slipped into Jack's hospital room while he was recuperating from an alcohol-related collapse and ingratiated herself.[14] Her future suddenly writ large, she changed her last name to Barrie and surrendered to Jack's advances almost as soon as he left the hospital. In no time, they began turning up at Manhattan's most fashionable nightspots, where, as Elaine well knew, reporters would be waiting in ambush. Dolores wasn't fooled for a minute by Jack's assurances to the press that Elaine was merely his protégé. Neither were the newspapers, who rightly assumed there was something more going on between them than acting lessons.

In the wake of the Michael Strange episode, Dolores focused her accumulated wrath first on Jack's wallet, tightening the terms of their upcoming divorce settlement. Then, except for his animal trophies and other items she considered valueless, she emptied the Tower Road house of his belongings. When Jack returned in the fall, he found the place just as she had left it: walls denuded of artwork, bookshelves emptied, wires protruding where sconces and chandeliers had previously hung.[15]

Dolores's anger only intensified when Jack publicly announced that he could no longer be responsible for his debts, which also meant hers. The next day she retaliated with an announcement of her own: she was suing her husband for divorce, she told the press, on grounds of "habitual intemperance and extreme cruelty."[16] He had struck her, the complaint alleged, causing "great pain and bodily injury." Twenty years after Mae Costello had branded her husband a wife-beater, Dolores had done the same thing to Jack. "He is cruel, drinks too much and deserted me," she told reporters. "Besides, I am being dishonored by his amorous meanderings."[17]

For most of the time they spent apart, the hypocritical Dolores was as guilty of having an extramarital dalliance as Jack—she was just better at hiding it. Exactly when she and her gynecologist became lovers, neither of them would ever reveal. According to Helene's timetable, Dolores and John Vruwink were already involved when she returned from Cuba in February, a month before Jack met Elaine. She and Dolores had "never been particularly close," Helene wrote, "but they were sisters, and she had been hearing some odd things."

> She took the boat again, cabling Dolores when she would arrive at San Pedro Harbor. Instead of Dolores, Ebba Webb, daughter of Warner Brothers' Producer Gordon Hollingshead, met her. Dolores, it seemed, was seeing her attorney that morning. . . . After they met, Dolores went to her dentist and had a tooth pulled. Dolores had a big party scheduled for Helene that night, but Dolores, because of her tooth, had to go to bed. She told Helene archly, "You know, we're going to have a very special guest tonight." Helene asked who, and Dolores said, "Uncle." That was her code name for Dr. Vruwink. Helene asked who Uncle was and Dolores explained, adding softly, "I'm very fond of him."
>
> "Yes I know," Helene said. "Ebba told me all about that in the car." Dolores sat straight up in bed, forgetting her tooth. "She's a god-damned liar!" she said. Helene shortly learned how bad things had become between Jack and Dolores. She found bottles hidden all over the house, although Jack had been long gone from it.[18]

Dolores's furtive announcement to Helene that she and Vruwink were seeing each other occurred in February, about the same time that Jack's farewell letter arrived. So, unless she and Vruwink just happened to fall in love around the time the letter came, their romance had been going on for some time.

By the time the Barrymores were officially divorced on October 9, 1935, both were well established in other relationships. Jack's was already going badly—in September, Elaine filed suit to recover the canary diamond ring he had given her when he moved into her parents' apartment and had taken back when he moved out. That was also the week he signed Dolores's financial settlement, which he must have known would bankrupt him. With every part of his life in disarray, Jack sat down at his desk at the Essex House and composed a telegram on the occasion of Dolores's thirty-second birthday:

> DEAR WINKIE, HAPPY BIRTHDAY AND LOVE TO THE CHILDREN. I WOULD LOVE TO THINK THAT YOU ARE AS LONESOME AS I AM, BUT THAT IS AS IT MAY BE. ANYWAY, MY LOVE TO YOU AND THE BABIES. YOU MUST ALWAYS REMEMBER THAT ONCE WE HAD LOTS OF FUN AND DON'T LET ANYTHING EVER MAKE YOU FORGET IT.

PLEASE BELIEVE I MEAN THIS, BABY, AND WE WILL BOTH FEEL BETTER. MUCH LOVE.

JACK[19]

Dolores had only just been awarded custody of her children when she found herself saddled with a second pair of dependents. For more than a year, Dolores had been sending money to her father to help him make ends meet.[20] He had worked only a few weeks in the last six years, and had no choice but to ask his daughter for help. If father and daughter were ever going to put the past behind them, there was no time like the present. No doubt it had occurred to Dolores that Maurice had been right about Barrymore all along—as it occurred to Maurice that Dolores was no longer out to get him. That Maurice would never again pose an existential threat to Dolores's love life did much to soften her feelings toward him. That Dolores was paying his rent each month did much to soften his feelings toward her.

Helene left Cuba in February with the ball still in Mussie's court. Faced with the choice of losing his wife or staying on his mother's payroll, Cora's money held sway. What Helene did not share in her memoir was that there was more to their separation than the Del Barrio fortune.[21] In one of Mussie's drawers she found a photograph of a woman she discovered to be his mistress. She also learned that they had children together, yet even then she refused to rule out the possibility of a reconciliation.

Helene's financial prospects were now almost as bleak as her father's. Whatever hope she still had that the public's memory of her scandalous divorce trial had faded was dashed by some boating friends of Mussie's: "They had heard of Lowell Sherman's death on the ship's radio. One woman had been a fan of Lowell's. She said how much she admired his plays, how much she would miss him, cutting herself off midway to say, 'By the way—who was his last wife—the one with those awful books?' Deep silence, and then Helene said sweetly, 'I was. Another drink, dear?'"[22]

From then on, whenever Maurice or Helene had nowhere else to turn, they turned to Dolores. Both had been careless with money, Maurice especially. But Dolores took after Mae. "He was a bad business man," she said of her father. "My mother was a very good business woman. My mother and I worked things together. I didn't have an agent. Now you have to have [one]. My mother and I did things together. Dad wouldn't listen. . . . My mother said 'leave them, start your own company.'" Her father, she suggested, had stayed with Vitagraph out of a misplaced sense of loyalty: "If someone wanted to form their own company, he said, 'Look I can't leave Smith, he took me in and gave me the opportunity.'"[23]

Dolores was like Mae, but not at all like Maurice, who either spent or gave away every cent he had. And now, without Jack compulsively throwing their money away, Dolores could hope for the best but plan for the worst. Unlike her father and sister, she hadn't forgotten what it was like to go hungry. "She shopped almost every day," her grandson Dore Bedell remembered. "She had this huge freezer that was like a coffin, but it was waist high. It would have ten, twenty pound hams and turkeys inside, and all sorts of other things. I had friends who survived a concentration camp and hoarded food, but nothing like my grandmother."[24]

Outweighing Dolores's financial insecurity was her sense of family obligation. This had been the case ever since she handed over the first money she made posing for James Montgomery Flagg. The Costello sisters had supported their parents from the time they joined the *Scandals* company, but now that Helene was without an income, Dolores was the only bankable commodity she and Maurice had left. Whatever resentments Helene still harbored toward her older sister would have to remain on hold, so long as Dolores's generosity was the only thing standing between herself and oblivion.

19

Daddy Butch

Not incidental to the lives of the surviving Costellos and their Barrymore progeny, was the Michigan-born, Los Angeles–bred gynecologist and obstetrician, John Vruwink. Devoid of his predecessor's Rabelaisian charm and movie-star sex appeal, he was the perfect antidote to everything that had blinded Dolores to the real Jack Barrymore until it was too late. Vruwink was financially secure, emotionally stable, and best of all, though he enjoyed his evening cocktail, he was habitually sober. He was compassionate by nature, and by virtue of his profession, was attuned to the lives of women in ways few men of his generation could have been.

Unlike Jack, Vruwink did not have a rash or mercurial streak. Of humble Midwestern parentage, he was characteristically unpretentious and down-to-earth. His friends called him "Butch." At the University of Chicago he had been a star athlete in three sports—football, baseball, and basketball—and for years he was considered one of the two greatest athletes in the school's history. A man of strong moral character, he was the only member of his class to fully repay his student loans. He expressed himself openly and straightforwardly, which Dolores at times found disconcerting. When his mother died, Vruwink fled sobbing into an upstairs bedroom, tears streaming down his face. Unsure of how to console him, Dolores turned to her daughter for help. "Go in and put your arm around him and call him 'daddy,'" she pleaded. She couldn't, Dede said, because he wasn't her daddy—but she would if she could call him "Daddy Butch." Dolores agreed, and the nickname stuck.[1]

"He was a kind, thoughtful human being," Dede said of the only real father she ever had. "He was my anchor. He was nurturing and attentive to me. After dinner he would come to my room and we would talk. Once he told me that 'emotions are the greatest things we have if we can control them. They can either make us or break us.' I've never forgotten those words." He was handsome, she said, in "a John Wayne sort of way." Butch and her mother weren't physically demonstrative, nevertheless the bedroom door "was shut a lot. He would come in through the patio door, which was always unlocked, and disappear upstairs into her room."[2]

Dolores had purposely chosen substance over style. Ironically, this was mostly Jack's doing. Vruwink quipped that if her ex-husband hadn't prevented every man under the age of eighty from getting anywhere near Dolores, he wouldn't have stood a chance. Actually, he would have—Dolores had learned the hard way from her screen-hero father and former husband that beneath their shining armor there was nothing to hold on to. In Daddy Butch she had a responsible partner and a superb role model for her children.[3]

And with a prosperous Beverly Hills physician in the house, Dolores would never go hungry again. "She was a food junkie," Dede said. "My mother loved to cook, loved to eat, loved restaurants, loved to entertain with food. She spent most of her money on food." As a child of poverty, she could also be frugal: "My mother shopped for bargains, especially clothes. She saved Green Stamps during the war. She shopped in August for next year's Christmas presents."[4]

With Jack's support payments already in arrears, Dolores knew that if she was going to find a suitable home for herself and the children, she would have to go back to work. She had last appeared in a "three-star act" with Al Jolson before the divorce, but hadn't made a penny since. So when David O. Selznick offered her the coveted role of Dearest in the film adaptation of Francis Hodgson Burnett's *Little Lord Fauntleroy,* she gratefully accepted. Selznick, with his keen eye for casting, had chosen perfectly: Dearest's angelic nature and Dolores's angelic face couldn't have been better suited to each other. Production began Thanksgiving week 1935 and continued into the new year. On March 4, 1936, the picture debuted in the unlikeliest of venues: the Comerford Theater in Warm Springs, Georgia. Dolores had traveled alone cross-country to watch the film with forty polio patients from FDR's Warm Springs Foundation, most of them children. At a stopover in Tucson, when a reporter asked if there was any chance of a reconciliation with John Barrymore, Dolores replied with unusual candor. "Something within me died since last October," she said. "I have turned a page in my life's story. . . . No there will never be a reconciliation between my husband and me." Tellingly, though they had been divorced for six months, she was still referring to Jack as her husband.

Critics loved the film and adored Dolores, who hadn't been in front of a camera since *Expensive Women* five years earlier. "A triumph for everyone concerned," wrote a reviewer, "particularly for Freddie Bartholomew . . . and for Dolores Costello, whose 'come-back' performance as Lord Fauntleroy's mother is the best of her entire career."[5] That it was. Dolores's rich, expressive voice owed much to Jack's vocal training. She had come far as an actor since her swooning portrayal of Esther in *The Sea Beast,* alternately exalting and agonizing over young Fauntleroy's adventures without ever overacting. Dolores had her father's naturalness on screen, and like him (but not at all like the Barrymores) she wasn't a scene-stealer. Her scenes with Bartholomew, gently underplayed so her costar could shine all the brighter, are models of professional courtesy. Her off-screen affection for the ten-year-old star surely helped. "She adored him," Dede recalled, "and often talked about how easy and wonderful he was to work with."[6]

In the fall of 1936, Dolores fell in love with a stylish Mediterranean mansion in the posh Hancock Park subdivision of Windsor Square, and purchased it. To refurbish the interior she hired Hollywood decorator and upholsterer William Ledendecker. "My mother used to say he had 'lace on his cuffs,'" Dede said, "the word 'gay' wasn't used then."[7] With the bills piling up, Dolores had to keep working. After the release of *Little Lord Fauntleroy,* she went from the sublime to the mediocre in *Yours for the Asking.* As Lucille Sutton, she played a financially struggling society woman who falls for the owner of a gambling house. As Johnny Lamb, George Raft plots to exploit Lucille for her high-brow connections, but falls in love with her instead. During the filming, the mood turned funereal when two workmen were electrocuted on the set. It was reported that Dolores, Raft, and a youthful Bing Crosby tried unsuccessfully to revive them.[8]

With Dolores's star again on the ascent in the mid-thirties, interviews with the press were, as always, de rigueur. Only once did she share anything truly personal. "Do you know, this is the first time in my life I've ever been on my own?" she told *Screenland.* "The first time ever to be alone! First there was my mother, then Jack. I have a feeling now of waiting to see what happens. Anyway, I have never made a plan for myself that was lived up to. It always turned out that I went the other place or did the other thing."

During her busy year of home buying and picture making, Dolores and Vruwink barely saw each other. Dede didn't remember him coming to the Irving Boulevard house at all. No doubt this was because Daddy Butch was still married. Of particular concern was his wife Laura's spotless reputation as cochairman of the Women's University Club's *Motion Picture Reviews,* a monthly magazine ruled by a panel of society matrons dedicated to steering children away from unwholesome movie fare. *Hopalong Cassidy Returns,* for example, rated an unequivocal "no" due to a scene "that will bring shudders to many, the spectacle of an invalid dragged to his death in a wheel-chair." The reviewer declared, "Such a spectacle of wanton cruelty is unnecessary and to be deplored, especially in a picture which will attract junior audiences."[9] Under the circumstances, another scandalous Costello marriage would have thrown poor Laura to the tabloids. The press had been sniffing around for prospective suitors ever since Dolores's divorce became final, but so far they had turned up nothing. Hoping against hope to keep it that way, save for their occasional trysts at the Santa Ynez Inn near Santa Barbara, Dolores and Daddy Butch spent much of the year apart.[10]

In March, a fan magazine reported that Dolores and her former husband arrived separately at the Countess Di Frasso's party, neither knowing that the other was invited. The room "tightened up considerably" when a telephone call arrived from Elaine Barrie, whose cross-country romance with Jack had recently made headlines.[11] Doubly embarrassed, Jack beat a hasty retreat. Elaine later claimed that she and her mother, Edna, had tried to crash the party but were barred from entering.

A month later, Dolores was photographed escortless at Carole Lombard's gala, wrapped in a shimmering white dress, her head topped with a towering white wig.[12] "Sometimes Arthur Lubin escorted my mother," Dede said. "Everyone in Hollywood knew he was gay, so when single actresses wanted to go out on the town without attracting the gossip mongers, they called him."[13]

After years of virtual imprisonment, Dolores was out in the world again. She became a weekly fixture at ex-Democratic congressman Thomas Patten's Sunday salons, hosted by his wife and sister at the Patten's Vine Street bungalow. Their teas were well attended by members of the film colony, with guests crammed onto benches so close together "their rear ends touched." Dolores often brought Dede along, and occasionally John Blyth. "You had to be there exactly at 3 p.m.," Dede said. "Patten's sister-in-law, who I called Aunt Jakey, served the tea. My brother and I liked to go into the backyard to feed their pet turtle." But not on the day Douglas Fairbanks

Jr. came to tea. "I was about six and I remember the four of us were sitting together—Fairbanks, my mother, and someone I don't recall. We were drinking our tea and he was smiling this beautiful smile from ear to ear, flashing these beautiful white teeth. He was wearing a dark blue suit and had this gorgeous dark complexion. My jaw just dropped." When Dolores saw her daughter's expression, she said, "'Dede go outside and play with the turtle.' I looked her straight in the eye and said, 'I can't mother—I am drinking my *tea*!' She threw her head in her hands as if to say 'oh god,' while Aunt Jakey, who was proud of her tea, laughed uproariously."[14]

Daddy Butch kept a low profile in the weeks before Christmas 1936. With press photographers snapping away, Dolores and the children boarded the *Queen Mary* in mid-December to begin a five-month-long vacation that first took them to Switzerland for the holidays, then to France, and finally to England. Just before their departure, the children's rarely seen grandfather put in an appearance at Dolores's newly decorated showplace at 454 Windsor Boulevard. Apparently, Maurice had taken up electronics in his spare time, which he now had in endless amounts, as he spent much of the day running a buzzer from the kitchen to Dede's bedroom. "I was sick in bed and my mother came in and said 'your grandfather is making you a present in the garden.' He made a hole in two pieces of balsa wood and strung an electrical wire through it, and there was a big red button in the middle of it. He handed it to me and said to me very sweetly, 'if you need something to eat, press the button and we'll come running.' I think it was his way of showing his love. You could see he took pride in his work."[15]

Dolores brought with them to Europe a nurse and a governess, both of them named Margaret, to care for the children in her absences. The "Bad Margaret," as Dede called her, went along in a much different capacity than the one originally intended. Shortly before they left, Dede entered four-year-old John Blyth's room to find the woman touching the boy in places that even a six-year-old knew she should not. Dede told her mother, who ordered the pedophilic Margaret to accompany the family to England, where she was sent home to her native Ireland with strict instructions never to return to the United States. The "Good Margaret" stayed on to look after Dede and John Blyth, while Dolores attended numerous social functions.[16]

With London's pre-Coronation festivities going full blast, British novelist Dennis Wheatley threw a party for Dolores. A few days later a cable arrived with an urgent message that would cut their vacation short by a month. Dolores, the children, and the remaining Margaret had to return home at once to deal with a family crisis almost a decade in the making.[17]

Helene had her first lung hemorrhage in 1927. At the time the cause was thought to be rough handling by a costar while they were filming a scene, probably for the movie version of Maurice Barrymore's great stage vehicle, *The Heart of Maryland.* A few weeks later, the *Film Daily* reported that actress Edna Murphy had replaced Helene in the film *Black Diamond Express,* due to a bad case of influenza.[18] Years later, Helene told Deirdre that being tied to a tree in the rain while Cuban thieves stole her jewelry had caused her disease, though she had probably contracted it years earlier.[19] It was only when an old lesion on her right lung broke open in early 1935, that her tuberculosis was officially diagnosed. After that, wrote Helene, she "was working where and when she could. I didn't sweep Darryl Zanuck's office [a reference to not having to sleep with him to get work], but he didn't ask me to."[20] She got a small part in Metro Goldwyn Mayer's *Public Hero No. 1,* but was cut out of the finished film. Dolores's friend and escort Arthur Lubin cast Helene as the main character's sister in Monogram Studios' low-budget *Hollywood Limited,* but again her scenes were deleted.

In July, Helene made her stage-acting debut as the fictitious Pulitzer Prize–winning poetess Ember Joyce in the Vine Street Theater production of *A Wilder Beauty.* To nobody's sorrow, playwright DeWitt Bodeen abandoned the theater shortly after that to write screenplays. "The play is bad, childish, written with an infant's hand," sniped a reviewer.[21] As for Helene's performance: "The ridiculous lines she reads with great dignity. She has fine poise and is graceful and unpretentious. If the role were anything at all, hers would be a very nice performance." Among opening night attendees were Norma Talmadge, who owed her first big break to Maurice Costello, and the now seventy-three-year-old Mrs. Leslie Carter, donning the trademark scarlet wig she had worn ever since *The Heart of Maryland* made its Broadway debut forty years earlier. Bad reviews and Hollywood audiences more attuned to film than theater forced the show's early closing, leaving Helene once again unemployed. She lost the opportunity to costar with Maurice Evans in the play *St. Helena* on Broadway, when the producers decided that, at five foot two and a half, Helene would make Evans's six-foot-one Napoleon look gargantuan.[22]

In October, she got a break. Jack Ruben, another director friend of the family, gave Helene a small speaking part in MGM's *Riff Raff,* starring Jean

Harlow. Though she was billed second to last in a cast of twenty-four, her scenes are some of the film's most memorable. In her three frantic minutes of screen time, Helene, as the escaped convict Maisie, races through a typhoon-like deluge, crawls through a drainpipe with water up to her chest, and washes down a muddy embankment while being shot at with a machine gun, before she escapes with Harlow in the backseat of a getaway car. The Costello curse, which never permitted a success without a corresponding failure, arrived on cue. A few days before the rain scenes were scheduled to be shot, Helene's tuberculosis took a sudden turn for the worse. Once again the press referred to it, in their veiled way, as influenza. "But she will be on hand today to take the role," the *Los Angeles Times* reported, "nevertheless and notwithstanding. The unfortunate part about the whole thing is that the sequence in which Miss Costello must work calls for rain and lots of it. . . . Her doctors have kept her home and in bed to obtain all strength possible to combat the added danger of a relapse."[23]

The escape scene, which required numerous takes, put Helene out of commission until the middle of 1936. By then she felt healthy enough to give theater acting another try, only this time on more stage-friendly turf. In July, she checked into the Hotel Lombardy for a short stay in Manhattan, before heading north to play summer stock at the Berkshire Playhouse in Stockbridge, Massachusetts. In August, she appeared in *The Octaroon,* the well-worn nineteenth-century play in which her father had appeared in his first season on the legitimate stage. "There was talk of another Broadway play," Helene wrote, "and for a while she lived on promises. . . . It was all talk."[24] The trade papers reported that she and screen actor Monroe Owsley would appear together in the vaudeville playlet *Grease Paint,* but for reasons unknown their partnership never materialized.

Helene returned to New York in the fall in search of theater work and also to rendezvous with Mussie in a last-ditch effort to save their marriage. If she thought she could convince him to live in the States without his mother's money, she was mistaken. How much of the next eight months they spent together while she was still on the East Coast, Helene never shared, but when she returned to Hollywood in the spring of 1937, Mussie wasn't with her. By that point, their marriage was over in everything but name.

Dede wasn't privy to what the telegram said, but she knew what it did. Her mother's disappointment at having to miss the king's coronation must have been palpable, given that she had crossed the Atlantic Ocean to witness it. But her sister needed her. "She loved England and everything English, but my aunt Helene was very sick, so my mother turned in our tickets and we left a month early on the *Queen Elizabeth.*"[25] They arrived home in mid-April to find Helene in dire straits both medically and financially. A year of expensive hotels had used up every cent of her money. A $4,655 court settlement from Lowell Sherman's estate extended her stay—but, as Walter Winchell reported, she had "battered at the doors of the theatrical producers only to encounter the perfunctory expression of regret."[26] Now she needed care and hospitalization, but didn't have the money to pay for it. She lay in her bed, she remembered, "coughing blood for three days before she had Dolores call a doctor. It was all over then. She could not do a day's work, let alone stage an extended battle of a come-back. If she wanted to live six months, she would have to quit work immediately and go to bed in a sanitarium."[27]

Amazingly, Helene held off the inevitable for another seven months—tragically, just long enough to sign a contract with Twentieth Century-Fox that would have made her comeback a reality. Now it was an impossibility. Eighty years later, Dede vividly remembered the day that Helene left the Windsor Square house to check into the San Gabriel Valley Sanitarium: "I remember how sad she looked in my mother's bedroom as she was packing to leave—her beautiful black Irish coloring, china blue eyes, black eyelashes and eyebrows. Her black marcelled hair, hugging her beautifully shaped head. She wore it in a chignon, with a bun in the back that looked like a fancy doughnut. She looked so sad, like one of those SPCA ads where the dogs need a home and their faces are just begging you to help them."[28]

The death knell to Helene's film career sadly coincided with the end of her marriage to Mussie. In "almost suicidal despair" she wrote him to say it was over, but wouldn't tell him it was because of her illness.[29] It had taken two ceremonies to marry them—one in Havana, the other in Reno—now it would take two divorces to pull them apart. On May 11, 1937, Mussie filed for his in Cuba, citing "incompatibility of character." Helene waited another two years to get hers, until circumstances left her no alternative but to finally give him up.

20

The Lions at Bay

Dolores thrived, Helene languished, and Maurice rallied, albeit briefly, when Paramount Pictures took pity on twenty-five discarded movie stars and cast them as incidental players in the 1936 film *Hollywood Boulevard.*[1] Maurice and former archrival Francis X. Bushman played film directors and received full screen credits. Afterward, with nothing on his plate work-wise, he went back on the dole—Dolores's—collecting the $100 a month she had been sending him since their reconciliation. Without it he might have starved, as they had in Bayside, or just as unthinkably, found a job outside of acting.

Whatever warm feelings their rapprochement engendered faded quickly when Helene was hospitalized in November 1937. With her sister's medical bills skyrocketing, Dolores had to reconsider, among other things, her financial commitment to her father. She hadn't worked in a year, and with widespread health insurance coverage a thing of the future (especially for out-of-work actors), the burden of paying Helene's medical expenses fell squarely on her shoulders. With the availability of antibiotics still a few years away, doing nothing would have been preferable to the clinical methods still in use to treat a disease that was not yet curable. Over the next several months, doctors subjected Helene to a variety of surgical procedures, ranging from the barbaric to the ineffectual—Dr. Clifford Wood's "pneumothorax therapy," for example, which consisted of injecting air into the chest cavity to deflate the lungs.[2]

Dolores's increasing financial burdens must have terrified her. Why else, a month before Helene's hospitalization, would she have gone back to work for Jack L. Warner, a man she despised, whose company she believed had ruthlessly exploited her? In September, she returned after an absence of six years to play the second-billed part of a school teacher in *The Beloved Brat,* featuring teenage star-of-the-moment, Bonita Granville.

Daddy Butch had returned to the fold by then, to everyone's satisfaction, except for his soon-to-be-ex-wife, Laura. Dede adored him. He proposed to Dolores shortly before the England trip and she accepted—circumstances permitting. She was still abroad when the press got wind of their engagement and reported it, with a disclaimer attached stating that unnamed "friends" had denied the assertion.[3] Walter Winchell repeated the announcement in late April, though exactly who the actress was engaged to, he didn't say: "Dolores Costello Barrymore will marry a West Coast doctor, when his estranged wife stops retarding the divorce."[4] Unbeknownst to Winchell, columnist Ed Sullivan had filled in the blank a few days earlier: "Dolores Costello prefers John Vruwink. And that's not a typographical error."[5]

As she had with Jack, Dolores was having a secret romance with a married man and trying with ever-diminishing success to keep it that way. When the engagement story broke in the gossip columns, tongues must have wagged in the offices of the *Motion Picture Review,* though never in the presence of the magazine's cochairman, Laura Vruwink.

Probably the week before Dolores and the children left for England, Jack paid the Windsor Boulevard house a long overdue visit.[6] The tardiness of the occasion—he had seen his children only once since his return to Los Angeles the year before—owed entirely to the dictates of his most recent ex-wife. Nearly everyone who knew Jack and later wrote about him, told of how badly he missed his "babies." To be with them again, he told Elaine, was his sole reason for leaving New York.

Except that Dolores didn't want to have anything to do with Jack, or for Jack to have anything to do with the children. For one thing, she was afraid of how he would behave around them. Michael Strange had similar concerns about Jack's relationship with their daughter Diana, and shunned him accordingly. For another, at a time when divorced fathers could more easily be cast aside, Dolores saw Vruwink as the childrens' father-to-be and Jack becoming an increasingly distant memory. She knew from the newspapers that he was going downhill. Indeed, his mental and physical capabilities had declined sharply in recent months. He had been under relentless pressure—from his creditors, from Dolores and her attorneys, and from the equally litigious Elaine Barrie, whose threatened lawsuit to get her diamond ring back nearly kept him from leaving New York.[7] Despite his every attempt to stop drinking, Jack's alcoholism had proved unconquerable. Since his separation from Dolores, a parade of doctors, nurses, and caretakers had tried and failed to dry him out.

He had crossed the continent twice—the first time on the run from Dolores, the second from Elaine. Having tasted the limelight and found it intoxicating, the former Hunter College student, whom Jack had seduced with promises of wealth and stardom, wasn't about to give him up without a fight. "So started the madness of the famous Caliban and Ariel cross-country flight," she wrote in her aptly titled memoir, *All My Sins Remembered.* "It wiped everything off the front pages for days, and fed radio comedians and vaudeville stars with enough material for three seasons."[8] Trailing reporters in her wake, Elaine boarded Jack's train in Chicago and, amid the popping of flashbulbs, pounded on his stateroom door. "John, this is your Ariel!" she shouted. "John, John, I love you!" She didn't know it, but he had slipped off the train before her arrival. Undaunted, Elaine traveled alone to Kansas City, where she took to the airwaves. "I address this appeal in an effort to reach John Barrymore, whom I love dearly," she told the radio audience. "I also address this to the people of Kansas City and the Middle West who have been so sympathetic and understanding. John, dear, I know you need me now—more than ever before. . . . Please, please, dear John, don't think I have deserted you. I am here in Kansas City waiting for your call. Please come to me. I am waiting. We have each other. That's all that matters."[9]

Impressed with her audacity, Jack called Elaine from New Mexico and agreed to a reconciliation. In triumph, she told the press they were getting back together, and returned to New York to await Jack's final divorce decree. As soon as he was legally free of Dolores, Jack moved Elaine and her mother, Edna, into a small house he rented for them in Hollywood.[10] Now she could devote herself to the twin tasks of launching her film career and becoming the fourth Mrs. Barrymore. The latter she accomplished within the year—but Elaine had confused fame with notoriety and would have no better luck becoming a successful screen actress than she had crashing the Countess Di Frasso's party.

Helene and Dolores joined in the cacophony of ridicule, playing a prank on Elaine that took considerable time and effort to pull off. When the sisters learned from a reporter that Elaine was about to leave town on the Super Chief, Dolores jokingly said she wanted to get her autograph for the children. Donning servant's clothes and wigs, Helene and her close friend, the character actress Minna Gombell, caught a cab to the station and tracked Elaine to her compartment. "Your autograph, Missus Barrymore—my daughter is deaf and dumb—it would mean so much of her!" Minna begged, while Helene crossed her eyes and sucked her fingers. Elaine signed her name with a flourish.[11]

The Caliban and Ariel affair only added to Dolores's revulsion at the prospect of ever having to see her former husband again. Tragically, this evolved into a policy of preventing his children from seeing him, which would do them lasting, irreparable harm. Dede was six and a half when her father appeared on her doorstep in early December 1936. Dolores wasn't home, not surprisingly, but for unknown reasons neither was John Blyth. Jack came loaded down with gifts, his longtime Japanese gardener, Mark Nishimura, doubling as his chauffeur. Vruwink greeted her father at the door, Dede recalled: "They kissed each other on both cheeks, French style. Something was whispered, but I couldn't hear what it was."

"My father looked in through [the] open front door into the entry hall and saw the oil painting of my brother he had commissioned. My guess is that he was told 'Johnny's not here,' because he walked into the living room, sat down in his chair, which my mother took from Tower Road, and threw his head in his hands."[12] Jack had brought presents for the children, and a huge straw wheel of candied fruit as a housewarming gift, which was placed on the piano. "George, our Japanese houseman, asked, 'Would anyone like anything to drink?' Nishi said 'No! No!' While this was going on, I was standing in the curve of the piano about four feet away from where my father was sitting. He never lifted his head. I never saw his face, because his head was buried in his hands. I don't think he saw me. We never said a word to each other. I don't think he even knew I was there."

The visit, if it could be called that, would be the one and only time she remembered seeing her father after her parents' separation. Jack's Christmas present to Dede proved as evanescent as their meeting: "It was an exquisite apricot ostrich-feathered bed jacket that went around the whole top of my body. I planned to wear it to bed that night and my mother said, 'you can sleep in it, but I'm taking it back to the store tomorrow.' When I asked why, she said 'it's too old for you.' She had *spoken,* so I realized there was nothing more I could do. But I've loved that gorgeous color ever since."[13]

The encounter was a disaster for everyone concerned—except for Dolores, of course, who had successfully ostracized the man she considered a mortal threat to her well-being. In the process, tragically, she deprived her four-and-a-half-year-old son of the only conscious memory he might have had of the towering figure he would forever be compared to, but would never be allowed to know. As for Dede, the last time she saw her father he was slumped over in a chair, too overcome with grief even to acknowledge her presence.[14]

In true Costello fashion, another opportunity for healing had died in a hail of bitterness and resentment that crippled everyone in the end. For Jack it was another coffin nail, one Dolores was only too happy to drive home at her children's expense. Elaine divorced him four months later (charging him with, among other offenses, calling her "vile, violent, obscene, indecent, profane and opprobrious" names), only to dissolve the interlocutory decree after two months and take him back.[15] She would witness the best and worst of his remaining years, as would Helene. "She read his scripts for him, and he relied on her for her advice," wrote his ex-sister-in-law with what sounded like a pang of regret. "She was his 'kid sister' to the end, and there was more companionship between them than there had ever been with Jack and Dolores. She read his scripts with an eye toward parts for herself, but he never volunteered to help her get one. Shortly before he died, after he divorced Elaine Barrie Jacobs, she asked him why he had never given her a break in pictures. 'Helene, beauty is never competition—talent always will be,' he said. She flared at that; it not only failed to excuse him but reflected upon her looks. Jack only grinned and shrugged."[16]

The more money Dolores was required to spend on Helene's medical treatments, the less she had left to give to her father, and the more terrified of homelessness Maurice was becoming. To save money, he moved out of his North Wetherly bungalow into a smaller apartment, but soon he couldn't afford that. Then came Dolores's announcement that she was cutting him off, and Maurice's response was extreme, even for him. Certainly, it was not unprecedented. Freddie Bartholomew's parents had tried to wrest control of their son's estate from his Aunt Millicent, who raised him.[17] The Langhankes, Mary Astor's parents, sued their daughter for support and were awarded $100 per month.

In May 1938, Maurice filed suit against Dolores for "non-support." He was "destitute and unable to work," he told the *Los Angeles Times*. His daughter had been supporting him, but thirty days ago "served him with notice that she would make no further contributions." As ill-health now prevented him from finding employment, he was asking the court to award him $200 a month—twice what Dolores had been paying. "I'm as poor as a church mouse," he told a reporter. "If it rained soup, I'd have a fork in my hands."[18]

Before he could be evicted from his current residence, Maurice absconded in the dead of night to an apartment a friend had rented for him in Los Feliz, then one of Los Angeles's humbler sections. It was a part of town Maurice did not know well. He awoke the next morning to find himself staring out of the window at none other than the old Vitagraph lot, bustling just as it was in 1925, before Blackton and Smith sold the property to Warner Bros. "I thought to myself, 'wouldn't it be just my luck to move to a place where the surroundings are such to bring back memories of old times.' Believe me the last ten years of my life have been very tough. That's the way things happen and I don't know why. I've been an actor for 48 years and that's all I know. If I can't get a part on the stage or screen there is nothing else I could possibly do, except drive someone's car."

Up to that point the Costellos, both singly and severally, had been parties in some twelve court cases—seven times as plaintiffs, five as defendants, four of those times against each other. Each was reported in the national press. "I am sorry this matter has become public," Dolores told the newspapers, sickened by the prospect of having to appear at yet another legal proceeding. She tried to get him to budget his expenses, she said, but he refused. "Father told me 'One should support one's father and if he does not the publicity is sure to be unfavorable.' This sounded like a threat and I do not like to be threatened. I cannot comply with his demands and that's all there is to it. Father has been given enough right along, though he has thought otherwise."[19]

If Dolores really wanted to cut him off, rather than spout schoolmarmish platitudes, she might have simply stated that she could no longer afford to pay him. Now she could either give in to his demands, or do nothing and watch him get evicted as the whole country looked on. She could have thwarted him when she had the chance, but now it was too late. Maurice had won. The amount she agreed to pay him wasn't revealed, but it would be enough to keep a roof over his head for the time being.

Making the matter public had other, larger benefits for Maurice. If ever Hollywood had an opportunity to show it had a conscience, this was it. In October, the Associated Press reported that Maurice was "playing his first feature in a talking role. . . . It's a 'speaking part,' which means $25 a day and is good for three days."[20] While he was appearing in the MGM short subject *Nuts and Bolts* (which paid him a lifesaving $82.50 for six days' work), Director W. S. Van Dyke offered him a part in *Stand Up and Fight,* featuring Robert Taylor.

It wasn't a speaking part, unfortunately—just a day or two's work in a pair of setups, for which Maurice appears in an antebellum entry hall, lost in a crowd of well-heeled visitors. He probably wasn't paid more than $50, but he couldn't complain. "I'm trying to get in the back door," he said. "I simply had to have a job. . . . I don't want to be dependent on others. Whether I get anywhere or not, this is better than sitting around my room all day."[21]So began Maurice's part-time stint as an unbilled bit player and movie extra. Ironically, he had Dolores to thank for her unintentional role in getting the studios to feel even sorrier for him than they already did—sorry enough to finally start hiring him. Her actions also forced him to join the Screen Actors Guild and get his Central Casting card, neither of which he had done, probably because she was supporting him.

In May, the court put the support matter on hold, around the time Maurice's snowy head began popping up in a variety of films for a number of Hollywood studios.[22] He played a staff member in Columbia's *I Am the Law,* a town councilor in RKO's *A Man to Remember,* a juror in Paramount's *Disbarred.* He was an actor at a dress rehearsal in Warner Bros.' *Comet over Broadway,* with Dolores and Helene's close friend Minna Gombell in a supporting role.

Maurice was working again, but his paychecks from Central Casting, combined with what Dolores was sending him, were barely enough to cover his expenses. Once he had owned a closet full of dress clothes; now a single black-checked blazer and wing collar shirt would have to suffice for every occasion.

21

A Trio of Marriages

In August 1938, Maurice landed a bit part in the RKO release *Breaking the Ice,* with his daughter Dolores second-billed as the mother of the boy singing star, Bobby Breen, who was then cresting the wave of his brief stardom. Unlike most child actors, he was doubly cursed: Breen's appeal wasn't based just on his little-boy cuteness but also on a soprano voice that was about to deepen with the onset of puberty. Maurice is nowhere to be found in the completed film, in which Dolores reprises the long-suffering mother part she played to perfection in *Little Lord Fauntleroy.* This time, however, perfection was not attainable. This wasn't Dolores's fault—the film's low budget and lower production standards crippled it from the beginning. Still, the sight of Dolores Costello playing a bonneted Mennonite widow was worth the price of admission to at least one movie critic: Laura Vruwink thought highly enough of the film to give it an unqualified "Yes" in the October edition of *Motion Picture Reviews* (the same issue also gave a thumbs-up to John Barrymore, now in professional free fall, in Fox's inane *Hold That Co-ed*).[1] For Dolores, the film was proof that her work-when-I-want-to relationship with Hollywood hadn't succeeded. She had watched from the sidelines as a succession of harder-working actresses fought their way to the top, starting with Bette Davis, who Dolores claimed had "carried on where I left off" at Warner Bros.

Until the release of *The Beloved Brat,* Dolores thought she could maintain her status as part-time movie star. "There is no disputing the fact," she told a reporter, "that even a short absence from the screen is dangerous. But with the right spirit, an actress can win her way back."[2] After two months, one lawsuit, and a Bobby Breen picture, her outlook had darkened considerably. "The public forgets you very easily," she said. "I broke my contract with Warner Brother's by mutual agreement eight years ago when my first baby was coming. I never intended then to return to the screen. But circumstances have changed since that time. I remained off the screen for a couple of years and among other things made a trip to Europe. That probably was a mistake. The people soon forget you when you don't appear before them all the time."[3] Hopefully, added Dolores, she wouldn't have to play too many more mother parts.

Nevertheless, her next role was a mother part. United Artists' *King of the Turf* starred Adolph Menjou as a down-on-his-luck horse trainer who takes in a runaway boy (played by Roger Daniel, whose movie career never quite got off the ground). By an unfathomable coincidence, the boy turns out to be the trainer's long-lost son, which makes his mother, Dolores's character, his ex-wife. After that she appeared in Columbia's *Whispering Enemies,* starring Jack Holt as the hero, with Dolores second-billed as his nemesis-turned-love interest. Holt's early days as a movie actor reached almost as far back as Maurice Costello's, but thanks to his own canny career management, he kept working until his death in 1951.[4]

Given the Costellos' ongoing history of scandal and litigation, it's astonishing that Dolores still had a screen career at all. Added to her own legal entanglements, she had been linked to a pair of lawsuits that weren't hers—John Barrymore's tardy divorce from Michael Strange, which she indirectly caused, and John Vruwink's ongoing divorce suit, now moving toward its inevitable conclusion. Adulterous though it was, the arrangement seems not to have disquieted the upright Laura to any noticeable degree. "My father came to see me every day," her daughter Jane recalled, "but he would never spend the night. My mother never discussed their divorce with me. Those things just weren't talked about."[5]

Daddy Butch wasn't spending the night at Dolores's either, but at his apartment in the Los Altos on Wilshire Boulevard. Late afternoons and evenings, however, he could be found at Fifth and Windsor. "When he came over I would jump on him and wrap my legs around him," Dede recalled. "He would call me Charlotte [after Charlotte Greenwood, the popular actress and dancer known for her unusually long legs]. Then he would go up the stairs and into my mother's room and I wouldn't see him again for the rest of the night. I know he didn't stay over because he wasn't there in the morning when I woke up."[6]

According to Dede, what hastened her mother's marriage to Vruwink as much as his divorce, was Dolores's growing fear of the unknown. In 1939, the year that all of Europe erupted into war, an appeaser's pro-Hitler diatribe at the Patten's dinner table left Dolores shaken and in tears. "We were leaving and the door was open. My mother was at the threshold and she was sobbing, and this bastard was standing there while we were saying goodnight to Aunt Jakey and Uncle Tom. I said to Daddy Butch 'why is my mother crying?' and he said, 'Because this man is pro-Hitler, and they're taking the Jews' homes away from them.' I stuck my tongue out at the man so hard, and this jerk just laughed."[7]

With the coming war in Europe and the demise of Dolores's movie career, Vruwink's divorce couldn't have come at a better time. On November 29, two and a half years after Ed Sullivan had announced their engagement in his column, the couple slipped off to Prescott, Arizona, and were quietly married.[8] That they loved and needed each other, Dede had no doubt. Even Laura's daughter Jane conceded that Dolores gave her father something her "straight arrow" mother could not. This was, of course, glamour—of the dazzling Hollywood kind that staid, professional men like John Vruwink weren't supposed to think twice about, much less end their marriages over. Truer to form, Laura Vruwink kept a stiff upper lip during the entire affair, waiting patiently for the inevitable. "My mother was cool and collected," said Jane. "She was the polar opposite of Dolores."[9]

By then, Vruwink couldn't have cared less about the social register, but not so Dolores. The more distance she could put between her downtrodden childhood and the decorous life she aspired to, the happier she was. "Don't be common," she once admonished a grandchild, though few had been cut from commoner cloth than she. Being feted and fussed over by prominent Londoners during the coronation festivities in 1936 lit the spark: from then on, said Dede, her mother loved everything English.[10] Now, as the ex–movie star wife of a prominent Beverly Hills physician, whatever remained of the Brooklyn-bred hoofer who had stepped off the train from Chicago in 1925 would never show its face again.

Respectability wasn't in the cards for Maurice, then or ever. Even at the height of his fame as America's original film celebrity, movie actors were still seen as glittering anomalies that fit into no particular mold. By the time that changed, the business had left him behind. From then on, he would be seen as a tragic figure—belligerent and beaten down, weak but resilient, a ne'er-do-well who deserved better, given what he had done for movies early on. Now that he had revived his working relationship with the studios, perhaps what he needed in order to stage a proper comeback was to follow Dolores's lead and pursue the staid and conventional.

Marrying well might have done it, if Maurice hadn't put his usual dystopian stamp on the relationship from the very beginning, starting with his choice of partners. Thirty-year-old Ruth Reeves, the daughter of federal judge Albert Reeves, came from a respectable family.[11] She had a desk job at Central Casting and, like Maurice, occasionally appeared as a movie extra. If she hadn't been half his age, her good name might have rubbed off on him before he had a chance to tarnish it. To downplay the disparity, Maurice gave his age on their marriage license as fifty-four, though he was almost sixty-two. The newspapers blithely catered to this falsehood, but any moviegoer over the age of fifty would have known he was fibbing.[12]

Ruth and Maurice were married in Tijuana on August 29, 1939. The next day the groom told reporters that they had also tied the knot in a previous ceremony, though he wouldn't say when or where. "It's a retake," Maurice chuckled. "We were married two months ago but our friends didn't know it. It will be a big surprise to a lot of people." When asked why they married twice, he said they "weren't satisfied" the first time and wanted to do it again.[13] Much easier to fathom than why someone would elope with the same person twice, is why Maurice cooked up such a ridiculous story to begin with. Most likely it was because they were living together out of wedlock at Ruth's North Alfred Street apartment, and were trying to cover it up.

Ruth's parents were thunderstruck at the news—sixty-five-year-old Judge Reeves especially, who must have blanched at the realization that his new son-in-law was just four years younger than he was. The Reeves had arrived a week earlier to pay their daughter a visit, but somehow didn't learn of the first or the second ceremony until they heard about it from the press. "We just met him casually," a dazed Mrs. Reeves told reporters.[14] If she knew anything about the groom, she knew that her daughter had taken a huge leap of faith.

By marrying Ruth, Maurice lost the only moral leg he had to stand on. The justification he had so often used for divorcing Mae and leaving his family—that Jack was too old for Dolores and his wife and daughter had openly defied him—was now as meaningless as it was hypocritical. He had done exactly what he had excoriated Jack for doing: married someone too young and naive to know what they were getting into.

Not to be outdone by anyone's rashness when it came to matrimony, if it wasn't for Helene's readmittance to the hospital in early 1939, all three

Costellos would have been married the same year. Indeed, there could have been no farer cry from Mussie Del Barrio than the twenty-four-year-old bartender George Lee Le Blanc—a depression-era drifter who was working in his aunt's club when he and Helene met. He had been married and divorced. He had a child but had signed over his parental rights to his ex-wife, Antoinette, and her new husband. "He was a clumsy youth with no paternal feeling," Helene wrote. "Yet he had a fine drawing talent, and in his blind, yearning way burned to be an artist. I married him thinking I was Pygmalion, but it turned out Frankenstein."[15] When asked what her father might have seen in the chronically ill, penniless Helene Costello, Deirdre cited both love and opportunity in roughly equal measure: "Once when dad was in Los Angeles, I asked him if he ever loved my mother and he said 'Of course I did!' However, I have to divulge his inherent bent toward opportunism. My mother was, after all, his entry into working at the studios, even though it began with just an inking job for Loony Tunes."[16]

They began writing a children's book, to be called *Animalore,* with Helene creating the text and Lee Le Blanc drawing the illustrations. "[He] begged her to marry him," Helene wrote, "but she refused. 'I won't marry anyone while I have one foot in the grave,' she told him. He replied: 'Helene, whether you've got thirty years or three days left, I want you to spend them with me.' Her comment now: 'If I didn't have any money to spend, at least I could spend my days on him, and my nights under him.'"[17]

Early in the new year they slipped off to Tijuana and were quickly married. Helene didn't tell Dolores, who was still paying her hospital bills and who she thought wouldn't approve, until they were married a second time in the small but respectable town of Salome, Arizona. Maurice "disapproved of Mexican weddings, and . . . nagged her until she went through it again," Helene recalled.[18] Exactly why he disapproved, having recently been married in Mexico himself, he didn't say. For Helene this was par for the course: by the time she was thirty-four she had been married seven times to four different husbands.

In September, the newlyweds got incredible news: Helene was pregnant. Over the years more than a dozen doctors had told her she could never have a baby, and three previous marriages had seemed to confirm the diagnosis. The couple didn't have money for food much less to raise a child—Lee's aunt had fired him and Helene was back in a sanitarium. To stay afloat until the baby came, Helene sold what was left of her jewelry—a gold shoe horn and the wedding bands from her last two marriages. The seventy-five dollars she got from the sale would see them through. On February 18, 1941, Helene gave birth to a baby girl. After considerable discussion, the couple settled on the name "Deirdre Ann." "Dad wanted to name me either Daphne or Gabriella, but my mother didn't like the nicknames they engendered—Daffy and Gabby. She had read James Stephens's *Deirdre of the Sorrows* and fell in love with the name. Mother told me that my name wasn't decided upon for a couple of days, and I was put in a basket with a pink ribbon and a label saying, 'Baby George.' So, for a couple of days, I was called George."[19]

Wrote Helene in triumph: "It gave her something to live for. Broke and tubercular, with a husband six years younger than she, who had no earning power at all, yet Helene Costello Regan Sherman Del Barrio Le Blanc was happier than she had ever been."[20]

Maybe the real reason that Maurice was against Mexican marriages was that his was going so badly. It took him less than a month to transform poor, unremarkable Ruth Reeves into the unfaithful, conniving, dishonest Jezebel he imagined her to be. Their relationship quickly collapsed under the weight of Maurice's oppressive jealousy, which was one of several marriage-killing traits he shared with John Barrymore. Jack's pathological mistrust of women was mostly confrontational. Police-style interrogations that lasted until the wee hours had been the ruin of Jack's last two marriages—his final split with Elaine occurred in September 1940. Maurice, on the other hand, preferred to grumble and stew before blowing his top, which he did in spectacular fashion in front of dinner guests one evening while he rifled through his mortified wife's handbag. As always, he found nothing incriminating. On another rampage he telephoned the wives of her employers at Central Casting to tell them that his wife was sleeping with each of their husbands.[21] But what impressed itself most on Ruth was the .22 pistol he once waved at her in a fit of accusatory outrage.

Maurice was also engaged in passive activities. He hunkered down in his car outside their Hollywood apartment, straining to catch a glimpse of Ruth doing something illicit through the bedroom windows. His behavior had taken a sinister turn in the late twenties, when he began spying on Dolores and Jack. Now he was combing through Ruth's things, looking for telltale signs of the assignation he was sure was taking place under his nose. He began monitoring her supply of Lysol disinfectant, one of the most common forms of birth control in the 1930s, to see how much of it was being used. Where once he had written fragmented observations in ledgers and diaries, he was now typing lengthy, police-style documents. By December, two months into their marriage, Maurice was in full-blown surveillance mode:

> I arrived home at 6:50 PM—Big reception when I got home. Ruth told me she had been to the Bank, and also to the State Unemployment Agency. Said she left at Noon, 15 miles on the Speedometer for trip. Reticent when questioned. The Douche-bag wet—Lysol Douche had been freshly used. WHY? First time she has used Lysol since we have been Married. I wonder how she stayed in Hollywood. Ruth was reluctant to say when she got home, or what she did the rest of the afternoon, or what time she did get home. Could it be possible that she and Jack Howe have been coming into Hollywood, and that they have a secret meeting place? And WHY a Lysol Douche in the afternoon? And also on the nite of the 19th she was too tired to play. Wanted to sleep. If She is not seeing Jack Howe, who is she seeing? . . . This whole thing has got my Goat.[22]

A month later, Maurice was still grasping at straws:

> Ruth had a Luncheon engagement at Ariane's home—948 Stone Canyon Rd. She left at 11:30 A. M. I had to push her car to get it started—I watched her go up La Cienega to Sunset Blvd. She turned EAST on Sunset, again WHY?
>
> At 1:25 P. M. I saw her Car in front of 948. Almost Two Hours later. Question is, what time did she get there, and what Time did she leave? She got Home at 5:30 P. M. Wearing a Gardenia—she said SHE bought it. No sign of drink. She said she didn't have a drink, and that Ariane didn't even Smoke on account of her condition. BUT, when I looked in her Car, I found the Ash-receiver full of cigarette BUTT's & Burnt Matches. The right door Glass is broken, so why use the Ash receiver? I've never seen Ruth use the receiver before. When I asked her why she turned East on Sunset, she told me that she went to a Florist. (I doubt it) I wonder Who she picked up? And WHO did buy that gardenia? Told me she saw

> me watching her through her rear Mirror—WHY was she watching me if she wasn't up to some mischief? I wonder where she went when she left 948? She seemed very HURT when I asked her some questions.[23]

If Maurice had gone to such lengths to gather evidence in a divorce case, his actions might at least seem comprehensible. But when Ruth filed for divorce on September 3, 1941, he made no counterclaim. If nothing else it was a lesson in looking before you leap—not for Maurice, who was too far gone to make a success of any romantic attachment, but for Ruth. She eventually remarried, to a former army private and ex-candy salesman from Louisiana named Harold Cripps. The couple moved to Van Nuys, where they spent the rest of their days in welcome obscurity. After her day in court, she would never again utter another word publicly against Maurice Costello, or their ill-fated marriage.

22

The Magnificent Ambersons

In 1942, the chaotic genius Orson Welles chose as a follow-up to his brilliant but financially unsuccessful *Citizen Kane* the Booth Tarkington story of a wealthy Victorian family slowly coming apart at the seams. For the heroine of his screen adaptation of *The Magnificent Ambersons,* Welles cast the thirty-nine-year-old, long-out-of-work Dolores Costello, for reasons he made abundantly clear in the film's first five minutes. Like every other director she had ever worked with, Welles can't take his, or his camera's, eyes off of her. Like David O. Selznick, Welles knew exactly what it was about Dolores that made her so perfect for the part of Isabel Amberson Minifer: she had a chaste, Madonna-like beauty that could send any young man into paroxysms of oedipal longing—as in the case of the effete, humorless George Minifer, played by Tim Holt.[1] "I'd thought of Mary Pickford," Welles told Peter Bogdanovich in the 1970s. "I talked to her a lot and she almost did it—and I'm glad she didn't. I don't think she'd have been right. Finally, we thought of Miss Costello. Brought her out of total retirement."[2]

Early in the film, Welles freezes his camera on Dolores's Gibson-girlish silhouette and holds it there for a full twelve seconds, as the action quickly recedes into the background. Added to the mélange of Wellesian touches (seeing the world from above and below; craning his camera up and down the Ambersons' four flights of stairs), he positions Dolores's perfect profile in frame like a floral centerpiece and sets the drama swirling around it.

It's a testament to Dolores's skill as an actress that her Isabel runs out of gumption so convincingly, to the extent of forsaking the man she loves to pacify her son's obsession, à la Hamlet, with keeping her celibate.[3] Even on her deathbed (few actresses of the period looked quite so moribund), she lets George come between them.

The real Dolores would have tolerated no such interference. The men in her life were there because she wanted them there—and when she wanted them gone, she didn't need a George Minifer to send them packing.

The man she wanted, but had lost despite everything she had done to hold on to him, collapsed during a rehearsal for Rudy Vallee's Sealtest radio show—fittingly, while reading lines of Shakespeare. "I guess this is one time I miss my cue," John Barrymore whispered as he fell into Vallee's arms.[4] He died at Hollywood Presbyterian Hospital nine days later, on May 28, 1942. The cause of death, his doctor reported, was "myocarditis, a heart ailment, complicated by chronic nephritis, cirrhosis of the liver and gastric ulcers."

Dr. Vruwink was more to the point. "He told me all my father's organs were literally floating in alcohol," Dede said.[5] "My mother cried all day. I met her in the hall upstairs and tears were streaming down her face. She said, 'Dede, your father died today,' and went back into her bedroom." The newspapers reported that Dolores spoke with Jack before his death, and that during the conversation, as she later confirmed, he said he was sorry. She knew he was gravely ill, yet she waited until he was breathing his last to ask his brother if she should bring the children. "No," Lionel answered, "I want them to remember him as he was."[6]

Dolores could have overruled him, but she didn't. As a result, Jack wouldn't see any of his children in his last days. Decades later, his drug-addled son shared a garbled memory of visiting his dying father at somebody's house when he was ten—but Jack died when John Blyth was nine, and in a hospital not a house, so no such meeting could have occurred. "There's no way that happened," Dede said. "If Johnny had visited him, you can be sure he would have told me about it."[7] In the late 1940s, columnists Louella Parsons and Bob Thomas asked John Blyth on separate occasions if he had any memory of his father, and both times he said he didn't.

Diana Barrymore was set to attend the premiere of *Eagle Squadron,* in which she was romantically paired with Robert Stack, when Gene Fowler telephoned. "Get out to the hospital right away," he said, "I believe your father is dying."

"I can't possibly do it," she said, "I have a very important appointment."

"So has your father."[8]

She attended his funeral, at least, helping the wheelchair-bound Lionel Barrymore hobble into the chapel on his own two feet. Ethel was in Boston with her hit play, *The Corn Is Green,* only because Jack had insisted she not close the show and rush to his bedside. Among the pallbearers was W. C. Fields, who quipped, "The time to carry a pal is when he's alive" but carried his great friend anyway.[9] The kings of Hollywood were there in force: Spencer Tracy, Errol Flynn, Fredric March, Herbert Marshall—and the king of kings, Clark Gable. Still grief-stricken over the death of his wife, Carole Lombard, five months earlier, Gable sat behind a pillar with his face in his hands.[10]

Of Jack's four ex-wives, only Elaine came to his funeral. "He is my buried treasure," she wrote. "There will never be another." His first wife, Katherine Corri Harris, had died in 1927. Michael Strange sent flowers and a get-well telegram while he was in the hospital. Helene attended (in her mind, she was always the next best thing to any of Jack's wives), accompanied by the unlikeliest of mourners—her father. All had paid their respects—even Jack's archenemy Maurice—except for Dolores. She might at least have sent Dede and John Blyth in her place, giving them an opportunity to bid their father a posthumous farewell.

Dolores's tears for Jack dried quickly. There was a lot going on in her life in the summer of 1942: most importantly, the imminent release of *The Magnificent Ambersons.* The production had faced innumerable challenges, none of them more serious than the derisive reactions of preview audiences. Trying to avoid another box-office disappointment, as *Citizen Kane* had been, Welles's bosses at RKO cut forty minutes of footage from the film, to the director's utter mortification. Critics didn't quite know what to make of the finished product—some raved, many scoffed, most praised Welles's penchant for innovation. The *New York Times* noted his "eloquent, if at time grandiose, flair for the dramatic which only the camera can fully capture." The reviewer thought Dolores underused in the film, being "too beautiful and capable an actress to remain inactive for such long periods."[11] He could not have known that this wasn't the director's fault—Welles's overlords had cut several of her biggest scenes.

Dolores enjoyed working with Welles, Dede said. She was grateful to him for giving her the part, but his "huge ego" annoyed her. "Between shots when they were sitting around the set, he did his magic tricks and nobody wanted to watch them. He did this for the entire film." To retaliate, Dolores bought Welles a huge stuffed bear with a zipper in the back and filled it with dime-store novelties and magic tricks.

Dolores made clear in interviews before the picture's release that she was no longer trying for a comeback—the implication being that because she no longer needed the money, she no longer wanted the work. Her obvious lack of interest in his ground-breaking production puzzled Welles. "You might have thought she'd want to watch what we were up to. In rehearsals, I mean. But she was quite unfocused. Nothing naughty—just not wanting to be an actress."[12]

Now she wanted it less than ever. By the early 1940s, John Vruwink was one of the most sought-after physicians in Hollywood, counting among his celebrity patients Olivia de Havilland, Joan Fontaine, and Hedy Lamarr. More than *The Magnificent Ambersons,* Dolores wanted to talk about the piece of property she and her husband had recently purchased a hundred miles south of Los Angeles, on the hilly outskirts of Fallbrook, California. "It's a farm, not a ranch," she explained. "Out here in the west, people speak of having ranches. But I say that 42 acres where you have an orchard, a vegetable garden, chickens, turkeys and cows and pigs is a farm." She was through with "keeping up with the Joneses," she said. "There is nothing on the Lord's lovely green footstool so dear to my heart as that farm."[13]

In September 1941 an historic event took place on the set of the King Vidor film *H. M. Pulham, Esq.,* though no one but the director, an MGM photographer, and the film's star, Robert Young, took the slightest notice of it. Working together for the first time since their days at Vitagraph were Maurice and Helene, playing a pair of uncredited wedding guests at Young and Ruth Hussey's nuptials. Their scenes never made it out of the cutting room, but they were used to that. All that mattered was the $10.50 per day Central Casting was paying them. In the photograph, a white-haired Maurice stands in three-quarter profile, looking worn but handsome in his Western Costume tails, vest, fob, and cravat. The famous dimples had, by then, turned to deep, permanent creases. Radiant in her own finery, Helene looked surprisingly healthy for a woman who had been in and out of sanitariums for the last four years. For the moment, she was doing well. She was between hospital stays and, that year, had received the surprise gifts of marriage and motherhood. Her husband was, at last, gainfully employed. "She got him a job at Warner Brothers as a mail boy," Helene wrote, "and then as a student cartoonist with Schlesinger's *Loony Tunes.* He started to where he was earning $15 dollars a week, and by the fall of 1942, he'd worked up to where he was earning $35 a week as a cartoonist. Helene herself had gone back to work too [as a script reader for Darryl Zanuck], and between them they could keep alive and even pay Dolores something now and then for keeping the baby."[14]

The idyll would be short-lived. In early 1943, Helene's doctors told her that "her only chance was surgery, the painful series of three operations in which seven ribs are removed and the lung collapsed so it will remain static while the lesion heals."[15] With the widespread use of streptomycin for tuberculosis patients only a year in the future, she was at the mercy of the ghastly surgical methods still in use. After the operation she was transferred to Barlow's Sanitarium in Echo Park, for what promised to be a lengthy recovery.

It was then that Dolores realized her inner penchant for taking in wayward family members. She agreed to take care of two-and-a-half-year-old Deirdre while Helene was recuperating, as Lee Le Blanc would be gone most of the time, and Dolores had servants to care for the child round the clock. Helene wanted Deirdre to live with her sister while she was in the hospital, rather than return to the couple's cramped apartment near Fox Studios, where she had found her husband a job. The arrangement might have worked if Lee Le Blanc and his sister-in-law had not been at loggerheads from the beginning. He had promised to pay Dolores twenty-five dollars a month for Deirdre's care, but weeks went by and the money never came. Dolores, being Dolores, insisted he settle accounts. "She thought him *déclassé,*" Deirdre said, "and Dad thought she was a spoiled snob. Dad got along with Vruwink quite well. Dolores had a grasping hand when it came to money or things she thought were owed to her. I'm sure most of that came from being deprived when she was a child. Really, the two sisters were black and white. My mother would give you the last dime she had if she thought it would help you or make you happy. That's why one of them was worth over a million when she died, and the other was a pauper."[16]

In response to Dolores's demands, Lee Le Blanc removed his daughter from her care and placed her in a Catholic orphanage run by French nuns. Dolores's close friend, the ex-stage actress and vaudevillian Queenie Cawthorn, somehow learned of the child's whereabouts and told Dolores, who resolved to get her back as soon as possible. "I remember that despicable place and it being where my nightmares began," Deirdre said.

> Then I remember a beautiful blonde woman picking me up and seating me on her lap. In my child's eye she was an angel. I didn't want her to leave without taking me with her, but she promised she would be back and would then take me away. Which she did. I am sure that Dad put me in that place. He was always putting me away somewhere for other people to take the responsibility of caring for me. I wouldn't be surprised if he didn't tell Mother that he had taken me from Dolores. These are the first recollections I have of Mum Mum, who I thought was my mother. She told me she wasn't my mother, but that I could call her Mum Mum—Mum Mum Dolores.[17]

"Mum Mum" had been Jack's childhood name for his beloved grandmother, Louisa Drew, who rescued him from parental loss and uncertainty, much as Dolores now had Deirdre. He was heard muttering "Mum Mum" in his delirium shortly before his death. For reasons she never shared, Dolores had decided to carry the name forward.

Helene returned home after her release from Barlow's in February 1944, to find a dirty apartment and a heated tug of war going on between her husband and Dolores over custody of Deirdre. Helene fired the housekeeper and, despite her weakened condition, took over childrearing duties herself. The antibiotic revolution of the midforties had caught up to her—never again would she stay in a tubercular sanitarium for any length of time. But years of physical suffering and depression had taken their toll. The young woman who in her early twenties had been "mildly tight only once" was drinking heavily in her late thirties, ruining what was left of her already troubled marriage. The Le Blancs had found precious little to like about each other during their four years of matrimony and were barely hanging on as a couple. It had dawned on Helene while she was vacationing with her husband in San Francisco, that his feelings for her were mostly conditional on how often she went to bat for him at Fox. "They returned . . . with his plea to her to 'write Zanuck' ringing in her ears. She said, 'I got you every job you ever had in your life. Up to a point a man's wife can help him. After that he's got to rustle for himself. It won't help you with Zanuck to have mama coming to him all the time.'"[18]

In March 1945, with massive labor unrest rocking the film industry, Lee Le Blanc went on strike with the rest of his cartoon colleagues. Based on his revised employment status, his draft board reclassified him 1-A. Thus, in the final months of World War II he was sent off to join what was left of the fray. Hoping to stay out of harm's way, he enlisted with the Merchant Marines.[19] There would be nothing to fear as it turned out—by the time he finished basic training, the war was over.

So, too, was his marriage. He had broken his promise to send Helene six hundred dollars, which forced her to return Deirdre to Dolores's care and move in with her friend June Warlock, the former wife of director Jack Ruben. Except for a brief, feeble attempt by Lee Le Blanc to "try it again," they would have nothing more to do with each other until the start of their custody fight, the likes of which not even the Hollywood press had ever seen before.

23

Deirdre, Johnny, and Jane

Exactly when Hollywood's star obstetrician learned that he, of all people, was unable to father a child, neither he nor Dolores would ever confide.[1] Had it somehow not occurred to Daddy Butch—who refused to wear a wristwatch for fear of looking effeminate—that it was he, and not his former wife Laura, who couldn't have children? Had Dolores known this beforehand, would she have married him anyway? It's hard to believe she didn't know, though it would explain a lot: Why, for example, after all she'd been through with alcoholics, she started drinking. Why she and Vruwink were having marital problems, and why she had started to think of Deirdre as her child, not Helene's.

As Dede and John Blyth grew into adulthood, Dolores looked to her own childless future with growing despair. "My mother told me many times she wanted ten children," Dede said. "She loved children, so you can be sure that not being able to have any more after she married my stepfather was a huge disappointment to her." Dolores cherished her role as family matriarch, presiding dowager-like over breakfasts, afternoon teas, and family dinners. "My stepfather once asked me not to interrupt her at the dinner table. 'Let her do all the talking,' he told me. My mother was a raconteur, she would tell us about her day. She had stories about everybody."[2]

In summer 1945, with Lee Le Blanc training with the Merchant Marines, Helene was offered permanent residence at the Motion Picture Country Home—Hollywood's almshouse for retired performers. Because children were prohibited from living at the facility, Dolores agreed to become Deirdre's legal guardian until one or the other parent was in a better position to take care of her. Lee Le Blanc consented to the plan, once again promising to pay Dolores a set amount every month for Deirdre's support. Dolores already knew what his promises were worth, but she would look to the greater good—the rescue of her four-year-old niece, which would be her own rescue as well.[3]

Deirdre remembered bits and pieces of living with her parents in the months before they went their separate ways: her mother's dog Pixie, along with occasional visits to the Le Blancs' Ilona Avenue apartment by the increasingly irascible Maurice Costello. His lawsuit against Dolores, long since dropped, had permanently estranged them. At least he and Helene were on good terms. "Grandpa did a lot of cussing, and apparently this little pitcher with big ears recorded it," Deirdre said. "One day a policeman came to the door to check the dog's licenses (something they did back then). I was right behind him when he opened the door, and I said, 'Goddamn, it's a cop!' I asked Dad what he did, and he said he just looked sheepishly at the cop and smiled, shaking his head, as if to silently say, 'out of the mouths of babes.' The cop shrugged and Dad got the licenses to show him."[4]

She remembered going with her parents to see *The Song of Bernadette,* the story of a young woman who has visions of the Virgin Mary. It was her only memory of the Le Blancs ever doing anything together as a family. "They told me years later how afterward I would run to the bathroom to grab a towel for a veil when anyone came to visit, kneel on the floor, raise my eyes to the ceiling and rapturously say, 'I see her, I see her!' My first applause."[5]

Then Helene went into the Motion Picture home, and Deirdre was returned to her surrogate family on Windsor Square. "Dolores was very mothering," she said. "You were one of her favorite dolls. If I woke up from a nightmare I knew she would always allow me to climb into bed between her and Daddy Butch. When she kissed me goodnight, she once said, 'sweet dreams,' and it kept me from having nightmares. From then on, I made sure she said it to me every night."

"I always got my 4 1/2-minute soft-cooked egg in an egg cup," Deirdre added, "with toast soldiers (remember, Dolores was an Anglophile), and at night in winter the maid was instructed to place a hot-water bottle in my bed, with a small pitcher of water and a glass on the nightstand. The maid probably did that for everyone, but I cannot attest to that."[6]

Thanks to Vruwink's thriving medical practice, the family kept its head well above water during the war years. Dolores did her part for the Allies, converting their Fallbrook ranch into a rabbit farm to supply meat to nearby Camp Pendleton.[7] She had not worked since 1943, when Warner Bros. signed her to play a small part in *This Is the Army,* a revue-style tribute to America and its wars, featuring a host of patriotic songs composed by Irving Berlin. In her final film appearance, Dolores reaped what she had sown after a decade of keeping Hollywood at arm's length. At her old studio, with Michael Curtiz directing, it should have been Old Home Week. They might have featured her in one or more of the picture's *Scandals*-era dance numbers (though most involved soldiers in drag). Instead, she was relegated to a minute-long cameo, playing yet another adoring mother of yet another adoring son. It was a sorry send-off—though not undeserved given the ambivalence she had shown for a career that other actresses would have killed for. At least her remaining fans got to see the still-lovely actress go out in a blaze of Technicolor.

Some have attributed the demise of her film career to the appearance of skin damage said to have been caused by "Max Factor's poison"—a kind of caustic studio makeup that played havoc with delicate complexions.[8] The marks on her cheeks are clearly visible in *The Magnificent Ambersons,* though they seem not to have bothered Orson Welles a bit. They are no longer noticeable in *This Is the Army,* filmed a year later, thanks to brighter lighting and better makeup. So, career destroying they weren't. Long before Max Factor was ever accused of ending Dolores's film career, she was well into finding her own way out of the profession.

Family attention began shifting away from Dolores in the early 1940s, to refocus on the increasingly worrisome behavior of the bouffant-haired, teenage heir to the Barrymore throne—the Royal Family, as they were called, most famously in the play of that name by George S. Kaufman. "Johnny was a scary kid," Dede said. "He was a child bully. He used to torture me to the point where I had to call my friend Hillary across the street to save me from him. He could be really frightening. Think of Jack Nicholson in *The Shining* and you get the idea. When he was fifteen or sixteen, he would steal my mother's car and go drag racing."[9]

When Johnny needed money, he simply reached into Dolores's handbag and took it. Attempts to discipline him were ineffectual. A furious Daddy Butch once threw him in the shower stark naked and scrubbed him down hard with a bar of soap. Years of military schooling did nothing to improve Johnny's rebellious disposition. "He needed the love of two people, his parents," Dede lamented. "Neither were available to really show him they cared about him."[10] His biological father had been kept well away from him. Unlike his older sister, Johnny flatly refused to accept Daddy Butch as an authority figure. This left Dolores, who never had much control over him to begin with. Ethel Barrymore found his ungovernable behavior exasperating. "Who does he think he is," she once exclaimed, "Christ?"[11] Johnny loved to get on people's nerves, especially his mother's. At dinner he would run his index finger through the candle flame until she was ready to throttle him.[12]

"Johnny loved to pretend he was sword fighting on the stairs and then slide down the banister," Deirdre recalled, "and that drove Dolores nuts. He drove Husa, the cook, to near insanity by entering stealthily into the kitchen, opening the refrigerator and grabbing the bottle of buttermilk. I watched in disgust as he took a big gulp. Husa would chase Johnny out of the kitchen, brandishing his chef's knife, screaming threats in Japanese. I can't even count how many times Dolores wanted to go shopping and we would walk outside to see her Lincoln was gone. Yup, Johnny took it. He loved to sit at the grand piano in the living room and dramatically pound out Beethoven's 5th Symphony. I thought it was magnificent."

Johnny became aware of his Barrymore heritage early on. When Vruwink's college-age daughter Jane came to live with them after her mother's death, she once walked past his bedroom to find him admiring his profile in the mirror. "I've always thought he never got over the loss of his father," she said.[13]

Something else that he never got over happened around this time—almost the same thing that had happened to his father, and at almost the same age. Sitting in a Hollywood hotel room with his cousin Deirdre in the 1980s, Johnny confessed to having lost his virginity to his father's daughter—his stepsister, Diana. He didn't say when it happened, but it had to have been before his fifteenth birthday. Diana wrote of meeting Dolores for the first time on her first trip to Hollywood in 1942, also her half sister and brother, who she described as "a mischievous boy of ten."

"John told me it happened in his bedroom on Windsor," Deirdre said, "while she was on one of her trips to Los Angeles, and was staying there as a guest." Diana traveled to the West Coast twice in 1946, the second time in mid-December, so it was probably then that the encounter occurred. Diana was twenty-five years old, and Johnny was fourteen. Dede recalled that Diana spent a considerable amount of time with her family that year: "She called my mother 'mommie.' My mother loved the fact that Michael Strange's daughter would call her that." Dede didn't remember anything strange or untoward about their relationship, except, perhaps, that they liked to wrestle, and that once while they were rolling around on the floor "the crepe-silk wrap she was wearing fell open, exposing her breasts."[14] Diana left for New York just before Christmas that year, right after announcing her engagement to tennis player John Howard. So, whatever happened between her and Johnny had to have occurred before that. She wouldn't return to Hollywood for another six years. By then Johnny was an adult, and Diana was well into her much-publicized decline, which became the central theme of her autobiography, *Too Much, Too Soon.*

Like Jack, like Diana. On January 25, 1960, she died in her Manhattan apartment at the age of thirty-eight, her health destroyed after years of heavy drinking.[15] Like Johnny, like Jack. Their early encounters with sexual abuse instilled in both of them a mistrust of women that destroyed each of their marriages (they had four apiece), leaving their stranded offspring to fend for themselves in the best and worst traditions of their respective families.

Into the storm of Johnny's adolescence strode a resurgent Lee Le Blanc, waving a detailed plan to terminate not only Dolores's custodial rights to Deirdre, but also Helene's. Having been returned to Zanuck's good graces (thanks mostly to Helene), he could afford to hire an attorney and declare war on the Costello sisters for reasons having more to do with his wallet, than doing what was best for his daughter.[16] He must have known what he was up against: Dolores's lingering cachet as an ex–movie queen, combined with Helene's inherent credibility as the child's mother, would surely work against him in court.

No matter that he had to drag his penniless, long-suffering wife through the mud to avoid paying child support, Lee Le Blanc began his legal assault with the serving of subpoenas on July 3, 1947. "I would say he was in a fight to the death with my mother and her sister," Deirdre said. "He told me when I was twelve or thirteen that he thought my mother would have been an irresponsible parent, and that is why she shouldn't have had custody. In actuality, I think he was more concerned that, had she won custody of me, he would have to give her much more money to house, feed and provide for me in addition to her support, which he didn't want to do. Whatever the reasons, and there were many, dad fought for my sole custody like he had to win some triathlon or die."[17]

By that time, Helene had traded one chronic illness for another. Had it been anything besides the one Lee Le Blanc planned to use against her in court, he wouldn't have had a leg to stand on. But alcoholism was another matter. During the preliminary hearing in September, he responded to the judge's order that he pay his destitute wife fifty dollars a week, by telling the court the only reason he let Dolores keep Deirdre in the first place, was because his wife "was nearing the coma stage of alcoholism." Helene later testified that although she was drinking at the time, she had given up alcohol and had been sober for a year. "I want my child more than anything in this world," she sobbed on the stand, "and I'll fight for her to the end."[18] The magistrate's response was to order her tightfisted husband to pay Dolores seventy-five dollars a month on top of the fifty-dollar payment he was supposed to be giving Helene.

By mid-December the case was making national headlines. On the seventeenth, the *Los Angeles Times* reported that Dolores had asked to be relieved of her custodial duties, citing Lee Le Blanc's refusal to send her the court-ordered support payments.[19] Amazingly, with her six-year-old niece's future hanging in the balance, Dolores couldn't bring herself to forgive a debt any more than Lee Le Blanc could bring himself to pay one. When the judge asked her if she would agree to retain her guardianship until the divorce case could be heard, she relented—but not before lambasting her brother-in-law in open court. "I can feed and clothe your daughter and see that she has medical attention," she shouted, "but I can see no reason you should shirk your responsibility. I have no respect for you. I'm fed up, fed up, fed up!"[20]

Opening arguments in the custody case began two days before Christmas 1947. Helene testified that she was no longer living at the Motion Picture Home, and now was not only jobless, but homeless. The reason she hadn't seen Deirdre more than a dozen times in the last two years, she said, was because Dolores "didn't like us to see the child too often, because it upset Deirdre."

Lee Le Blanc's attorney then called to the stand Helene's former nurse, who claimed she had seen the plaintiff intoxicated several times at the Motion Picture Home. "Last October she left for several days," the nurse testified, "and when she returned she had a man with her. I had to take her to her room, and the man followed. They were telling each other how much they loved each other. I undressed Helene and put her to bed, and then the man left."[21]

There had been cheerier Christmases at 454 South Windsor Boulevard. Stuck inside with a broken collarbone, Johnny wreaked havoc on the women of the house, which included Daddy Butch's twenty-year-old daughter Jane. "I especially remember how Johnny would steal the vinegar Jane poured into a glass to pour on her blonde hair," Deirdre said, "which she used as a final rinse when she finished washing it in the sink. Johnny would put his finger to his lips to warn me to be quiet, then pick up the glass, drink down the vinegar and put the empty glass back. That always made me cringe, and it ticked off Jane."[22]

Dolores's drinking increased markedly after the onset of the trial. Deirdre recalled, "I remember her coming home one night—she and Vruwink were fighting, and her drunk and stumbling, then falling down on the floor in the entry. I had been wakened and crept to the balcony to witness this at least once, then Johnny came and got me and put me back to bed."

The fact that Dolores had limited Helene to just twelve visits with her daughter in two years should have clued her in to the fact that Lee Le Blanc wasn't her only adversary. Helene knew as well as anyone what she was up against where her sister was concerned. History showed, and would continue to show, that those who ended up on the wrong side of Dolores, ended up with nothing. Her father had tried to get rid of Jack and lost everything. When Jack sought to reenter his children's lives after the divorce, he found his way forever blocked.

The trial resumed on December 27, with Lee Le Blanc taking the stand to give an exhaustive account of his finances. He argued feebly that although he had earned $15,819 during the last two years, he couldn't afford to pay Helene's court-ordered alimony and, therefore, hadn't sent it. "I don't have enough money to pay it and besides I have other obligations," he brazenly told the judge.[23] What he didn't say was that he had also stopped paying Dolores. A quick bit of figuring by the court would have shown the two payments together added up to only $1,500 a year. He made sure to take a swipe at Helene, claiming she was "drinking heavily while she was an expectant mother [having spent much of her pregnancy in a sanitarium, how could that have been true?] and many times since."

Testifying for Helene on the thirtieth were two of the earliest actors of film history—both elderly, one forgotten, and the other coming to the end of a long and illustrious screen career. It was an historic moment—the surviving patriarchs of the first families of the American stage and screen—the Barrymores and the Costellos—coming together to help one of their own. Following seventy-year-old Maurice Costello into the courtroom was the no-longer-ambulatory Lionel Barrymore, preparing to testify the way he did everything nowadays—from his wheelchair. He seemed relaxed and at ease under questioning from Helene's lawyer, Robert A. Neeb Jr.:

"Do you know Mrs. Le Blanc?" Neeb asked.

"Oh yes, surely," Lionel replied. "Ever since she was born practically."

Had he ever seen Helene intoxicated?

"Never did. I asked her for a drink—wanted one myself—and she said there wasn't anything in the house."[24]

When it was Maurice's turn to testify, he made sure to tell the judge that he and Helene went to church together every Sunday while she was living at the Motion Picture Home.

"While they were living in Sierra Madre, after the birth of Deirdre, did they visit you in your home?" Neeb asked him.

"Yes, I remember that very well," Maurice replied.

"Did your daughter use liquor at that time?"

"No, no liquor. But I asked them to leave. I couldn't get into the kitchen to prepare a meal," Maurice joked. "Pans and bottles all over the place—nursing bottles, that is."

Dolores took the stand to corroborate her father's testimony, capping off what seemed like a good day for the Costellos.[25] Neeb had produced three credible witnesses. Each had refuted the nurse's charges in no uncertain terms. So far, Lee Le Blanc hadn't proven anything other than that he had defied the court's support order. His case seemed on the brink of collapse.

If it wasn't for the nurse's damning testimony, it probably would have been. But on the last day of the year, Judge Byron J. Walters declared Helene Costello "not a fit and proper person" to raise a child, and so ordered that physical custody be given to the father. No doubt he considered the testimony of family members inherently biased (not unreasonable in this case, as Maurice knew perfectly well that Helene drank), and the nurse's account, by virtue of her professional status, entirely trustworthy. What he didn't know was that Lee Le Blanc and his star witness were friends, perhaps even lovers. "Not that they had an affair," Deirdre said, "I can't testify to that, but she had a couple of dachshunds she loved, and after the hearings Dad painted their portrait for her. A painting for another debt owed?"[26]

Neeb instantly appealed the decision, and a new trial date was set for January 7, 1948. This time Dolores brought her own attorney, for reasons she soon would make clear. The hearing got off to a promising start for Helene, when Judge Newcomb Condee told Neeb that he would be open to reversing the lower court's decision and allow Dolores to retain her guardianship for the time being. This would have been a godsend for Helene—she would have had three more months to find a job and a permanent place to live. Most importantly, she would have had additional time to prove that she could stay sober.[27] At that moment, she was a court decision away from changing the course of her thus far luckless life. For Deirdre, staying with Dolores while her mother got back on her feet would have been her salvation. For Lee Le Blanc, having to pay thousands of dollars in alimony and child support would, if nothing else, have been character building. And, as for Dolores, if nobility meant *behaving* nobly, the moment of her rebirth was at hand.

Lee Le Blanc's lawyer strenuously objected to any decision that would have allowed Dolores to retain custody of her niece, even temporarily. Then, just as Condee was about to overrule him, the unthinkable happened: Dolores's attorney rose to tell the court that due to the previous judge's decision to award custody to the father, his client wished to be relieved of her guardianship immediately. "Both steps were taken over the tearful protests of Deirdre's mother, whose attorney wanted Mrs. Vruwink to keep Deirdre for the time being," reported the *Los Angeles Times.*[28]

As Deirdre's temporary guardian, Condee explained, Dolores had the right to resign, and because the custody issue could not remain "in a vacuum" until April, he had no other choice but to uphold the lower court's ruling and place the child in the care of her father. The courtroom erupted—Helene, Deirdre, and, inexplicably, Dolores sobbed in unison as the verdict was read. Dolores's attorney tried to shield his client's grief-stricken face with his briefcase as the news photographers rushed forward, but one of them slipped around him and captured Dolores's contorted expression for all the world to see. Partially hidden, but plainly visible in her aunt's lap, is the back of Deirdre's small, blonde head. "I hated the reporters and their flashing Graflexes," Deirdre recalled seventy years later. "I did break away from Dad as we were leaving and ran to Mum Mum to crawl into her lap and hide my face. Dolores told the reporters to back away. 'You're frightening the child!' she said. Dad couldn't have forcibly tried to hold on to me because the reporters would have captured him on film and in print."

As Dolores stood up to leave, the *Times* reported, "Diedre [*sic*] wept unabashedly on the shoulder of her aunt. Mrs. Vruwink wept too. After a while Le Blanc walked over to the two, picked up Diedre in his arms and left the courtroom. Photographers made a picture and Diedre tried a smile, but her cheeks were still wet."

Money had trumped love—or was it the other way around? What was Dolores *really* crying about when the verdict was announced? She had gotten what she had asked for after all—the relief of her guardianship. Was it because she had knowingly turned over her beloved niece to a man she despised, whose custody she knew was the worst possible choice the court could have made? Or was she grieving for the little girl she had grown hopelessly attached to, but would eventually have lost no matter which parent won the case?

Helene rushed weeping from the scene of her greatest humiliation—greater even than being branded a collector of pornography—before the cameras could steal what was left, if anything was left, of her dignity. Her spirit broken, a lifetime of doctor-prescribed anesthesia seemed to be all she had left to look forward to. To ease the pain of her surgeries, Helene had been getting regular injections of barbiturates, and probably morphine as well.[29] Maybe if Deirdre had been there for her to care for, and to care for her, she could have dealt differently with the pain.

On April 10, the court ordered Lee Le Blanc to pay Helene a one-time settlement of $1,800 (around $20,000 in modern currency). In return, Helene agreed to end the custody fight.[30] No doubt it was just as well: the San Fernando Valley motel room where Helene was living could hardly have been considered a proper place to raise a child.

To boost her sagging spirits, Helene wrote a pair of outlines for a family memoir she planned to call *The Fighting Costellos,* and went in search of a publisher. She pitched the shorter of the two to the *American Weekly,* a nationally syndicated Hearst newspaper supplement, which, to her delight, agreed to publish it in serial form beginning in October 1948. Normally, a national preview would have piqued the interest of any number of publishers, but for reasons unknown Helene's literary aspirations never went any further. Her efforts weren't for naught, however—the money she earned from the Hearst papers helped get her through the winter, both financially and emotionally. But the real beneficiary of Helene's one and only writing endeavor was, and is, posterity: at forty-four breezily written pages, the longer of the two manuscripts survives as the single most important source of personal information that exists about the family. Without it, no contemporary biography of the Costellos could have been written. Scarcely to her benefit, Helene had again made history. Some thirty years after being voted America's most popular child star, and twenty years after heading the cast of the first all-talking picture, she had preserved for all time her family's remarkable legacy.

After the custody fight and the loss of Deirdre to the hated Lee Le Blanc, Dolores was left with all the guts but none of the glory of child-rearing. Loving and being loved by a sandy-haired child was a far cry from raising two volatile teenagers, each on the verge of a difficult adulthood. While vacationing with his family near Watertown, New York, Johnny quietly vanished, but not before snatching $300 out of Dolores's purse. "My mother dragged my stepfather across country to Thousand Lakes," Dede recalled, "which she had always wanted to see, though he couldn't have been less interested. One day my brother decided he missed his friends, so he reached into my mother's purse, which he was always doing, and stole the cash she brought along for the trip."[31] Not long after Vruwink contacted the police, an officer found Johnny milling around La Guardia airport, waiting to board the next flight to Los Angeles. He recognized the son of John Barrymore, he told a reporter, by his profile.

Johnny was detained pending his stepfather's arrival. Dolores, who must have been livid, stayed behind. Johnny and Butch spoke briefly at the airport before speaking to the press. Afterward, an AP photographer snapped what looked more like a mug shot than a newspaper photograph: Johnny stares straight into the camera, his greased-back hair combed up high on his head, sporting a look of utter defiance. Vruwink had decided to let him return to Los Angeles, rather than risk an unpleasant scene in the airport, or worse, having him face his mother in Watertown. "Asked as he watched the plane take off if his stepson had acting ambitions," reported the Associated Press, "Dr. Vruwink replied: 'He has everything his father had—plus.'"[32] What he meant by that would soon be crystal clear.

Dolores was doing her best to keep her teenage son out of the movie business, but forces beyond her control were conspiring to make John Barrymore's son and namesake a star in his own right. In one of his first newspaper interviews, Johnny was asked why he wanted to become an actor. "I guess it's because you always want the things that are denied you," he answered. "My mother always wanted me to be a doctor or a lawyer or something like that. When I decided I wanted to be an actor, she told me 'it's a filthy business.'"[33]

Somehow it hadn't occurred to Dolores that Johnny wasn't cut out for the social register. Besides his smoldering good looks and the Barrymore name, he shined as an actor from his very first scene in his very first picture. From the moment he canters into the opening shot of the cowboy potboiler *The Sundowners,* he isn't just playing the scene so much as living it. What he lacked in formal training (his only acting lessons, he said, had taken place "alone before a mirror") he more than made up for in raw talent. Perhaps no other actor of his generation had, at the start of his career, so much of what it took to carve out a lasting place for himself in the annals of film. Skill, pedigree, ambition—"Everything his father had," as Vruwink put it, "plus." Within his reach were all the bounties of his birthright. All he had to do was reach out and pluck them.

24

Here Lies the Mick

Maybe he was tired of working for peanuts as a movie extra, or maybe he was just tired. Around the time of his seventieth birthday, Maurice gave up trying to live on his weekly pittance from Central Casting and applied for residency at the Motion Picture Country Home in Woodland Hills, California.[1] His qualifications for admittance were impeccable: he was the king of the ex-kings of the original movie stars. Helene had preceded him there by several months; his former Vitagraph leading lady, Florence Turner, by several years. How they ended up in such a place—sunny, quiet, and comfortable though it was—they would have nothing but time to consider. To appear solvent for the trial, Helene moved out of the facility a few weeks after Maurice moved in—but he would have no shortage of company. Filtering in, month after month, were the forgotten, the washed-up, the cruelly cast-aside of filmdom's formative years. Clara Kimball Young, Maurice's diminutive leading lady and costar, spent her last years there, as did such early screen notables as Viola Dana, Mack Sennett, Billie Dove, and H. B. Warner.

Maurice's family paid him occasional visits—sans Dolores, of course; when she was done with someone, she was truly done. "I think I saw him more than once, when I was eight and when I was nine," Deirdre said. "Seems I also remember, while still in the Valley, we visited 'Uncle Hugh,' Hugh Herbert, who was Mother's friend. He would always give me a handful of nickels so I could play the one-armed bandit in his recreation room while he and Mother visited." Maurice's Irish alter ego, the master of many a tent show monologue, also put in an appearance: "I remember sitting on Grandpa's lap and him telling some Irish tale in an Irish brogue. Of course he did it so well, bringing up the way his mother used to talk, I imagine."[2]

For Deirdre, the shuffling began. With Helene powerless to stop him, Lee Le Blanc palmed her off on a succession of caretakers: first a woman named Annabelle, and then he imported his parents from Michigan to look after her. After that came summer camp. In September 1948 he enrolled her as a full-time student at the Villa Cabrini Academy, a Catholic school in Burbank. “I was shown to the merry-go-round where some other girls were, and when I looked up to see Dad, who had been talking to the principal, he was gone. Not even a goodbye.”

> I created a bomb scare the first night I was there. By this time I was sure Dad was just trying to get rid of me. I turned eight while at Cabrini. I do not recall Mother ever visiting me while I was there. After school let out, Dad took me to stay with an older couple someplace. I don’t remember who they were or where it was. I was sure they were going to murder me, which I imagined was arranged by my father. For a few days I refused to eat anything, and for some cockamamie reason, I thought they wouldn’t kill me in my sleep if their little dog was allowed to sleep with me. They turned out to be a very nice couple, and I was sorry to have to leave them when Dad came and fetched me away again. It was then that I was allowed to move in with mother at the Wolff Sanitarium.[3]

Helene was back in a sanitarium again, only this time not for tuberculosis, but for the administration of various medications. The more drugs she was prescribed, the more dependent on drugs she became. It also provided a much-needed roof over her head and, to her great joy, over her daughter’s. The thrill of victory had rapidly dissipated for Lee Le Blanc. In mid-1949, he agreed to let Deirdre move with her mother into the small health-care facility run by German émigrés Marie and Otto Wolff. Among the couple’s live-in guests was retired vaudeville and silent film star Trixie Friganza, who rented a cottage behind the couple’s white-frame, two-story house.

Mom-and-pop caregivers like the Wolffs thrived by the thousands in the pre-Medicare days of the rest home. “There were patients there who needed care, and some were retired on a pittance and needed assistance,” said Deirdre. “Marie Wolff had been a nurse in Germany and met and cared for her husband, Otto, who had been shot in the leg during WWII.”

> Otto's leg was a continuous problem. Shrapnel was often coming to the surface, and he was in a lot of pain. He had to lie on the couch in their living room during the day where Marie could attend to him. I called them Oma and Opa. They had an old German Shepherd called Liebchen. I wish I knew where Marie got the energy she had. I'd like an nth of it. She not only kept track of and meted out medicine for everyone, she cooked three meals a day and delivered the trays to all. Then she got hired by the local bakery where she had been using their ovens to bake her cakes for the odd wedding, a birthday or other celebration orders she got. She refused to give them her buttercream frosting recipe, but she continued to take orders for the cakes from the bakery—*in her spare time.* Her cakes were the best I've ever had, and she used to bake me a birthday cake until I was 13 or 14.[4]

Her father's actions were, as always, self-serving. He married again, to a Russian tourist he met in an art gallery. Only when Rosalya Platanova (later discovered to be a pseudonym) refused to consummate the marriage did he realize that she had only married him to stay in the United States. Unable to get an annulment, he sued her for divorce. "He had attorney's fees because the Russian was always getting him hauled into court; he had no place to house me or anyone to give me supervision while he was at work six days a week."[5]

Thus, mother and daughter were happily reunited under the Wolff's nurturing roof:

> I very much liked it there. There was a girl next door I was friends with for a while, but I didn't want anything to do with her after she stole an amethyst geode that one of Mom's friends had given me. Sometimes Mom had some spare money so we could go into town to the Jewish deli where we'd get turkey wings or drumsticks, potato salad, kosher pickles and coleslaw, then go back to the apartment and turn on a radio program while we ate our feast, sitting cross-legged on our beds. Mom listened to *Sam Balter's Sports Desk* every day, read the green racing forms on her bed, along with the newspaper, the *Reader's Digest, Look* magazine, and books. Maybe she had won a race when we could afford to go to the deli.[6]

Their idyll would continue for another two years, until Lee Le Blanc enrolled Deirdre in yet another Catholic school—Flintridge Sacred Heart Academy, where she spent the next seven winters of her life.

On October 14, 1950, Maurice suffered a massive heart attack. He was rushed to Cedars of Lebanon Hospital and put in an oxygen tent, which was standard procedure in those days for cardiac patients. There was nothing else they could do. For the next two weeks he clung to life in a semiconscious state. Unlike John Barrymore, no coterie of cronies gathered at his bedside, no heartbroken relatives posted all-night vigils—as Lionel had done for Jack—to field telephone calls from ex-wives and newspaper reporters. Maurice died in his hospital room on the morning of October 29.[7] As no one claimed to have been with him at the end, he might have died alone.

The wire services praised his accomplishments, to the extent that they could remember them. Because Maurice peaked so early in the scheme of things, they relied on their own ancient reportage for information—much of it either woefully inaccurate or downright false. The *Los Angeles Times* claimed that Maurice went "from stock companies to Broadway, and on to Broadway stardom—that was the Costello story."[8] It was somebody else's story, maybe, but not Maurice's. He went from stock companies straight into making movies, bypassing Broadway entirely. The Associated Press said he had "joined the movies in 1905 [as this was his busiest year on the stage, that would have been impossible], leaving a successful stage career [if second or third billing in Maude Fealy's road company could be considered successful] to take a job with the old Vitagraph Co." Unlike most sources, at least they didn't say that he started with Edison.

Some of it they managed to get right. He was correctly identified as "the first of the great screen lovers; the first to receive fan mail, and the first to show temperament."[9] With so little information to go on, they could only scratch the surface. With the cult and culture of movies still in its infancy when Maurice burst onto the film scene, it went largely unchronicled. In 1907, the year he scoffed at set-building to make himself the first bona-fide screen actor, the outside world was paying little attention.

Maurice would have been furious at Dolores for burying him in the plot next to Mae's. No doubt the thought of her parents lying side by side for eternity comforted her. Perhaps the thought that it would have galled him no end comforted her also. On October 31, a requiem mass was held for Maurice at the Immaculate Heart of Mary Church in East Hollywood. Family members in attendance were Helene, Dolores, and John Barrymore Jr., looking somber but chic in his crisp, dark suit. Nine-year-old Deirdre wasn't told of her grandfather's death until after the funeral. "I didn't even know Grandpa Costello had died until I saw his photo and read about it in the newspaper the next day. Somebody came and picked up Mom to take her to the funeral. I thought she was going out to lunch with them."[10] Dede was in no condition to attend. Ten days earlier, as Maurice lay dying, she gave birth to her first child, named Hillary in honor of the childhood friend who often rescued her from Johnny's tyrannical pranks.[11]

After the service, about fifty mourners joined family members at Calvary Cemetery for the interment. Buried nearby were a number of stars of the early silent era, including Mabel Normand, Owen Moore, and one of the original successors to Maurice's throne, King Baggot. Once known as "the King of the Movie Stars," like Maurice he had fallen from favor, taken to the bottle, and ended up as an uncredited extra.

Sadly, the actor who had won the Popular Player Contest by a hundred thousand votes couldn't drum up the requisite number of pallbearers to carry him to his final resting place. A trio of mourners volunteered—Ed O'Neill and Jack Casey from Maurice's early days at Vitagraph, and his friend Bert Dorris, who gave him moral support during his first torturous year in Hollywood. Following the service, Pierce Brothers had to supply the additional manpower to take him the rest of the way.[12]

Dolores had just lost her father to heart disease, her daughter to matrimony, and her son to the movie business. Helene had shunned her for resigning as Deirdre's custodian at the worst possible moment and tipping the judicial scales in favor of Lee Le Blanc. The sisters arrived at Maurice's funeral in separate cars, neither one speaking to the other.

Then came the end of her marriage. Daddy Butch had done everything he could to handle Dolores's drinking—from avoiding confrontation, to paying for treatment in an out-of-state facility. "She was like Dr. Jekyll and Mr. Hyde when she drank," Dede said. "She had an allergy to alcohol. She simply couldn't tolerate it. It turned her into a completely different person. Some people are happy drunks. She wasn't."[13]

The catalyst, as Dolores later testified, was a roast chicken. She was scolding her stepdaughter Jane for keeping dinner in the oven too long, she said, when Vruwink erupted. "I said, 'Look here, why didn't you watch this?' and with that he went after my son. . . . He went on and on, and the man became so incensed that a terrible row ensued." Upon entering the kitchen, her husband flung open the swinging door with such force that when it swung back it hit her hard in the head. "It hurt me terribly," she testified, placing her gloved hands on her temples. "Then he went after me. It was the end of everything. He pushed me with his elbows and I went out completely. I was picked up off the floor and was very ill afterward. I had been very ill before that, too."[14]

The implication was that he had been physically abusive before that night. Slander was an integral part of the process before the advent of no-fault divorces, and truth took a backseat to expediency. Therefore, Dolores had to come up with something sufficiently damning to get a favorable judgment. Dede was living in Beverly Hills at the time and was often in touch with her mother, but knew nothing of the incident. Neither did Jane, who Dolores claimed was there when it happened. Seventy years later, Jane was emphatic in her insistence that her father would never have done such a thing—to Dolores, or to anyone.[15]

Regardless of what did or did not happen, the marriage was not ended by a single occurrence but by any number of alcohol-fueled incidents that had made life with Dolores impossible. Finally, Vruwink walked into Jane's room and told her to pack her bags. She did, and off they went to an apartment her father had rented nearby. She would never see the Windsor Square house or her stepmother again.[16]

Their divorce case went to trial in mid-July 1951. Before that the parties bickered, reconciled briefly, and then returned to their respective corners to hammer out a final settlement. At her worst, Dolores threatened to expose Vruwink for performing abortions. At her best, she consented to a fairer distribution of assets than in her previous divorce. When she was through with John Barrymore, the Tower Road house was cleaned out down to the sconces. She made off with most of Jack's treasures: rare books, prints, paintings, and objets d'art of every description. Years later, Dolores said she only took them because she knew that he would have nothing to leave his children. As it turned out, she was right.[17]

This time she agreed to a more equitable split. Dolores got the ranch and the Windsor Boulevard property. As she could no longer afford the house, she would have to sell it at once and move to Fallbrook. Vruwink got the commercial property they owned jointly—a five-story medical building adjacent to Good Samaritan Hospital. By the time the case went to court, the press had none of the usual ingredients from which to cook up the usual Costello divorce scandal. That is, not until Dolores took the stand. By simply repeating the accusations stated in the original complaint, she could have reduced the matter to a blurb in the *Los Angeles Times.* Instead, she went into lurid detail about how her husband had caused "the end of everything," hitting her with the swinging door and knocking her to the floor.[18] One only had to follow the newspaper trail leading to matters financial, to see what she was really up to. Besides what they had already agreed on out of court, Dolores was asking for additional support in the amount of $1,390 a month.

What she got in the end wasn't alimony, but a clean slate—devoid of husband, parents, siblings, children, career. All either had passed on or moved away, and now she was alone for the first time in her life. If losing Daddy Butch wasn't devastating enough, there was the loss of Deirdre, her alienation of Helene, the death of her father, and her children's absences—all of which occurred over a three-year period. When it was over, Dolores fell into a deep depression that reached its nadir about the time she very publicly hit bottom.

She decided to act again, for the first time in a stage play. In *The Great Man,* Dolores costarred opposite Albert Dekker, best remembered for his portrayal of the mad scientist in *Dr. Cyclops.* She said that they had asked her "out of the blue" and that she had agreed because she liked the script. The real reason was that she needed the money. When a reporter asked her in February 1951 why she had decided to come out of retirement, she said she hadn't retired at all: "I don't remember when I wasn't in show business and I'll never be out of it. . . . Any announcement of retiring is so stupid. What you want to do today you might not want to do tomorrow."

Dolores knew that if she was going to make a comeback after a decade out of the public eye, she could no longer give her usual short shrift to reporters. For the first time publicly since their separation, she spoke of Jack without sadness or rancor: "I was his third wife. . . . I held the record—seven years!—at least under the same roof [actually it was six years]. What a character he was! He could have been in the gutter, but if you helped him he would get up on his feet and bow. He had a beautiful face, yes, but a beautiful face is one thing and not the most important, I think it was his mentality that fascinated me most of all. . . . He could write divinely, was an excellent poet. I treasure the memory of his few moments of contentment. . . . The truth about John Barrymore would be a greater story than the one the world knows."[19]

The Great Man was written by Harold M. Sherman, whose forte was writing books on mental telepathy; the reviewer for the *Los Angeles Times* described the play as a "faltering stage event." It featured a life-after-death sequence that confounded reviewers and audiences alike: "Only little Eva ascending into heaven was missing, but that couldn't be fitted in. . . . For the rest, *The Great Man* is pretty dreary for entertainment."[20] Dolores played Dekker's estranged wife—hardly a stretch, given that she had filed for divorce from Daddy Butch a week earlier. The reviewer praised Dekker as "a highly competent actor" and gave a nod to Dolores's "sympathy and wifely qualities" and "warmth as a personality" (surely her truest gift as an actress). But she lacked theater training, and he found her to be "uncertain in her stage work."

Perhaps if she had found a better part in a better play, or better yet in a really good play, her revived career aspirations might have stood a chance. But at a time when movie actresses far more famous than she were dropping like flies in the onrushing age of television, it is unlikely that her phone would have started ringing under any circumstances. The play's failure, coupled with her recent divorce, literally leveled her. At the end of March, she checked herself into Good Samaritan with a bad case of shingles, for which stress is a known trigger. A week later she came home to an empty house, which for Dolores meant an empty life. Without husband, career, and family, all she had to look forward to was the relative solace of her drinking.

25

A Minor Kidnapping

Sixty-five years after the fact, Dede's memory of the events of June 18, 1953, was clear in some places, spotty in others. According to the newspapers, she was the one who called the police—but she insisted that it had been the neighbors who called. What is indisputable is why they were called and what they encountered at Dede's Beverly Hills apartment when they got there. Officers found Dolores "in an advanced state of intoxication, argumentative and belligerent." According to her daughter, she had drunk an entire bottle of wine and gone haywire, lashing out in ways that were both frightening and dangerous.[1]

Dolores was arrested, booked, and released on twenty-five dollars bail. Whether or not they dared put Hollywood's "Madonna of the Screen" in a jail cell, Dede couldn't, or wouldn't, recall. For the second time in a month, Dolores's alcohol-related transgressions had caught the attention of the national press. In early May, she plowed her car into the back of another vehicle, seriously injuring the owner. Then came the altercation with Dede, and when she didn't show up for her arraignment the next day, the *Los Angeles Times* ran a story tagged with the inglorious headline: "Miss Costello Forfeits Bail in Drunk Case."[2]

Even for the Costellos, who never misbehaved in a small way, this was extreme behavior. Dolores had intimidated everyone in her family at one time or another, but now her daughter was afraid to come near her. Whether her next act of desperation was premeditated or a spur-of-the-moment decision, Dolores did what she had always done when there was no other alternative—she went for broke. She had done it twice with Jack: first tricking him into entering Good Samaritan's psychiatric ward, and then marooning him aboard the *Infanta* in one of her ill-fated attempts to dry him out. Now came the pièce de résistance of last-ditch efforts, culminating in a display of audacity that made the others seem tame: Dolores decided to end her childlessness, even if it meant taking a toddler away from his mother.

While Dolores was publicly reaching the end of her rope, Dede was privately divorcing Thomas Fairbanks, née Fuchs, the dysfunctional son of the renowned Los Angeles voice teacher, Viktor Fuchs. He had treated her cruelly, and after two years of emotional abuse, she left him. Her second child, Antony, was a year old when they separated. Dede had never worked, so when Tom's support payments abruptly ceased after their divorce, Dolores, as always, came to her financial rescue. She was already paying half her daughter's expenses, now she would have to carry the entire load.[3]

Dolores's money, Dolores's childlessness—both her Achilles' heels were straining in unison. When Antony was eighteen months old, mother and son were invited to Fallbrook for a visit, and then when it came time to leave, Dolores picked Tony up in her arms and refused to let him go. He would be better off at the ranch, she told her incredulous daughter. "What do you have to offer Tony?" she snorted over his mother's horrified protests. Not knowing what else to do, Dede left without him.[4]

Daddy Butch tried to explain to Dede what she was up against. Dolores was suicidally depressed, he told her. She had tried to kill herself by swallowing pills. If Tony were taken away from her, she would certainly try it again. Having a child to love and care for would be her salvation. "I had no choice but to let him go," Dede said. "She needed Tony so desperately."[5]

Seven decades later, when asked which domicile he would have chosen to grow up in, Tony answered without hesitation: "I would have stayed with my grandmother." He was glad to have grown up in Fallbrook, surrounded by dogs, farm animals, and the rural countryside: "With all her foibles, she was the real deal and I miss her. I remember putting my head against her back, hearing that rich, resonant voice and feeling comfortable. She was my Mum-Mum and I loved her."[6]

Johnny's increasingly aberrant behavior showed itself publicly for the first time when he was arrested and charged with ignoring a battery of traffic citations. These included driving without a license, changing lanes in traffic unsafely, and not carrying a registration in his car. Five days after Dolores's traffic accident, Johnny pled guilty to his charges and was given a choice of paying twenty-five dollars or spending five days in jail. He paid the fine and was released.[7]

Dolores was not only paying her daughter's bills, she was supporting Johnny and his new wife—the blue-eyed, red-haired television actress Cara Williams. Just as his popularity was beginning to soar, Johnny quit RKO over a disagreement involving Cara's frequent visits to the set. "He was extremely insecure," she explained. "At home we would rehearse his lines and he would go into another room, because he didn't want me to see him act. He asked me to coach him on the set, so I would stand out of camera range and signal him if I thought he was emoting too much. The director didn't like that, so the studio forbade me from coming to the set. That's why he quit."[8]

Almost seventy years later, Cara revisited the story of their fractured courtship with equal parts sadness and mirth: "Dede Barrymore insisted I meet her brother, but at first I said no. Finally I agreed, I don't know why I did these things—I wanted him to think I was French, so the first time we met I began speaking to him in a French accent. It went on for weeks when we were together, then one day out of nowhere I reverted to perfect English. He ran into the next room and didn't come out for hours."[9]

Cara was seven years older than Johnny and had been married once before. She had her career to think about. "When I told him I didn't want to see him anymore he became very quiet and walked out of the room. When he came back, as I hugged him goodbye, I saw blood on his arm. I looked down and saw he had slashed his wrist." This was no superficial wound—Johnny had sawed through a tendon. "I told him he needed to call his mother and that we had to go to the hospital. I'll never forget the conversation. He told Dolores what happened and she said, 'I don't have time right now, why don't you come to Fallbrook?' I couldn't believe how cold she was to him."

"So that's why I married him," she said. "He had no one. No one loved him."[10]

Like father, like son—and also like his grandfather Maurice, Johnny's mistrust of women was marrow deep. Cara told Hollywood columnist Erskine Johnson in the 1950s that "in his frantic desire to be assured of my love," Johnny "misunderstood things. His father, I have learned, was exactly the same way. He feels we should be together all the time. I have to turn down things that would take me out of town." Sixty-five years later she could be more forthcoming: "He was insanely jealous. I used to play poker and he wouldn't let me go unless I agreed to sleep with him that night."[11]

Dolores's financial burdens eased a bit when the Barrymores left for New York in early 1954. With no reason to stay in Hollywood, Johnny decided to try his hand at stage acting on the East Coast, his father's old stomping ground. His first encounter with live theater had ended disastrously when, in a paroxysm of stage fright, he walked out on a company of summer-stock players a week before opening night.[12] This elicited a stern rebuke from Actors' Equity, also from his Aunt Ethel. Before heading east with Johnny, Cara introduced her new sister-in-law Dede to Lew Bedell, a stand-up comic, and it was love at first sight. When Lew had to leave town to host a television show in New York, he took Dede and her four-year-old daughter, Hillary, with him. They moved into Cara's empty apartment (the Barrymores had returned home prematurely when Johnny again got into trouble with Actors' Equity) to begin an exciting three-month stay in Manhattan.[13]

Dolores had only two dependents left: her sister Helene, whose medical bills she was still paying, and her live-in grandson. Vruwink was right—Tony *had* given her a reason to go on living. Dolores was still drinking, but not as much, and not as destructively. To ease her conscience, perhaps, she compared her own solid circumstances to those of her wayward daughter, headed off on an eastern fling with a man she wasn't married to, seemingly without a care in the world.[14]

26

An Old Spanish Custom

"I was allowed to visit my mother only once a year, at Christmas and New Years," Deirdre recalled. "The last New Year's I spent with Mother she was staying at the Hollywood Garden Court Apartments. Her room looked down on Hollywood Boulevard. We had gone out earlier to get a cab to take us to two different restaurants where we ordered food to go: spaghetti with meat sauce from Villa Capri, then Musso & Franks for lamb chops."

As they stopped to hail a cab, two men walked toward them. One was a childhood chum of Helene's, who greeted her by name. "Tell me, Helene," he asked as they chatted, "why do you always wear black?"

"I'm in mourning for my life," she replied.

"Well, I thought that was just the greatest line I had ever heard, thinking it was original," said Deirdre. "It wasn't until several months later that I read Chekov's *The Seagull,* and realized it was a line from the play that she had remembered. The night was to be a grand example of her eidetic memory."[1]

While Helene heated up their takeaway dinners in the hotel room's tiny kitchenette, Deirdre watched late-night revelers strolling along Hollywood Boulevard, gazing out of "a large window that cranked open and had a very deep ledge on the outside. On the side street people were walking up and down, and in a group of four young men, one of them looked up at me and invited me to join them. He was on the other side of the wooden fence that separated the pool area from the side street. I told him I couldn't because we were going to be eating dinner soon. During all of this, he had climbed the fence and made it to the window ledge."

"You're just now eating dinner?" he asked. "It's almost midnight."

"Yes. It's an old Spanish custom," shouted Helene from the kitchenette door. "Now, Romeo, get down before you fall and break your neck." The young man, it turned out, was an acting and theater student at Michigan

State. Their football team, the Spartans, was playing the UCLA Bruins at the Rose Bowl that year, and he and his friends had come to see the game. "He immediately began to recite the beginning of the balcony scene from *Romeo and Juliet,* and Mother blithely took over Juliet's part. As I recall, he began with 'But soft! What light on yonder window breaks? It is the east and Juliet is the sun . . .' Mother kept coming back with Juliet's responses so he kept right on going. I'm not sure when it ended, but it seemed to me they did the whole scene." At the end, the young man asked who she was, and Helene answered, "Never mind. Now, get down and let us eat our dinner. And good luck on your acting career." When the young man continued to ask for permission to take Deirdre out for a Coke, "Mother was adamant and he finally climbed down and rejoined his friends. Oh, by the way, the line about dining so late being an old Spanish custom is from an old movie, with Dick Powell, I think."[2]

If Helene was going to survive her addictions, she would have to do it the way she had beaten TB—in a specialized facility with round-the-clock care. She was now the hardest of cases. Unlike illegal drug users, her morphine supply was legally prescribed by a doctor. By the end of 1956, as Dede witnessed, she was injecting herself numerous times daily, probably with morphine, and desperately needed help.[3] With no income of her own, Helene had only her sister to depend on.

"You're wondering who paid for all of this? I think it must have been Dolores," said Deirdre.

> After all, she had made a promise to their mother that she would always look after Helene, which she reminded me of many times. I know that Dad gave Mom money to buy me presents for birthdays and Christmases, because he liked to throw in that she couldn't have afforded to get me something without his help. However, both Dolores and Dad refused to pay for a private sanitarium when Mom wanted to kick the drugs, and that's why she ended up in a state hospital. She told me this that last New Year's Day before Dad picked me up, and she told me she might die there because of it. My first true bout with denial.[4]

In the nineteenth century, mental institutions like Patton State Hospital were known as lunatic asylums. In the 1880s, progressive thinkers like

Philadelphia psychiatrist Thomas Kirkbride resolved to change both the perception and treatment of mental illness; for starters, they wanted them to be called hospitals instead of asylums, and their occupants referred to as patients. The so-called Kirkbride Plan, the system on which Patton and many other state facilities were patterned, was predicated on the belief that well-ventilated, light-filled spaces were beneficial to mental health and were an integral part of the patient's recovery.[5]

Plan or no plan, the term "hospital" was a misnomer. In point of fact, Patton wasn't a hospital at all, but a state-sanctioned repository where psychotic criminals, indigent drug addicts, alcoholics, epileptics, and those with mental and genetic disorders, such as autism, Down syndrome, schizophrenia, and dementia, could be locked away and forgotten. Helene wasn't exaggerating when she told her daughter that if she went in, she very well might not come out.

A few days after Deirdre returned to Flintridge, a very pregnant Dede got a frantic telephone call from Helene. Her doctor had died suddenly and left her without a prescription. She needed a place to stay until she could straighten things out, she said, otherwise she would have to commit herself. But Dede had nothing to offer her. There had been a fire in the lower half of their Hollywood duplex, she told Helene, where several members of Lew's family were living. They had moved upstairs into his grandmother's apartment, where Dede, Lew, and Hillary were also living, so there wasn't room for another person. Dede was also seven months pregnant, so caring for her aunt in both their conditions would have been impossible.[6]

With no place else to go and no one to turn to, Helene threw herself at the mercy of the state mental health-care system. "She committed herself to kick a drug habit and that hospital only practiced cold turkey treatment," Deirdre said. "That meant off *all* drugs, whatever she had been on, without any thought or consideration that some were not part of the addiction but what relieved an actual physical ailment. Dolores and I had a conversation about this sometime in the 70s, and this is what she thought had happened, and what we both could determine had caused her death."[7]

With her condition already critical, Helene was driven by bus to San Bernardino and admitted to Patton. She died two days later, on January 26, 1957. The cause of death was given as pneumonia—but that was the effect, not the cause. Deprived of her medications, the trauma quickly weakened her. More than anything, Deirdre said, "It was the inept doctor at Patton who withheld the adrenaline that murdered my mother. It helped clear her one remaining lung. That's what I was told when Marie Wolff showed me how to administer it intramuscularly by injection into Mother's thigh when she couldn't breathe. I gave it only when Mom fought for breath, and it cleared her bronchial tubes, or whatever, almost instantly."[8]

Withdrawal from narcotics can be fatal, evidence shows, especially among incarcerated users, due to inadequate medical care. A convergence of circumstances, and substances, had taken her life, but mostly it was the fault of a medical community still in the Stone Age in their treatment of substance abuse.

At least she did not die alone. Dolores arrived on the twenty-sixth to find her sister lying in a hospital bed, an oxygen mask covering her nose and mouth. Helene looked up and mutely tapped the side of her head. Dolores had just ordered glasses for driving, and Helene hadn't seen them. Or maybe she was admonishing her for not taking them off—a cardinal sin for a movie star in public, even a former one.[9]

Deirdre was at school the day her mother died. It had not snowed in Los Angeles in over a decade, but two inches fell at the foot of the San Gabriel Mountains that Sunday. "I was wearing my white uniform, kneeling in the Flintridge chapel while attending mass. On one of the walls of the chapel there were windows looking outside. As a surprise to all of us it began to snow. A rare sight indeed in Pasadena, California, and I immediately thought of Mother and how she would like to see the snow, coming as she did from New York. I wished that I could call her, but I had no phone number with which to reach her."[10]

After mass, the students filed into the dining room to have breakfast. While they were eating, one of the older girls told Deirdre that the headmistress wanted to see her. She found Sister Benigna standing in the hallway handing out permission slips to the girls who wanted to go into town. "When she was finished, she looked at me and said to come with her. She led me back into the dining room and we sat in two side chairs against the wall, and I knew."

"There's no good way to tell you this," the Sister began.

"My mother is dead," interrupted Deirdre.

How did she know? wondered the headmistress.

"The snow. I just knew."

> She then told me they had been trying to reach my father. He had been in Pala, in San Diego County, but was on his way back and he would be picking me up around noon. I asked her how she knew my mother had died, and she said that my aunt had been calling since midnight, drunk, and wanting to pick me up herself, but Sister Benigna said she couldn't allow that. It all went downhill from there.

Helene's funeral was held on the thirtieth in the chapel at Calvary Cemetery. Only twelve mourners attended, among them former screen heartthrob Gilbert Roland, who acted as Dolores's escort. A tug of war ensued over Deirdre, who ended up going with her father and was, therefore, consigned to the rear of the chapel. During the service, the *Times* reported, Dolores shook as she wept.[11] No matter how dismal Deirdre's circumstances had been at times, until now she had always had something to look forward to. "My dream had been that when I turned 18, I would go live with Mother and take care of her. I was a naive child with no knowledge of what was really going on; protected and ignorant. Yes, my mother was in mourning for her life. She knew what she had already set in motion when she said that. Hers was a tragedy danced to an Irish jig. She loved acting and was as spontaneous as ever. Think of the last performance of hers at the window with that young Romeo. That's how she would like us to remember her."[12]

The year 1957 tore gaping holes in the ranks of Hollywood's Old Guard: Humphrey Bogart died of lung cancer in January, two weeks before Helene. That year saw the passing of Oliver Hardy, Louis B. Mayer, Erich von Stroheim, and Josephine Hull and also of silent stars Gene Lockhart, George Cleveland, Harrison Ford (no relation to the current actor), and Norma Talmadge, with varying levels of attention given to them in the press. Newspapers across the country carried Helene's obituary, as erroneously compiled by the Associated Press. She died of pneumonia at the age of fifty-three, the AP reported, and "once earned $3,000 a week starring in films with the late John Barrymore."[13] Working for the miserly Warner Bros., Helene never got anything close to $3,000—nor had she ever starred in a picture with her ex-brother-in-law. Worst of all, she wasn't fifty-three when she died, she was fifty. This most inglorious of parting shots would have both appalled and amused her.

If only they had recognized Helene for what she *had* accomplished. She was the first woman to star in a feature film without title cards, without a single word of silent dialogue. Literally, a talking picture. When the line between the silent and sound eras was finally crossed, she had been the first leading actress to cross it. That she gave a coherent performance at all, racing against Brian Foy's time constraints, and with little or no time to rehearse, was in itself a monumental accomplishment.

But her greatest triumph was not professional. As part of the first wave of tuberculosis patients to survive one of history's worst killers, she had endured twenty years of torturous surgeries, dashed hopes, financial disasters, and romantic disappointments, capped off by the loss of her daughter; and she had emerged with, if not her health, then her sense of humor intact.[14]

27

Mum Mum

With nothing to keep her in Hollywood, Dolores gave up her apartment on Wilshire Boulevard and retired to her Fallbrook ranch to grow avocados and, more importantly, to raise her grandchild far from parental threats to her guardianship. For the moment, she needn't have worried. Tom Fairbanks was unaccounted for, and Dede had resigned herself to the situation for her mother's sake and even given her power of attorney so she could make legal decisions in Tony's behalf. It took more than a little chicanery on Dolores's part to bring this about. She had called Dede to tell her that the boy needed an ear operation right away, but first she would need written authority from the mother. When Dede asked for the doctor's phone number, Dolores said that he was performing an operation out of town and couldn't be reached. During their conversation, Dede could hear Tony playing energetically in the background, so he was obviously not sick at all. Still, she signed the papers and thus handed over the lion's share of her parental authority.[1]

Dolores had power of attorney, but she wasn't taking any chances. She made sure to keep mother and son well apart (as she had tried and failed to do with Helene and Deirdre), disinviting Dede to the ranch whenever family gatherings were scheduled. The first time Hillary and her mother came down on the train, Dolores met them at the station with startling news: citing "doctor's orders," she declared that only Hillary could come back with her to the ranch. Dede would have to return home. Docile to the end, she departed on the next train to Los Angeles.

Dede's obedience under the circumstances is hard to fathom. Or is it? Like Tony, when asked if she would have done things differently, she said she would not have. "I really think she would have died without him, and I loved my mother dearly. I worried about her constantly. I was a mamma's girl and she was a dominant figure. I was passive and let her be the boss. She could be generous, on the other hand she had the balls to make a success of herself in this town. I didn't realize how much it would hurt Tony at the time, but we can't change what we've done, or who we are."

The last of the Costellos found a last measure of tranquility in Fallbrook, California, cut off from the world in her rural paradise, surrounded by forty acres of rolling hills, ancient trees, and native shrubs. At the top of the long, steep driveway stood a white clapboard ranch house half-hidden in a tangle of Cecile Brunner roses, ferns, live oaks, and a Deodar cedar that towered over it. Family members, save for Dede, made their pilgrimages, along with the occasional journalist, historian, or biographer, for whom Dolores would put on lipstick and her best finishing school accent. When Diana Barrymore died in January 1960, Dolores told a visiting reporter that her stepdaughter had been "badly treated all her life."[2]

"The last time I talked to Diana, I scolded her," she said. "It was for speaking unkindly of her father on a television show. I also upbraided her when she published that book [her autobiography, *Too Much, Too Soon*]. I told her never to be unkind to the memory of her dear father. She sent me a copy of the book, because I never would have bought it." By the early fifties, Dolores had softened considerably when it came to Jack, to the extent of re-adding Barrymore to her last name.[3]

Adding to Dolores's peace of mind, the court finally granted her custodial rights to her grandson. In 1958, Tom Fairbanks had the temerity to sue Dolores and Dede for custody of Tony. All his former wife had to do, however, was tell the court that he owed $6,313 in back child support to have the case thrown out.[4] At last the issue was settled—what began as an abduction had become an adoption. As a parent, Dolores did the best she could, given the person she had become. Hard as it would have been for her grandchildren to imagine, there had been a time when she could love openly and trust unreservedly. In the honeymoon diaries, like a giggly schoolgirl, she wrote of nothing more often or more effusively than her love for Jack. But this wasn't the Dolores they knew. "Whenever I tried to hug her she would recoil," Dede recalled.[5] After Jack, she was suspicious of anyone who might try to draw her feelings back into the open. When her grandson Dore would tell her he loved her on the phone, Dolores's standard reply was, "No you don't."

She showed her affection in other ways. Hillary remembered her warm glances, her pale blues eyes "crinkling up around the edges" when she smiled. "When she gave me those looks I knew I was loved," she recalled.[6] In moments of crisis, Dolores was there when no one else would have been. When Hillary was struggling to find herself in the early 1970s, she took her in and helped plan out her future. What followed was a Montessori class, paid for by Dolores, which led to a lifelong career in early education.[7] She tried to focus her grandson's attention along academic lines, but by the late 1960s Tony had another direction in mind—north. At the age of fifteen, he went to live with his mother and stepfather in Los Angeles, eventually to be subsumed by the raging counterculture and the corrupting influence of his Uncle John.

Johnny had officially changed his name to John Drew Barrymore in 1958, thinking the junior suffix put him at a disadvantage.[8] But he had burned his bridges by then. He had broken contracts, riled his bosses, and been punished by Actors' Equity. He twice went to jail on drunk-driving and domestic abuse charges. His troubled seven-year marriage to Cara, which produced a son, John Blyth Barrymore Jr., ended in divorce when he jetted off to make low-budget Italian films and refused to come back.

In Italy, he got into street brawls, one of which landed him and his new wife, Gabriella Palazzoli, in jail for several days. In late 1960, he brought Gaby and their infant daughter Blyth to Los Angeles to meet his family.[9] Four years later the marriage was over and Johnny was back in Hollywood looking for work. He appeared in several episodes of *Gunsmoke* and *Rawhide,* which under more favorable circumstances might have relaunched his career. In 1966, Hollywood columnist and Barrymore aficionado Erskine Johnson found him living in a shack in the Mohave Desert. A few months later Johnny was arrested and charged with possession of narcotics, as part of a San Bernardino sting operation.

Still, he garnered praise as an actor. In a review of the TV movie *Winchester '73,* the writer decried its "terrible acting by some of the great old pros such as Dan Duryea, Joan Blondell and Tom Tryon," while praising that of "the three Johns—Saxon, Dehner and Barrymore—who hold it all together."[10] Before that came the offer of cult immortality that only a guest spot on the new *Star Trek* series could have given him. As the time traveler Lazarus, the script called for him to kiss a black female crewman on the *Enterprise* (the scene was cut due to the producer's worries over how it might play in the South) and engage in a fistfight with Captain Kirk.

At his wardrobe fitting, Johnny was handed a copy of the script, and that was the last anyone saw of him. With the first of his scenes scheduled for the next day, he called the casting director and told him he was quitting the episode. A mad scramble to find another actor ensued and threw the production into almost irreparable chaos. "One of the reasons Johnny was a no show," said his nephew, Dore Bedell, "was that one of his friends told him it would ruin his career because it was a kids' show. In fact, it would have helped it in countless ways." The Screen Actors Guild suspended him for six months and fined him $1,500 for nearly derailing the episode and putting the future of the series in jeopardy. "Ricardo Montalban and Chuck Heston went to bat for him, but in the end SAG banned him. He couldn't get work and his phone stopped ringing."[11]

Johnny was all but washed-up as a working actor. His friend David Carradine hired him for the part of the Scottish sculptor Alex McGregor in a 1974 episode of *Kung Fu,* but after that no other important offers were forthcoming. In Johnny's current state, none of it seemed to matter. "Acting is just a thing with me," he said. "I do only parts that appeal to me. . . . So much in the world today conditions rather than reveals. I cannot care about being part of anything that conditions."[12]

For the first time in a century, there were no Barrymores or Costellos actively treading the boards or emoting in front of a camera. Dolores spent the last decade of her life with little connection to the industry she had been part of since its beginning. How deeply, or how often, she thought about the past, she never revealed. If not for the occasional disparaging comment about Jack Warner, one would never have known who she was and what she had accomplished.

Because she shared so little of herself, her grandchildren remember her for the most part anecdotally. Deirdre tells of the time she brought a boyfriend to meet Dolores, who admonished the young man to "stand when a lady enters the room." Hillary's boyfriend had the reverse effect, eliciting a seductive, almost flirty response. Once she likened a woman she considered promiscuous to a "filling station." And once, when one of her dogs gave a jealous growl, Dolores quipped: "I haven't had a look like that since Jack Barrymore."

Dolores went on one last terrible binge after Tony left and then quit drinking for good. According to Hillary, she had been sober for perhaps a dozen years before that. She would not stop smoking, however, and in the early 1970s was diagnosed with emphysema. Like her mother, she had suffered two heart attacks—unlike her, she survived the second one. She had seen the ravages of tobacco use firsthand: Mae was a chain smoker who died of heart disease in her late forties. Laura Vruwink and Daddy Butch both died from emphysema ten years apart. Still, when one of her doctors told her she would have to stop smoking, Dolores replied: "Would you mind if I have one while you're telling me that?"[13]

She was on oxygen as she gave interviews for the *Hollywood* series in 1977, during which her difficulty breathing was noted. A year later Dolores was so short of breath that she had to attend Tony's wedding ceremony in a wheelchair. He had returned to the ranch in the early 1970s and was living there with his wife, Dianne, when they learned she was pregnant. As the due date approached, Dolores was afraid she wouldn't live long enough to meet her new grandchild. She "found her spirituality" in her last years, Tony said. "She saw some kind of mystic and they had a session together. She said she wanted to be a better person." In her final weeks, struggling for breath, she told Dore and Hillary that she loved them. In late February 1979, when she could no longer breathe unassisted, she was taken the short distance from the ranch to Fallbrook Hospital. Family members began filtering in. "It was hard watching her struggle for every breath," Tony recalled. "It was like you were breathing with her."[14]

Early on the morning of March 1, 1979, Dede was fast asleep in the hospital waiting room when Dolores's nurse woke her up and said, "Hurry." "I left my purse and my book and ran in and sat on her bed. She sat up without a word, then looked past me, somewhere over my left shoulder. Then she said—very clearly—'mother,' and fell back on the pillows. It was as if Mae had come to get her."[15]

Epilogue

On March 4, 1979, Fallbrook's tiny St. Peter's Catholic Church held a rosary service for Dolores Costello Barrymore. At one o'clock on the following day, family members gathered at Calvary Cemetery for her funeral and burial service—minus Johnny, who had left the ranch for parts unknown.[1] His relationship to the aspiring actress Ildiko Jaid Mako had already come and gone, but not before the arrival of his fourth child, named Drew to honor the venerable acting family whose name the Barrymores had absorbed a hundred years before. Drew, four when her grandmother died, was two and a half years shy of her appearance in the Steven Spielberg blockbuster *E.T.* The film made her an overnight star and reintroduced the Barrymore name to a new generation of Hollywood moviegoers and celeb-watchers. Johnny had unwittingly produced an heir, a female heir amazingly, to bring the dynasty forward.

If Dolores hadn't given Jack a son, the Barrymore name would have died with him. (Lionel Barrymore had no surviving children.) Instead, the family went on to become the oldest and perhaps the greatest of American dynasties, the Kennedys notwithstanding. Giving Jack an heir was the easy part—for all her shortcomings, it was Dolores who kept the Barrymores together as a family in something other than name. When she died, her heirs split into warring factions over both the terms and the authenticity of her will, into which was inserted a questionable codicil dated shortly before her death and signed with an "X." Like everything the Costellos had ever done publicly, the ensuing legal battle made national news, especially when fisticuffs broke out between family members on the Vista courthouse steps.[2] Exactly who got what from Dolores's $1.3 million estate scarcely mattered in the end—the ordeal created a family schism that took fifteen years to repair. By then, all her money and most of her possessions were scattered to the winds. Johnny bartered his father's valuable collection of rare books, artifacts, and antiquities for untold quantities of Quaaludes and cocaine, until there was nothing left to barter.[3] By the time Johnny succumbed to cancer in 2004, he had worn out his welcome with nearly everyone in the family save for Drew, who graciously paid his living expenses during his last years. Like Maurice Costello, when Johnny had no one else to turn to, his daughter came through. Also like Maurice, despite Johnny's famously infamous behavior, his loved ones never completely abandoned him. "He was lovable, like a charming, handsome, bad child," said his niece Hillary, "so you forgave him."[4]

The same upbringing that had crippled her brother left Dede Bedell relatively unscathed. As of this writing she is alive and well, notwithstanding the infirmities of age. Lew Bedell, her husband of thirty years, died in 2000, leaving Dede alone in their ivy-covered house in the Beverlywood section of Los Angeles. At age eighty-nine, she remains the last living link to the Royal Family: Ethel, Lionel, and John. She shares with Deirdre the honor of having known all three of the Costellos' principal actor-members: Maurice, Dolores, and Helene.

Jack's disappearance in Dede's early childhood produced in her none of the rage and resentment it did in her brother. Unlike Johnny, Dede chose to love the father she had, rather than pine for the one she lost.[5] As a teenager, having briefly considered the idea of taking up "the family curse," as Jack called their stock-in-trade, his delightfully photogenic daughter opted instead for a life of mostly quiet domesticity—of cooking, gardening, keeping house, and raising children. Like her father, she has a passion for books and a love of the decorative arts bordering on the obsessive—of which those closest to her remain the beneficiaries. But given her perfect placement at the confluence of America's two great acting families, hers has not been a life without turbulence.

Despite the loss of her mother and the trials of being raised by a callous, neglectful father, Deirdre Le Blanc survived her childhood to become a thriving, successful adult. She married and had a child. For twenty-three years she worked for MGM as a secretary and an assistant matte artist, before she retired to write television scripts and paint. She moved to the East Coast in 2009, to be near her daughter, her grandchildren, and her great-grandchild Rachel, who at age three was the spitting image of Helene Costello at the time she was the country's most popular child star.

"There will be no more Costellos after dad and Dolores and I are gone," Helene wrote in the last paragraph of her all-too-brief memoir. "So even the blood will be thinned out by intermarriage, and be gone with the name."[6]

But the name is not gone, nor will it ever be, so long as movies confer immortality on all who appear in them. "This was the first family of the film industry, there at its birth, and very much a part of its history," Deirdre said. "When audiences see cast and crew credits today, they should thank Maurice Costello. The actors themselves should thank him. As soon as actors were no longer required to perform duties outside their craft, other jobs in the industry were created, like grips, gaffers, set decorators, property masters, etc." Beneath the kohl and greasepaint, after all, they were just people: "The gods and goddesses created by the camera, these motion picture stars, aren't any different than the folks who buy popcorn and sit in a theater, or cozy at home to watch their marvels on the screen. To be entertained, to watch someone we can admire and love. It's all make believe—but then, everyone loves a fairytale, don't they?"[7]

Acknowledgments

A thousand heartfelt thank-yous—to the multifaceted Richard Day Gore, whose boundless knowledge, patience, and enthusiasm saw me through the writing of this book from beginning to end; to the staggeringly versatile historical writer Michael F. Blake, for his unflagging interest and encouragement; to Leonard and Alice Maltin for their help and generosity; to Denise Barrymore for giving me full access to her private collection of Barrymore artifacts and memorabilia; to Kevin Brownlow for the full transcript of his interview with Dolores Costello for the incomparable *Hollywood* series; to UCLA Emeritus Professor Gerald Goodman for his insights into the deep chasm of Maurice Costello's psyche; to Faye Thompson, photo archive coordinator at the Academy of Motion Picture Arts and Sciences, for her industry and resourcefulness during the photo selection process; to the Carnegie Library research staff for steering me through the turbid waters of Pittsburgh history; to the Library of Congress film librarians for making the LOC's massive collections so easily accessible; to the EYE Filmmuseum of Amsterdam for posting so many of Maurice's films online; to John Blyth Barrymore Jr. for his help and generosity early on; to Patti Scheck Creative for coming through in a pinch; to Jane Vruwink Palmer for sharing her memories of John Vruwink, and Vince Pirolli for bringing us together; to Rex Coughenour for contributing his cache of newspaper transcriptions; to authors Vanda Krefft, Tracey Goessel, Alan K. Rode, and Mark Alan Viera for their invaluable assistance; to Thomas Hume for his tech and marketing savvy; to Helmut Filacchione for his indexing skills. Last but not least, to Antony Barrymore for sharing aspects of his grandmother's life and character as only he could share them. To all of you, once again, thank you.

Notes

1. Mise-en-Scène

1. Grace Kingsley, *New Movie Magazine,* January 1931, 91.

2. Jacqueline Boles, *Life upon the Wicked Stage: A Sociological Study of Entertainers,* (Bloomington: iUniverse, 2010), 16–17.

3. Deirdre Le Blanc, email message to the author, September 2014.

4. Ibid.

5. Charles Musser, *Before the Nickelodeon: Edwin S. Porter and the Edison Manufacturing Company* (Berkeley: University of California Press, 1991), 326.

6. Frank Cullen, with Florence Hackman and Donald McNeilly, *Vaudeville, Old and New: An Encyclopedia of Variety Performers in America* (New York: Routledge, 2006), 900.

7. Ibid.

8. Musser, *Before the Nickelodeon,* 374.

9. John L. Fell, *Film before Griffith* (Berkeley: University of California Press, 1983), 34.

10. Ibid.

11. *Moving Picture World,* June 1907, 226.

12. Simon Louvish: *The Man on the Flying Trapeze: The Life and Times of W. C. Fields* (New York: W. W. Norton, 1999), 24.

13. *New York Dramatic Mirror,* June 1908.

14. Musser, *Before the Nickelodeon,* 434.

15. Peter Decherney, *Hollywood's Copyright Wars: From Edison to the Internet* (New York: Columbia University Press 2013), 33.

16. Terry Ramsaye, *A Million and One Nights: A History of the Motion Picture* (Abingdon, UK: Frank Cass & Co., 1926), 396.

17. George Burns, *All My Best Friends* (New York: G. P. Putnam's Sons, 1989), 23.

18. Charles Musser, *The Emergence of Cinema* (Berkeley: University of California Press 1990), 417.

19. Don B. Wilmeth and Christopher Bigsby, *The Cambridge History of American Theater,* vol. 2, *1870–1945* (Cambridge, UK: Cambridge University Press, 1999), 201–202.

20. *New York Dramatic Mirror,* October 28, 1905.

21. *Oswego Daily Times,* June 5, 1914.

22. Kerry Segrave, *Actors Organize: A History of Union Formation Efforts in America, 1880–1919* (Jefferson, NC: McFarland, 2007), 154.

23. Burns, *All My Best Friends,* 23.

24. *Motion Picture,* 30th Anniversary Edition, February 1941.

2. Pittsburgh and North

1. Allen Dieterich-Ward, *Beyond Rust: Metropolitan Pittsburgh and the Fate of Industrial America* (Philadelphia: University of Pennsylvania Press, 2016), 53.

2. Stefan Lorant, *Pittsburgh: The Story of an American City* (Lenox, MA: Authors Edition, 1975), 178.

3. Goss, William Freeman Myrick, *Smoke Abatement and Electrification of Railway Terminals in Chicago,* (Chicago: Chicago Association of Commerce and Industry, 1915), 1107.

4. *Annual Report of the Board of Health of the City of Pittsburgh* (Pittsburgh: Best and Company, 1878), https://books.google.com/books?id=_XlIAAAAYAAJ&printsec=frontcover&dq=Annual+Report+of+the+Board+of+Health+of+the+City+of+Pittsburgh&hl=en&sa=X&ved=0ahUKEwjj5b3A4J3hAhXRKH0KHUWUCvwQ6AEILzAB#v=onepage&q=Annual%20Report%20of%20the%20Board%20of%20Health%20of%20the%20City%20of%20Pittsburgh&f=false

5. Ibid., 17.

6. Ibid., 50.

7. George Peter Gregory, "A Study in Local Decision Making: Pittsburgh and Sewage Treatment," *Western Pennsylvania Historical Magazine* 57, no. 1 (1974): 28.

8. *Pittsburgh Commercial Gazette,* August 6, 1877, 4.

9. National Archives online, 1880 Federal Census, https://www.archives.gov/research/census/microfilm-catalog/1790-1890/part-07.

10. Patricia McElligott, *Irish Pittsburgh* (Charleston, SC: Arcadia 2013), 24.

11. Howard Zinn, *A People's History of the United States* (New York: Harper Perennial Modern Classics, 2003), 233.

12. National Archives online, *1880 Federal Census.*

13. Stephen Albert Rohs, *Eccentric Nation: Irish Performance in Nineteenth-Century New York City* (Madison, WI: Fairleigh Dickinson University Press, 2009), 167.

14. *New York Clipper Almanac* (New York: Frank Queen, 1879), 29.

15. Robert M. Lewis, ed., *From Traveling Show to Vaudeville: Theatrical Spectacle in America, 1830–1910* (Baltimore, MD: Johns Hopkins University Press 2003), 95.

16. Andrew L. Erdman, *Blue Vaudeville: Sex, Morals, and Mass Marketing of Amusement 1895–1915* (Jefferson, NC: McFarland, 2004), 22.

17. John Gassner, ed., *Best Plays of the Early American Theater,* 1787–1911 (New York: Dover, 1967), xxxvi.

18. Lynn Conner, *Pittsburgh in Stages: Two Hundred Years of Theater* (Pittsburgh, PA: University of Pittsburgh Press, 2007) 50.

19. Ibid.

20. James Parton, "Pittsburg," *Atlantic Monthly,* February 1868, 34–35.

21. Conner, *Pittsburgh in Stages,* 41.

22. Ibid., 55.

23. Anthony Slide, *New York City Vaudeville* (Charleston, SC: Arcadia, 2006), 8.

24. *The Century Dictionary and Cyclopedia,* vol. 3 (New York: Century Company, 1900), 1580.

25. *Canadian Bookseller and Library Journal* 15, no. 1 (1902).

26. *St. Louis Star and Times,* March 14, 1929.

27. Jackson R. Bryer and Mary C. Hartig, *The Facts on File Companion to American Drama,* 2nd ed. (New York: Facts on File, 2010), 412.

28. John Bush Jones, *Reinventing Dixie: Tin Pan Alley's Songs and the Creation of the Mythic South* (Baton Rouge: Louisiana State University Press, 2015), 22.

29. Ibid.

30. *Pittsburgh Post-Gazette,* December 27, 1898.

31. Ibid.

32. *Motion Picture Magazine,* January 1916, 111.

33. Conner, *Pittsburgh in Stages,* 75.

34. Ibid.

35. *Pittsburgh Post-Gazette,* July 24, 1948.

36. James W. Kastner, *Where the Movies Played in Downtown Pittsburg[h]: 100 Years of "Going to the Show" 1896–1996* (Pittsburgh, PA: Rosedog, 2011), 25.

37. *Pittsburgh Gazette Times,* December 26, 1915.

38. James Kotsilibas-Davis, *Great Times, Good Times: The Odyssey of Maurice Barrymore* (Garden City, NY: Doubleday, 1977), 397.

39. Avenue Theater Playbill, June 1900, Curtis Theater Collection, University of Pittsburgh Library.

40. Kastner, *Where the Movies Played in Downtown Pittsburg[h],* 11.

41. Paul S. Moore, *Now Playing: Early Moviegoing and the Regulation of Fun* (Albany: State University Press of New York, 2008), 21.

42. Moore, *Now Playing,* 13.

43. Moore, *Now Playing,* 10

44. Tracey Goessel, *The First King of Hollywood: The Life of Douglas Fairbanks* (Chicago: Chicago Review, 2016), 35.

45. *Pittsburgh Post,* June 5, 1900.

46. Ibid.

47. Ibid.

48. Helene Costello, "The Fighting Costellos," unpublished manuscript, 3–4, personal collection of Deirdre Le Blanc (hereafter LBC).

3. Mae

1. Costello, "The Fighting Costellos," 3, LBC.

2. Ibid.

3. Dede Barrymore Bedell, interview with the author, December 2015.

4. Costello, "The Fighting Costellos," 2, LBC.

5. Letter from Mae to Maurice, March 1903, personal collection of Denise Barrymore (hereafter DBC).

6. Ibid.

7. Costello, "The Fighting Costellos," 2, LBC.

8. Carol Stein Hoffman, *The Barrymores: Hollywood's First Family* (Lexington, KY: University Press of Kentucky, 2001), 145.

9. Ibid., 146.

10. Costello, "The Fighting Costellos," 5, LBC.

11. *New York Dramatic Mirror,* July 4, 1903, p. 8.

12. William L. Slout, *Theatre in a Tent* (Cabin John, MD: Wildside, 2006), 75.

13. "When the show arrived"; *Pittsburgh Press,* February 2, 1931.

14. *Pittsburgh Daily Post,* May 17, 1914.

15. Ibid.

16. Helene Costello, outline published in Hearst newspaper supplement *American Weekly,* in serial form beginning October 1948 (hereafter, published outline), 3, LBC.

17. Costello, "The Fighting Costellos," 6, LBC.

18. Ibid.

19. Ibid.

20. Dede Barrymore Bedell, interview with the author, January 2016.

21. *Knickerbocker News,* October 29, 1950.

22. National Archives online, 1900 Federal Census, https://www.archives.gov/research/census/microfilm-catalog/1900.

23. Ibid.

24. Ibid.

25. Ibid.

4. East to Eden

1. *History of Pittsburgh and Environs* (New York: American Historical Society, 1922), 138.

2. Rose Goff, "Factors in the Drop in United States Infant Mortality: 1900–1940" (Dietrich College honors thesis, Carnegie Mellon University, 2010), 11.

3. Paul Underwood Kellogg, ed., *The Pittsburgh Survey: The Pittsburgh District* (Philadelphia: William F. Fell, 1914), 93.

4. Kellogg, *The Pittsburgh Survey,* 95.

5. S. J. Kleinberg, *The Shadow of the Mills: Working-Class Families in Pittsburgh, 1870–1907* (Pittsburgh: University of Pittsburgh Press, 1989), 111.

6. Kellogg, *The Pittsburgh Survey,* 407.

7. *Elmira Gazette,* April 23, 1903.

8. Costello, "The Fighting Costellos," 1, LBC.

9. Don B. Wilmeth with Tice L. Miller, *The Cambridge Guide to American Theatre* (Cambridge: Cambridge University Press, 1996), 361.

10. *Broadway Weekly,* February 11, 1904, 18.

11. *New York Dramatic Mirror,* September 17, 1904.

12. *New York Morning Telegraph,* September 6, 1904.

13. *Daily Standard Union,* October 4, 1904.

14. *New York Dramatic Mirror,* June 10, 1905.

15. Maurice Costello business ledger, 1905, DBC.

16. *Motion Picture Magazine,* January 1916, 111.

17. *Stars of the Photoplay* (Chicago: Photoplay Magazine, 1924), n.p.

18. Harry T. Brundison, unidentified newspaper clipping, November 8, 1929, Margaret Herrick Library (hereafter MHL).

19. Maurice Costello business ledgers, 1905, DBC.

20. *A Million and One Nights,* 1926, 441.

21. *Variety,* October 29, 1950.

22. Daniel Blum, *A Pictorial History of the Silent Screen* (New York: G. M. Putnam & Sons, 1953), 9.

23. Maurice Costello business ledgers, 1905, DBC.

24. Ibid.

25. Letter from Mae to Maurice, October 1906, DBC.

26. Costello, published outline, 7–8, LBC.

5. Chewing the Scenery

1. Albert E. Smith and Phil A. Koury, *Two Reels and a Crank* (Garden City, NY: Doubleday & Co., 1952), 29.

2. Ibid.

3. Charles Musser, "American Vitagraph: 1897–1901," *Cinema Journal* 22, no. 3 (Spring 1983), 6–7.

4. Anthony Slide, *The Big V: A History of the Vitagraph Company* (Metuchen, NJ: Scarecrow, 1987), 43.

5. Musser, "American Vitagraph," 6.

6. Ibid., 9.

7. Slide, *The Big V,* 7.

8. Musser, "American Vitagraph," 12.

9. Ibid., 13.

10. Smith and Koury, *Two Reels and a Crank,* 44.

11. Slide, *The Big V,* 9.

12. Smith and Koury, *Two Reels and a Crank,* 1.

13. Ibid., 66.

14. Ibid., 67.

15. Richard Abel, ed., *Silent Film* (London: Athlone, 1999), 92.

16. Musser, "American Vitagraph," 17.

17. Slide, *The Big V,* 12.

18. Kelly R. Brown, *Florence Lawrence, the Biograph Girl* (Jefferson, NC: McFarland, 1999), 18.

19. Richard DeCordova, *Picture Personalities: The Emergence of the Star System in America* (Chicago: University of Illinois Press, 2001), 74.

20. Costello, "The Fighting Costellos," 9, LBC.

21. Brown, *Florence Lawrence,* 8.

22. Donald Dewey, *Buccaneer: James Stuart Blackton and the Birth of the Movies* (Lanham, MD: Rowman and Littlefield, 2016), 114.

23. Brown, *Florence Lawrence,* 8.

24. Smith and Koury, *Two Reels and a Crank,* 187.

25. Letter from Mae to Maurice, December 11, 1906, DBC.

26. Vicki Callahan, *Reclaiming the Archive: Feminism and Film History* (Detroit, MI: Wayne State University Press, 2010), 78.

27. Costello, "The Fighting Costellos," 9, LBC. Additional corroboration of the date came from movie magazine writer Rosalind Shaffer: "Costello, who first gained fame in the old Vitagraph, was starred from 1907," *New Movie Magazine,* January 1929.

28. Letter from Mae to Maurice, November 26, 1906, DBC.

29. Letter from Mae to Maurice, November 1906, DBC.

30. Costello, "The Fighting Costellos," 9, LBC.

31. Agnes Kessler, "A Trip to Vitagraphville," *Moving Picture Magazine,* April 1915, 83.

32. Costello, "The Fighting Costellos," 9, LBC.

33. *Motion Picture,* 30th Anniversary Edition, February 1941.

34. Charles Musser, *The Emergence of Cinema,* 473.

6. A Lusty, Growing Thing

1. Anthony Slide, *The Big V,* 37.

2. *Brooklyn Daily Eagle,* June 27, 1915, 15.

3. Costello, "The Fighting Costellos," 9, LBC.

4. *Evening Leader* (Corning, NY), August 21, 1939.

5. *Motion Picture Classic,* January 1920, 73.

6. Smith and Koury, *Two Reels and a Crank,* 187.

7. Ira H. Gallen, *D. W. Griffith: Master of Cinema* (Victoria, Canada: Friesen, 2015), xiv.

8. *Movie Pictorial,* July 25, 1914.

9. Kevin Brownlow, "Silent Films: What Was the Right Speed?" *Sight and Sound* 49, no. 3 (1980): 164–167. Brownlow wrote: "Nevertheless, the fact that silent pictures were invariably shown slightly faster than they were shot was confirmed by historian David Shepard. When for example he worked on the restoration of *Nanook of the North* (1922), he found that Flaherty had shot the film at 16 fps, 'but the pace and rhythm of the edited feature was completely destroyed by [that] slow a speed.'"

10. Dolores Costello, 1977 interview, in *Hollywood: A Celebration of the American Silent Film.* Documentary series. Directed by Kevin Brownlow and David Gill. London: ITV network. Originally aired February 9 to April 1 1980 (hereafter Dolores Costello interview, *Hollywood* series).

11. *Movie Pictorial,* July 18, 1914.

12. *Pittsburgh Press,* February 2, 1931.

13. *Photoplay,* December 1917.

14. *Stars of the Photoplay*, n.p.

15. Gladys Hall, *Motion Picture Magazine,* February 1941, 26.

16. *Santa Cruz Sentinel,* January 22, 1939.

17. *Motion Picture Story Magazine,* February–July 1912, 133.

18. *New York Press,* October 12, 1912.

19. Hall, *Motion Picture Magazine,* February 1941.

20. Ibid.

21. Paramount Publicity Department Release, November 19, 1940, Maurice Costello Collection, MHL.

22. Musser, *The Emergence of Cinema,* 466, 470.

23. Ibid., 471.

24. National Archives online, Federal Census 1910, https://www.archives.gov/research/census/publications-microfilm-catalogs-census/1910; Brooklyn City Directory, 1910, Brooklyn Public Library online, https://archive.org/details/newyorkcityinclu1910newy/page/n8.

25. Costello, "The Fighting Costellos," 9, LBC.

26. Letter from Mae Costello to Maurice Costello, undated, DBC.

27. Hall, *Motion Picture Magazine,* February 1941, 60.

28. Ibid.

29. *New York Dramatic Mirror,* October 5, 1910.

30. *Moving Picture World,* November 26, 1910, 1223.

31. *Nickelodeon,* October 15, 1910, 228.

32. Ibid., 262.

33. Gregory D. Black, *The Catholic Crusade against the Movies, 1940–1975* (Cambridge, UK: Cambridge University Press, 1997), 1.

34. Pittsburgh City Directories, 1905–1907, State Library of Pennsylvania online, https://sshelco-primo.hosted.exlibrisgroup.com/primo-explore/search?query=any,contains,pittsburgh%20directory%201905&tab=default_tab&search_scope=default_scope&vid=STLIBPA&lang=en_US&offset=0.

35. Hall, *Motion Picture Magazine,* February 1941, 58.

7. Great Days

1. Frederick A. Talbot, *Moving Pictures: How They are Made and Worked* (Philadelphia, PA: J. B. Lippincott, 1912), 172.

2. *Cinema News and Property Gazette,* August 1912, 10.

3. *Motion Picture Story Magazine,* February 1911, 114.

4. Hall, *Motion Picture Magazine,* February 1941, 26, 60.

5. *Los Angeles Times,* November 6, 1929.

6. Smith and Koury, *Two Reels and a Crank,* 188.

7. Hall, *Motion Picture Magazine,* February 1941, 60.

8. *Brooklyn Daily Eagle,* April 24, 1927.
9. *New Movie Magazine,* January 1931, 115.
10. *Motion Picture Story,* May 1912, 135.
11. *Motion Picture Story,* June 1912, 132.
12. Deirdre Le Blanc, email message to the author, November 2016.
13. Ibid.
14. *Motion Picture Story,* June 1912, 146.
15. *Motion Picture Story,* May 1912, 142.
16. *Motion Picture Story,* June 1912, 146.
17. Costello, "The Fighting Costellos," 6, LBC.
18. Gallen, *D. W. Griffith: Master of Cinema,* 2015.
19. *Motography,* March 6, 1915, 372.
20. *Cinema News and Property Gazette,* August 1912, xii.
21. Hall, *Motion Picture Magazine,* February 1941, 60.
22. *Cinema News and Property Gazette,* August 1912, xii.
23. Hall, *Motion Picture Magazine,* February 1941, 58.
24. *New Movie Magazine,* January 1930, 100.
25. David J. Shepherd, *The Bible on Silent Film: Spectacle, Story and Scripture in the Early Cinema* (Cambridge, UK: Cambridge University Press, 2015), 144.
26. Maurice Costello travel ledger, 1912–1913, DBC.
27. "It was an experiment for this ambulatory studio"; Dewey: *Buccaneer: James Stuart Blackton and the Birth of American Movies,* 118.
28. *Motion Picture Story,* August 1913, 102.
29. Maurice Costello travel ledger, DBC.
30. Ibid.
31. *Motion Picture Story,* 102.
32. Ibid., 104.
33. Ibid., 105.
34. Ibid.
35. Costello, "The Fighting Costellos," 13, LBC.
36. Ibid.
37. Hoffman, *The Barrymores,* 157.
38. Maurice Costello travel ledger, DBC.
39. *New Movie Magazine,* January 1929, 100.
40. Dolores Costello interview, *Hollywood* series.
41. Undated fan letter, DBC.
42. *Motion Picture Story,* August 1913, 101.

8. Smashing Things

1. *Motion Picture Story,* October 1913, 109.
2. *Brooklyn Daily Gazette,* November 25, 1913.
3. Ibid.
4. *Brooklyn Daily Eagle,* April 12, 1914.

5. Ibid.
6. Ibid.
7. Smith and Koury, *Two Reels and a Crank,* 188.
8. *Motion Picture Story Magazine,* October 1913, 109.
9. *Movie Pictorial,* July 25, 1914.
10. Ibid.
11. Ibid.
12. Smith and Koury, *Two Reels and a Crank,* 188.
13. Costello, "The Fighting Costellos," 15, LBC.
14. Ibid.
15. Ibid., 18.
16. Deirdre Le Blanc, email message to the author, December 2016.
17. *Brooklyn Daily Eagle,* April 24, 1927.
18. Maurice Costello diary, December 6, 1925, DBC.
19. Deirdre Le Blanc, email message to the author, February 28, 2017.
20. Dolores Costello interview, *Hollywood* series.
21. *Motion Picture Magazine,* November 1915, 124.
22. *Stanford Daily Pictures and the Picturegoer,* November 6, 1915, 112.
23. E. J. Stephens and Marc Wanamaker, *Early Poverty Row Studios* (Charleston, SC: Arcadia, 2015), 67.
24. Blum, *A Pictorial History of the Silent Screen,* 111.
25. *Boston Globe,* March 5, 1935.
26. Marian Blackton Trimble, *J. Stuart Blackton, A Personal Biography by His Daughter* (Metuchen, NJ: Scarecrow, 1985), 39.
27. Dede Barrymore Bedell, interview with the author, November 2016.
28. *Picture Play,* September 1916, 41.
29. *Brooklyn Daily Eagle,* August 6, 1917.

9. Desperation

1. Costello, "The Fighting Costellos," 6, LBC.
2. Deirdre LeBlanc, email message to the author, March 2017.
3. Delores Barrymore Bedell, interview with the author, November 2016.
4. Costello, *The Fighting Costellos,* 18, LBC.
5. Dolores Barrymore Bedell, interview with the author, November 2016.
6. Goessel, *The First King of Hollywood,* 188.
7. *Wid's Daily,* June 29, 1919, 7.
8. *Film Fun,* August 1919, 5.
9. Deirdre LeBlanc, email message to the author, December 2016.
10. *Purdue Exponent,* September 21, 1907.
11. *Motion Picture Magazine,* June 1923, 10.
12. *Motion Picture News,* March 1922, 1447.
13. Ibid., 1055.
14. *Motion Picture News Booking Guide,* October 1923, 34.

15. *Motion Picture Magazine,* April 1923, 76.

16. Costello, "The Fighting Costellos," 18, LBC.

17. Ethan Mordden, *Ziegfeld: The Man Who Invented Show Business* (New York: St. Martins, 2008), 189.

18. Costello, "The Fighting Costellos," 18, LBC.

19. Letter from Mae to Maurice, December 24, 1925, MHL.

20. *Chicago Tribune,* April 3, 1925.

21. Letter from Mae to Maurice, December 24, 1925, MHL.

22. Letter from Mae to Maurice, January 3, 1925, MHL.

23. Letter from Mae to Maurice, January 6, 1925, MHL.

24. Letter from Mae to Maurice, January 7, 1925, MHL.

25. *Poughkeepsie Eagle-News,* March 31, 1925.

26. Dolores Costello interview, *Hollywood* series.

27. Letter from Maurice to Mae, March 22, 1925, MHL.

28. Costello, "The Fighting Costellos," 1, LBC.

29. Letter from Mae to Maurice, April 5, 1925, MHL.

30. Letter from Mae to Maurice, April 29, 1925, MHL.

31. *Brooklyn Daily Eagle,* April 24, 1927.

32. Letter from Mae to Maurice, May 13, 1925, MHL.

33. Letter from Mae to Maurice, April 29, 1925, MHL.

34. *Chicago Tribune,* April 23, 1925.

35. Letter from Mae to Maurice, June 2, 1925, MHL.

36. Ibid.

37. Ibid.

38. Letter from Mae to Maurice, June 10, 1925, MHL.

39. Letter from Mae to Maurice, April 29, 1925, MHL.

10. The Lion at Warners

1. John Kobler, *Damned in Paradise: The Life of John Barrymore* (New York: Atheneum, 1977), 177.

2. *New York Herald,* December 3, 1922.

3. Michael A. Morrison, *John Barrymore, Shakespearean Actor* (Cambridge, UK: Cambridge University Press, 1997), 365.

4. Kotsilibas-Davis, *Great Times, Good Times,* 321.

5. Louisa Lane Drew, *Autobiographical Sketch of Mrs. John Drew* (New York: Charles Scribner's Sons, 1899), 21.

6. *Motion Picture Magazine,* December 1920, 94. (John landed in twenty-first place.)

7. Kobler, *Damned in Paradise,* 92.

8. Mary Astor, *My Story: An Autobiography* (New York: Doubleday, 1959), 71.

9. Morrison, *John Barrymore, Shakespearean Actor,* 235.

10. Kobler, *Damned in Paradise,* 190.

11. Ibid., 199.

12. Morrison, *John Barrymore, Shakespearean Actor,* 247.
13. Ibid.
14. Ibid., 248.
15. Margot Peters, *The House of Barrymore* (New York: Alfred A. Knopf, 1990), 264.
16. Ibid., 202.
17. Letter from Mae to Maurice, May 13, 1925, MHL.
18. Letter from Mae to Maurice, May 20, 1925, MHL.
19. Letter from Mae to Maurice, May 26, 1925, MHL.
20. *Brooklyn Daily Eagle,* April 24, 1927.
21. Dolores Costello interview, *Hollywood* series.
22. Letter from Mae to Maurice, July 20, 1925, MHL.
23. Ibid.
24. Costello, "The Fighting Costellos," 19, LBC.
25. Ibid.
26. Dolores Barrymore Bedell, interview with the author, May 2018.
27. Astor, *My Story,* 87.
28. Ibid., 89.
29. Letter from Mae to Maurice, September 4, 1925, MHL.
30. Peters, *The House of Barrymore,* 280.
31. Kobler, *Damned in Paradise,* 43.
32. Lionel Barrymore, *We Barrymores* (New York: Appleton-Century-Crofts, 1951), 85.
33. *New York Times,* May 31, 1931.
34. James Kotsilibas-Davis, *The Barrymores: The Royal Family in Hollywood* (New York: Random House, 1982), 56.

11. Alone Time

1. Maurice Costello diary, October 23, 1925, DBC.
2. Ibid., December 26, 1925.
3. Ibid., December 29, 1925.
4. Ibid., November 2, 1925.
5. Ibid., November 3, 1925.
6. Ibid., November 8, 1925.
7. Ibid.
8. Mary Astor, *My Story,* 92.
9. Maurice Costello diary, November 25, 1925, DBC.
10. Ibid., November 20–25, 1925.
11. Ibid., November 29, 1925.
12. Ibid., December 1, 1925.
13. Ibid., December 2, 1925.
14. Ibid., December 24, 1925.
15. Ibid., December 15–20, 1925.
16. Dede Barrymore Bedell, interview with the author, February 2017.

17. Ibid., December 8, 1925.
18. Ibid., December 29, 1925.
19. Ibid.
20. Ibid., December 4, 1925.
21. Ibid., December 19, 1925.
22. Roy Liebman, *The Wampas Baby Stars: A Biographical Dictionary, 1922–1934* (Jefferson, NC: McFarland, 2000), 8.
23. *Motion Picture Magazine,* June 1926, 23.
24. *Motion Picture News,* February 27, 1926, 987.
25. Clive Hirschhorn, *The Warner Bros. Story* (New York: Crown, 1979), 48.
26. Ibid., 46.
27. *Picture Play Magazine,* August 1926, 69.
28. *Motion Picture Magazine,* January 1927, 17.
29. *Picture Play Magazine,* August 1926, 64.

12. Trial in Error

1. Gene Fowler, *Good Night, Sweet Prince* (San Francisco, CA: Mercury House, 1989), 286.
2. Kotsilibas-Davis, *The Barrymores,* 70.
3. Fowler, *Good Night, Sweet Prince,* 286.
4. Ibid., 271.
5. Ibid., 272.
6. Ibid., 276.
7. Maurice Costello diary, January 1, 1927, DBC.
8. Ibid., February 15, 1927.
9. *New Movie Magazine,* January 1929, 100.
10. Maurice Costello diary, March 21, 1927, DBC.
11. Ibid., April 21, 1927.
12. Costello, "The Fighting Costellos," 38, LBC.
13. Hirschhorn, *The Warner Bros. Story,* 56.
14. Ibid., 58.
15. Ibid., 53.
16. Maurice Costello diary, April 11, 1927, DBC.
17. Kotsilibas-Davis, *The Barrymores,* 69.
18. Peters, *The House of Barrymore,* 280.
19. Maurice Costello diary, May 10, 1927, DBC.
20. Ibid., undated entry.
21. Ibid.
22. Peters, *The House of Barrymore,* 314–315.
23. *Picture Play,* October 1927, 115.
24. Ibid., 115.
25. Ibid., 114.
26. Costello, "The Fighting Costellos," 20, LBC.

27. Costello, published outline, 10, LBC.

28. Tony Villecco, *Silent Stars Speak: Interviews with Twelve Cinema Pioneers* (Jefferson, NC: McFarland, 2001), 92.

29. Costello, "The Fighting Costellos," 20, LBC.

30. Ibid.

31. Maurice Costello diary, April 24, 1927, DBC.

32. Costello, "The Fighting Costellos," 45, LBC.

13. Xanadu and Vicinity

1. Dede Barrymore Bedell, interview with the author, December 2016.

2. Fowler, *Good Night, Sweet Prince,* 305.

3. Peters, *The House of Barrymore,* 297.

4. Ibid., 297.

5. Costello, "The Fighting Costellos," 21, LBC.

6. Fowler, *Good Night, Sweet Prince,* 301.

7. *Detroit Free-Press,* July 17, 1927.

8. Costello, published outline, 19, LBC.

9. Peters, *The House of Barrymore,* 297.

10. Dolores Barrymore Bedell, interview with the author, July 2016.

11. Dolores Costello interview, *Hollywood* series.

12. Ibid.

13. Ibid.

14. Ibid.

15. Ibid.

16. Scott Eyman, *The Speed of Sound, Hollywood and the Talkie Revolution, 1926–1930* (New York: Simon & Schuster, 1997).

17. *Movie Makers,* September 1928, 606.

18. Eyman, *The Speed of Sound.*

19. Costello, "The Fighting Costellos," 19, LBC.

20. *Movie Makers,* September 1928, 606.

21. *Exhibitors Herald and Motion Picture World,* December 29, 1928, 51.

22. Dolores Costello interview, *Hollywood* series.

23. Ibid.

24. Maurice Costello ledger, July 3, 1928, DBC.

25. Ibid., January 15, 1928.

26. Ibid.

14. Going South

1. *Brooklyn Daily Eagle,* November 21, 1928.

2. Ibid., November 23, 1928.

3. *Modern Screen,* September 1935, 32–33.

4. Ibid.
5. *Los Angeles Times,* November 25, 1928.
6. *Variety,* October 3, 1928.
7. Kotsilibas-Davis, *The Barrymores,* 94.
8. Goessel, *The First King of Hollywood,* 237–238.
9. Fowler, *Good Night, Sweet Prince,* 312–313.
10. Snackett's diary, December 1928, DBC.
11. Ibid., January 1, 1929.
12. Ibid., January 2, 1929.
13. Ibid., January 3, 1929.
14. Ibid., January 4, 1929.
15. Ibid., January 5, 1929.
16. Ibid., January 6, 1929.
17. Keystone diary, January 1, 1929, DBC.
18. Ibid., January 1, 1929.
19. Ibid., January 2, 1929.
20. Ibid., January 3, 1929.
21. Ibid., January 6, 1929.
22. Ibid., January 9, 1929.
23. Snackett's diary, January 13, 1929, DBC.
24. Keystone Diary, January 13, 1929, DBC.
25. Ibid., January 18, 1929.
26. Ibid., January 19, 1927.
27. Snackett's diary, January 19, 1927, DBC.
28. Ibid., January 24, 1929.
29. Ibid., February 3, 1929.
30. Ibid., February 4, 1929.
31. Ibid., February 5, 1929.
32. Ibid., February 11, 1929.
33. Ibid., February 19, 1929.
34. Costello, "The Fighting Costellos," 22, LBC.
35. Kotsilibas-Davis, *The Barrymores,* 96.
36. Dolores's own inscription on the back of Mendum's portrait, expressing her gratitude and the reason for it; from the collection of Dede Barrymore.
37. Costello, "The Fighting Costellos," 23, LBC.
38. Ibid.
39. Dolores Barrymore Bedell, interview with the author, December 2016.
40. Kotsilibas-Davis, *The Barrymores,* 96.
41. Dolores Barrymore Bedell, interview with the author, December 2016.
42. Kotsilibas-Davis, *The Barrymores,* 96.
43. Fowler, *Good Night, Sweet Prince,* 331.
44. Hollis Alpert, *The Barrymores* (New York: Dial, 1954), 336–337.
45. Peters, *The House of Barrymore,* 313.
46. Alpert, *The Barrymores,* 336–337.

47. Fowler, *Good Night, Sweet Prince,* 334.
48. Ibid.

15. Sherman and the Nut

1. Jon Tuska, *The Films of Mae West* (New York: Citadel, 1973), 93.
2. Costello, "The Fighting Costellos," 24, LBC.
3. Ibid.
4. Ibid.
5. Ibid.
6. Ibid.
7. Hirschhorn, *The Warner Bros. Story,* 80.
8. Frank Cullen, Florence Hackman, and Donald McNeilly, *Vaudeville, Old and New: An Encyclopedia of Variety Performers in America,* 2 vols. (New York: Routledge, 2006), 1:xxxiii.
9. Maurice Costello ledger, December 14, 1929, DBC.
10. *Brooklyn Daily Eagle,* December 11, 1929.
11. Ibid.
12. Maurice Costello ledger, September 1928, DBC.
13. Letter from Vivienne Sengler to Maurice Costello, November 5, 1928, DBC.
14. Ibid., September 20, 1928.
15. Ibid., July 30, 1929.
16. *San Bernardino County Sun,* May 21, 1932.
17. *Oakland Tribune,* May 23, 1932.
18. *St. Louis Star and Times,* March 14, 1929.
19. Ibid.
20. Ibid.
21. Ibid.
22. *Screenland,* July 1930, 110.
23. Costello, published outline, 26, LBC.
24. Ibid.
25. *Motion Picture News,* August 10, 1929, 56.
26. Dolores Barrymore Bedell, interview with the author, June 2017.
27. Ibid.
28. *Talking Screen,* February 1930, 52.
29. Fowler, *Good Night, Sweet Prince,* 337.
30. Dolores Costello interview, *Hollywood* series.
31. Fowler, *Good Night, Sweet Prince,* 341.

16. The Middle of the End

1. *Movie Classic,* August 1932, 24–25.
2. Costello, published outline, 10, LBC.

3. Costello, "The Fighting Costellos," 27, LBC.
4. *Brooklyn Daily Eagle,* May 10, 1932.
5. *Oakland Tribune,* May 10, 1932.
6. Ibid.
7. *Brooklyn Daily Eagle,* May 11, 1932.
8. Ibid.
9. Ibid.
10. Costello, "The Fighting Costellos," 28, LBC.
11. *Detroit Free Press,* February 28, 1932.
12. *Photoplay,* May 1932, 60.
13. *Modern Screen,* January 1932, 21.
14. Peters, *The House of Barrymore,* 324.
15. Fowler, *Good Night, Sweet Prince,* 342.
16. Ibid.
17. Kotsilibas-Davis, *The Barrymores,* 140.
18. Costello, "The Fighting Costellos," 29, LBC.
19. Ibid., 30.
20. Ibid., 32.
21. Ibid., 31.
22. Deirdre LeBlanc, email message to the author, July 2017.
23. Costello, "The Fighting Costellos," 32, LBC.
24. Dolores Costello interview, *Hollywood* series.
25. *Moberly Monitor-Index,* May 2, 1931.
26. Kobler, *Damned in Paradise,* 275.
27. Ibid., 177.
28. Dolores Barrymore Bedell, interview with the author, May 2017.
29. Costello, published outline, 21, LBC.
30. Dolores Barrymore Bedell, interview with the author, May 2017.
31. Kobler, *Damned in Paradise,* 257.

17. Over Her Head

1. Fowler, *Good Night, Sweet Prince,* 345.
2. Ibid.
3. Vincent Sherman, *Studio Affairs: My Life as a Film Director* (Lexington: University Press of Kentucky, 1996), 39.
4. Ibid.
5. Ibid.
6. Costello, published outline, 22, LBC.
7. Peters, *The House of Barrymore,* 359.
8. Alpert, *The Barrymores,* 336–337.
9. Ibid.

10. Ibid.
11. Ibid.
12. Ibid.
13. Ibid.
14. Fowler, *Good Night, Sweet Prince,* 357.
15. Ibid., 358.
16. Dolores Barrymore Bedell, interview with the author, January 2018.
17. Fowler, *Good Night, Sweet Prince,* 359.
18. Costello, published outline, 23, LBC.
19. Ibid.
20. Fowler, *Good Night, Sweet Prince,* 360–361.
21. Ibid.
22. Dolores Barrymore Bedell, interview with the author, July 2017.
23. *Los Angeles Times,* October 10, 1935.

18. Three on Their Own

1. Antony Barrymore, interview with the author, August 2017.
2. *Motion Picture Herald,* January 27, 1934, 37.
3. *Motion Picture Herald,* September 15, 1934, 56.
4. *Los Angeles Times,* September 22, 1954.
5. Costello, published outline, 9, LBC.
6. Fowler, *Good Night, Sweet Prince,* 363.
7. Ibid., 364.
8. Ibid., 365.
9. Ibid., 385.
10. Ibid., 393–94.
11. *New Movie Magazine,* April 1935, 47.
12. *Brooklyn Daily Eagle,* March 19, 1935.
13. Fowler, *Good Night, Sweet Prince,* 372.
14. Elaine Barrie, *All My Sins Remembered* (New York: Appleton-Century, 1964), 107.
15. *Pittsburgh Press,* April 16, 1935.
16. *Oakland Tribune,* May 26, 1935.
17. *Arizona Republic,* May 11, 1939.
18. Costello, "The Fighting Costellos," 33, LBC.
19. Fowler, *Good Night, Sweet Prince,* 394.
20. *Brooklyn Daily Eagle,* May 3, 1938.
21. Dolores Barrymore Bedell, interview with the author, October 2017.
22. Costello, "The Fighting Costellos," 32, LBC.
23. Dolores Costello interview, *Hollywood* series.
24. Dore Bedell, interview with the author, October 2017.

19. Daddy Butch

1. Dolores Barrymore Bedell, interview with the author, October 2017.
2. Ibid.
3. Ibid.
4. Ibid.
5. *Movie Classic,* May 1936, 22.
6. Ibid.
7. Ibid.
8. *Photoplay,* July 1936, 46.
9. *Motion Picture Reviews,* November 1936, 3–7.
10. *Movie Classic,* March 1936, 10.
11. *Screenland,* March 1936, 65.
12. *Modern Screen,* April 1936, 51.
13. Dolores Barrymore Bedell, interview with the author, October 2017.
14. Ibid.
15. Ibid.
16. Ibid.
17. Ibid.
18. *Film Daily,* November 6, 1927, 11.
19. Deirdre Le Blanc, email message to the author, October 2017.
20. Costello, "The Fighting Costellos," 37, LBC.
21. *Brooklyn Daily Eagle,* August 4, 1935.
22. Costello, "The Fighting Costellos," 37, LBC.
23. Ibid.
24. Ibid.
25. Ibid.
26. *Akron Beacon Journal,* October 6, 1937.
27. Costello, "The Fighting Costellos," 37, LBC.
28. Dolores Barrymore Bedell, interview with the author, October 2017.
29. Costello, "The Fighting Costellos," 37, LBC.

20. The Lions at Bay

1. *Motion Picture Herald,* August 22, 1936, 51.
2. Ibid.
3. *Tampa Times,* March 17, 1937.
4. *Akron Beacon Journal,* April 28, 1937.
5. *Minneapolis Star,* April 12, 1937.
6. Dolores Barrymore Bedell, interview with the author, September 2017.
7. Fowler, *Good Night, Sweet Prince,* 392.
8. Barrie, *All My Sins Remembered,* 98.
9. Peters, *The House of Barrymore,* 381.
10. Barrie, *All My Sins Remembered,* 109.

11. Costello, "The Fighting Costellos," 35–36, LBC.
12. Dolores Barrymore Bedell, interview with the author, September 2017.
13. Ibid.
14. Ibid.
15. *Salt Lake Tribune,* January 16, 1937.
16. Costello, "The Fighting Costellos," 34, LBC.
17. *San Bernadino County Sun,* May 5, 1938.
18. *Dunkirk Evening Observer,* May 4, 1938.
19. *Philadelphia Enquirer,* June 5, 1938.
20. *Des Moines Register,* October 19, 1938.
21. *Salt Lake Telegram,* October 18, 1938.
22. *Oakland Tribune,* August 30, 1939.

21. A Trio of Marriages

1. *Motion Picture Reviews,* October 1938, 4.
2. *Altoona Tribune,* April 21, 1938.
3. *Salt Lake Telegram,* June 21, 1938.
4. *Los Angeles Times,* January 19, 1951.
5. Jane Vruwink Palmer, interview with the author, November 2017.
6. Dolores Barrymore Bedell, interview with the author, September 2017.
7. Ibid.
8. *Cincinnati Enquirer,* December 3, 1939.
9. Jane Vruwink Palmer, interview with the author, November 2017.
10. Dolores Barrymore Bedell, interview with the author, September 2017.
11. *Oakland Tribune,* August 30, 1939.
12. Ibid.
13. Ibid.
14. Ibid.
15. Costello, "The Fighting Costellos," 39, LBC.
16. Deirdre Le Blanc, email message to the author, February 2018.
17. Costello, "The Fighting Costellos," 39, LBC.
18. Ibid.
19. Deirdre Le Blanc, email message to the author, December 2017.
20. Costello, "The Fighting Costellos," 40, LBC.
21. *Los Angeles Times,* September 4, 1941.
22. Maurice Costello typescript document, undated, DBC.
23. Maurice Costello typescript document, January 17, 1940, DBC.

22. *The Magnificent Ambersons*

1. Robert L. Carringer, *The Magnificent Ambersons: A Reconstruction* (Berkeley: University of California Press 1993), 24.

2. Orson Welles, Peter Bogdanovich, and Jonathan Rosenbaum, *This Is Orson Welles* (New York: Harper Collins, 1994), 114.
3. Carringer, *The Magnificent Ambersons,* 24.
4. Kobler, *Damned in Paradise,* 361.
5. Dolores Barrymore Bedell, interview with the author, December 2017.
6. Kobler, *Damned in Paradise,* 363.
7. Dolores Barrymore Bedell, interview with the author, December 2017.
8. Kobler, *Damned in Paradise,* 363.
9. Ibid., 364.
10. *Indianapolis Star,* June 3, 1942.
11. *New York Times,* August 14, 1942.
12. Kodar, Rosenbaum, and Bogdanovich, *This Is Orson Welles*, 114.
13. *St. Louis Star and Times,* June 15, 1942.
14. Costello, "The Fighting Costellos," 41, LBC.
15. Ibid.
16. Deirdre Le Blanc, email message to the author, February 2018.
17. Ibid.
18. Costello, "The Fighting Costellos," 43, LBC.
19. Ibid.

23. Deirdre, Johnny, and Jane

1. Dolores Barrymore Bedell, interview with the author, September 2017.
2. Ibid.
3. Ibid.
4. Deirdre Le Blanc, email message to the author, December 2017.
5. Ibid.
6. Ibid.
7. Dolores Barrymore Bedell, interview with the author, September 2017.
8. Ibid.
9. Ibid.
10. Ibid.
11. Ibid.
12. Ibid.
13. Jane Vruwink Palmer, interview with the author, October 2018.
14. Dolores Barrymore Bedell, interview with the author, October 2018.
15. *St. Louis Post-Dispatch,* February 7, 1960.
16. Deirdre Le Blanc, email message to the author, December 2018.
17. Ibid.
18. *Miami News,* September 16, 1947.
19. *Los Angeles Times,* December 17, 1947.
20. Ibid.
21. *Des Moines Register,* December 25, 1947.

22. Deirdre Le Blanc, email message to the author, October 2018.
23. *Greenville News,* December 28, 1947.
24. *Los Angeles Times,* December 30, 1947.
25. Ibid.
26. Deirdre Le Blanc, email message to the author, January 2017.
27. *Los Angeles Times,* January 7, 1948.
28. Ibid.
29. Deirdre Le Blanc, email message to the author, January 2017.
30. *Los Angeles Times,* April 20, 1948.
31. Dolores Barrymore Bedell, interview with the author, July 2018.
32. Ibid.
33. *Bakersfield Californian,* June 17, 1949.

24. Here Lies the Mick

1. *Los Angeles Times,* December 30, 1947.
2. Deirdre Le Blanc, email message to the author, January 2017.
3. Ibid.
4. Ibid.
5. Ibid.
6. Ibid.
7. *Los Angeles Times,* October, 1950.
8. Ibid.
9. *Baltimore Sun,* October 30, 1950.
10. Deirdre Le Blanc, email message to the author, January 2018.
11. Dolores Barrymore Bedell, interview with the author, October 2017.
12. *Los Angeles Times,* November 1, 1950.
13. Dolores Barrymore Bedell, interview with the author, October 2017.
14. *Los Angeles Times,* July 13, 1951.
15. Jane Vruwink Palmer, interview with the author, October 2017.
16. Ibid.
17. Dolores Barrymore Bedell, interview with the author, December 2017.
18. *Los Angeles Times,* July 13, 1951.
19. *Los Angeles Times,* March 4, 1951.
20. Ibid.

25. A Minor Kidnapping

1. Dolores Barrymore Bedell, interview with the author, April 2018.
2. *Los Angeles Times,* June 20, 1953.
3. Dolores Barrymore Bedell, interview with the author, April 2018.
4. Ibid.
5. Dolores Barrymore Bedell, interview with the author, April 2018.

6. Antony Barrymore, interview with the author, May 2018.
7. *Los Angeles Times,* May 14, 1953.
8. Cara Williams, interview with the author, March 2018.
9. Ibid.
10. Ibid.
11. Ibid.
12. *Terre Haute Tribune,* July 22, 1951.
13. Dolores Barrymore Bedell, interview with the author, April 2018.
14. Ibid.

26. An Old Spanish Custom

1. Deirdre Le Blanc, email message to the author, March 2018.
2. Ibid.
3. Dolores Barrymore Bedell, interview with the author, June 2017.
4. Ibid.
5. "The Kirkbride Plan; Architecture for a Treatment System That Changed." *Hospital and Community Psychiatry* 27, no. 7 (July 1976): 473–477.
6. Ibid.
7. Deirdre Le Blanc, email message to the author, April 2018.
8. Ibid.
9. Ibid.
10. Ibid.
11. *Los Angeles Times,* January 31, 1957.
12. Deirdre Le Blanc, email message to the author, April 2018.
13. *Star-Gazette,* January 31, 1957.
14. Deirdre Le Blanc, email message to the author, April 2018.

27. Mum Mum

1. Dolores Barrymore Bedell, interview with the author, April 2018.
2. *Tucson Daily Citizen,* January 26, 1960.
3. Ibid.
4. *Eureka Humboldt Standard,* February 19, 1958.
5. Dolores Barrymore Bedell, interview with the author, May 2018.
6. Hillary Bedell, interview with the author, February 2018.
7. Ibid.
8. *Eureka Humboldt Standard,* February 19, 1958.
9. Dolores Barrymore Bedell, interview with the author, April 2018.
10. *Pittsburgh Press,* March 14, 1967.
11. Dore Bedell, interview with the author, April 2018.
12. *Independent* (Long Beach, CA), March 14, 1967.
13. Dolores Barrymore Bedell, interview with the author, May 2018.

14. Antony Barrymore, interview with the author, February 2018.
15. Dolores Barrymore Bedell, interview with the author, May 2018.

Epilogue

1. *Chicago Tribune,* March 3, 1979.
2. *Los Angeles Times,* June 29, 1981.
3. Dore Bedell, interview with the author, June 2018.
4. Hillary Bedell, interview with the author, June 2018.
5. Dolores Barrymore Bedell, interview with the author, February 2017.
6. Deirdre Le Blanc, email message to the author, May 2018.
7. Ibid.

Bibliography

Collections

Curtis Theater Collection, University of Pittsburgh Library
Margaret Herrick Library, Beverly Hills, California (MHL)

Maurice Costello Collection

Personal collection of Dede Barrymore Bedell
Personal collection of Deirdre Le Blanc (LBC)

Outline published in Hearst newspaper supplement *American Weekly,* in serial form beginning October 1948
Unpublished manuscript, "The Fighting Costellos"

Personal collection of Denise Barrymore (DBC)

Keystone diary
Maurice Costello diaries
Maurice Costello travel and business ledgers
Snackett's diary

Documentary

Hollywood: A Celebration of the American Silent Film. Documentary series. Directed by Kevin Brownlow and David Gill. London: ITV network. Originally aired February 9 to April 1, 1980.

Selected Published Sources

Abel, Richard, ed. *Silent Film.* London: Athlone, 1999.
Alpert, Hollis. *The Barrymores.* New York: Dial, 1964.
Astor, Mary. *My Story: An Autobiography.* New York: Doubleday, 1959.

Barrie, Elaine. *All My Sins Remembered.* New York: Appleton-Century, 1964.

Barrymore, Lionel. *We Barrymores.* New York: Appleton-Century-Crofts, 1951.

Black, Gregory D. *The Catholic Crusade against the Movies, 1940–1975.* Cambridge, UK: Cambridge University Press, 1997.

Blum, Daniel. *A Pictorial History of the Silent Screen.* New York: G. M. Putnam & Sons, 1953.

Boles, Jacqueline. *Life upon the Wicked Stage: A Sociological Study of Entertainers.* Bloomington, IN: iUniverse, 2010.

Burns, George. *All My Best Friends.* New York: G. P. Putnam's Sons, 1989.

Callahan, Vicki. *Reclaiming the Archive: Feminism and Film History.* Detroit, MI: Wayne State University Press, 2010.

The Century Dictionary and Cyclopedia. Vol. 3. New York: Century Company, 1900.

Conner, Lynn. *Pittsburgh in Stages: Two Hundred Years of Theater.* Pittsburgh, PA: University of Pittsburgh Press, 2007.

Cullen, Frank, Florence Hackman, and Donald McNeilly. *Vaudeville, Old and New: An Encyclopedia of Variety Performers in America.* 2 vols. New York: Routledge, 2006.

Decherney, Peter. *Hollywood's Copyright Wars: From Edison to the Internet.* New York: Columbia University Press, 2013.

DeCordova, Richard. *Picture Personalities: The Emergence of the Star System in America.* Chicago: University of Illinois Press, 2001.

Dewey, Donald. *Buccaneer: James Stuart Blackton and the Birth of the Movies.* Lanham, MD: Rowman and Littlefield, 2016.

Dieterich-Ward, Allen. *Beyond Rust: Metropolitan Pittsburgh and the Fate of Industrial America.* Philadelphia: University of Pennsylvania Press, 2016.

Drew, Louisa Lane. *Autobiographical Sketch of Mrs. John Drew.* New York: Charles Scribner's Sons, 1899.

Gallen, Ira H. *D. W. Griffith: Master of Cinema.* Victoria, Canada: Friesen, 2015.

Erdman, Andrew L. *Blue Vaudeville: Sex, Morals, and Mass Marketing of Amusement 1895–1915.* Jefferson, NC: McFarland & Company, 2004.

Eyman, Scott. *The Speed of Sound, Hollywood and the Talkie Revolution, 1926–1930.* New York: Simon & Schuster, 1997.

Fell, John L. *Film before Griffith.* Berkeley: University of California Press, 1983.

Fowler, Gene. *Good Night, Sweet Prince.* San Francisco, CA: Mercury House, 1989.

Gassner, John, ed. *Best Plays of the Early American Theater, 1787–1911.* New York: Dover, 1967.

Goessel, Tracey. *The First King of Hollywood: The Life of Douglas Fairbanks.* Chicago: Chicago Review, 2016.

Hirschhorn, Clive. *The Warner Bros. Story.* New York: Crown, 1979.

Hoffman, Carol Stein. *The Barrymores: Hollywood's First Family.* Lexington: University Press of Kentucky, 2001.

Jones, John Bush. *Reinventing Dixie: Tin Pan Alley's Songs and the Creation of the Mythic South.* Baton Rouge: Louisiana State University Press, 2015.

Kastner, James W. *Where the Movies Played in Downtown Pittsburg[h]: 100 Years of "Going to the Show" 1896–1996.* Pittsburgh, PA: Rosedog, 2011.

Kobler, John. *Damned in Paradise: The Life of John Barrymore.* New York: Atheneum, 1977.

Kotsilibas-Davis, James. *Great Times, Good Times: The Odyssey of Maurice Barrymore.* New York: Doubleday, 1977.

———. *The Barrymores: The Royal Family in Hollywood.* New York: Random House, 1982.

Lewis, Robert M., ed. *From Traveling Show to Vaudeville: Theatrical Spectacle in America, 1830–1910.* Baltimore, MD: Johns Hopkins University Press, 2003.

Liebman, Roy. *The Wampas Baby Stars: A Biographical Dictionary, 1922–1934.* Jefferson, NC: McFarland, 2000.

Lorant, Stefan. *Pittsburgh: The Story of an American City.* Lenox, MA: Authors Edition Inc. 1975.

Louvish, Simon. *The Man on the Flying Trapeze: The Life and Times of W. C. Fields.* New York: W. W. Norton, 1999.

McElligott, Patricia. *Irish Pittsburgh.* Charleston, SC: Arcadia, 2013.

Moore, Paul S. *Now Playing: Early Moviegoing and the Regulation of Fun.* Albany: State University Press of New York, 2008.

Mordden, Ethan. *Ziegfeld: The Man Who Invented Show Business.* New York: St. Martin's, 2008.

Morrison, Michael A. *John Barrymore, Shakespearean Actor.* Cambridge, UK: Cambridge University Press, 1997.

Musser, Charles. *Before the Nickelodeon: Edwin S. Porter and the Edison Manufacturing Company.* Berkeley: University of California Press, 1991.

———. *The Emergence of Cinema: The American Screen to 1907.* Berkeley: University of California Press, 1994.

Peters, Margot. *The House of Barrymore.* New York: Alfred A. Knopf, 1990.

Ramsaye, Terry. *A Million and One Nights: A History of the Motion Picture.* Abingdon, UK: Frank Cass & Co., 1926.

Rohs, Stephen Albert. *Eccentric Nation: Irish Performance in Nineteenth-Century New York City.* Madison, NJ: Fairleigh Dickinson University Press, 2009.

Segrave, Kerry. *Actors Organize: A History of Union Formation Efforts in America, 1880–1919.* Jefferson, NC: McFarland & Co., 2007.

Sherman, Vincent. *Studio Affairs: My Life as a Film Director.* Lexington: University Press of Kentucky, 1996.

Slide, Anthony. *The Big V: A History of the Vitagraph Company.* Metuchen, NJ: Scarecrow, 1987.

———. *New York City Vaudeville.* Charleston, SC: Arcadia, 2006.

Slout, William L. *Theatre in a Tent.* Cabin John, MD: Wildside, 2006.

Smith, Albert E., and Phil A. Koury. *Two Reels and a Crank.* Doubleday, 1952.

Stephens, E. J., and Marc Wanamaker. *Early Poverty Row Studios.* Charleston, SC: Arcadia, 2015.

Trimble, Marian Blackton. *J. Stuart Blackton, A Personal Biography by his Daughter.* Metuchen, NJ: Scarecrow, 1985.

Tuska, Jon. *The Films of Mae West.* New York: Citadel, 1973.

Villecco, Tony. *Silent Stars Speak: Interviews with Twelve Cinema Pioneers.* Jefferson, NC: McFarland, 2001.

Welles, Orson, Peter Bogdanovich, and Jonathan Rosenbaum. *This Is Orson Welles.* New York: HarperCollins, 1992.

Wilmeth, Don B., and Christopher Bigsby. *The Cambridge History of American Theatre.* Vol. 2, *1870–1945.* Cambridge, UK: Cambridge University Press, 1999.

Zinn, Howard. *A People's History of the United States.* New York: Harper Perennial Modern Classics, 2003.

Index

JB refers to John (Jack) Barrymore. MC refers to Maurice Costello.

Screen Classics

Screen Classics is a series of critical biographies, film histories, and analytical studies focusing on neglected filmmakers and important screen artists and subjects, from the era of silent cinema through the golden age of Hollywood to the international generation of today. Books in the Screen Classics series are intended for scholars and general readers alike. The contributing authors are established figures in their respective fields. This series also serves the purpose of advancing scholarship on film personalities and themes with ties to Kentucky.

Series Editor

Patrick McGilligan

Books in the Series

Olivia de Havilland: Lady Triumphant
Victoria Amador

Mae Murray: The Girl with the Bee-Stung Lips
Michael G. Ankerich

Hedy Lamarr: The Most Beautiful Woman in Film
Ruth Barton

Rex Ingram: Visionary Director of the Silent Screen
Ruth Barton

Conversations with Classic Film Stars: Interviews from Hollywood's Golden Era
James Bawden and Ron Miller

Conversations with Legendary Television Stars: Interviews from the First Fifty Years
James Bawden and Ron Miller

You Ain't Heard Nothin' Yet: Interviews with Stars from Hollywood's Golden Era
James Bawden and Ron Miller

Von Sternberg
John Baxter

Hitchcock's Partner in Suspense: The Life of Screenwriter Charles Bennett
Charles Bennett, edited by John Charles Bennett

Hitchcock and the Censors
John Billheimer

A Uniquely American Epic: Intimacy and Action, Tenderness and Violence in Sam Peckinpah's The Wild Bunch
Edited by Michael Bliss

My Life in Focus: A Photographer's Journey with Elizabeth Taylor and the Hollywood Jet Set
Gianni Bozzacchi with Joey Tayler

Hollywood Divided: The 1950 Screen Directors Guild Meeting and the Impact of the Blacklist
Kevin Brianton

He's Got Rhythm: The Life and Career of Gene Kelly
Cynthia Brideson and Sara Brideson

Ziegfeld and His Follies: A Biography of Broadway's Greatest Producer
Cynthia Brideson and Sara Brideson

The Marxist and the Movies: A Biography of Paul Jarrico
Larry Ceplair

Dalton Trumbo: Blacklisted Hollywood Radical
Larry Ceplair and Christopher Trumbo

Warren Oates: A Wild Life
Susan Compo

Improvising Out Loud: My Life Teaching Hollywood How to Act
Jeff Corey with Emily Corey

Crane: Sex, Celebrity, and My Father's Unsolved Murder
Robert Crane and Christopher Fryer

Jack Nicholson: The Early Years
Robert Crane and Christopher Fryer

Anne Bancroft: A Life
Douglass K. Daniel

Being Hal Ashby: Life of a Hollywood Rebel
Nick Dawson

Bruce Dern: A Memoir
Bruce Dern with Christopher Fryer and Robert Crane

Intrepid Laughter: Preston Sturges and the Movies
Andrew Dickos

Miriam Hopkins: Life and Films of a Hollywood Rebel
Allan R. Ellenberger

John Gilbert: The Last of the Silent Film Stars
Eve Golden

Stuntwomen: The Untold Hollywood Story
Mollie Gregory

Saul Bass: Anatomy of Film Design
Jan-Christopher Horak

Hitchcock Lost and Found: The Forgotten Films
Alain Kerzoncuf and Charles Barr

Pola Negri: Hollywood's First Femme Fatale
Mariusz Kotowski

Sidney J. Furie: Life and Films
Daniel Kremer

Albert Capellani: Pioneer of the Silent Screen
Christine Leteux

Ridley Scott: A Biography
Vincent LoBrutto

Mamoulian: Life on Stage and Screen
David Luhrssen

Maureen O'Hara: The Biography
Aubrey Malone

My Life as a Mankiewicz: An Insider's Journey through Hollywood
Tom Mankiewicz and Robert Crane

Hawks on Hawks
Joseph McBride

Showman of the Screen: Joseph E. Levine and His Revolutions in Film Promotion
A. T. McKenna

William Wyler: The Life and Films of Hollywood's Most Celebrated Director
Gabriel Miller

Raoul Walsh: The True Adventures of Hollywood's Legendary Director
Marilyn Ann Moss

Veit Harlan: The Life and Work of a Nazi Filmmaker
Frank Noack

Harry Langdon: King of Silent Comedy
Gabriella Oldham and Mabel Langdon

Charles Walters: The Director Who Made Hollywood Dance
Brent Phillips

Some Like It Wilder: The Life and Controversial Films of Billy Wilder
Gene D. Phillips

Ann Dvorak: Hollywood's Forgotten Rebel
Christina Rice

Lewis Milestone: Life and Films
Harlow Robinson

Michael Curtiz: A Life in Film
Alan K. Rode

Arthur Penn: American Director
Nat Segaloff

Film's First Family: The Untold Story of the Costellos
Terry Chester Shulman

Claude Rains: An Actor's Voice
David J. Skal with Jessica Rains

Barbara La Marr: The Girl Who Was Too Beautiful for Hollywood
Sherri Snyder

Buzz: The Life and Art of Busby Berkeley
Jeffrey Spivak

Victor Fleming: An American Movie Master
Michael Sragow

Hollywood Presents Jules Verne: The Father of Science Fiction on Screen
Brian Taves

Thomas Ince: Hollywood's Independent Pioneer
Brian Taves

Carl Theodor Dreyer and Ordet: *My Summer with the Danish Filmmaker*
Jan Wahl

Clarence Brown: Hollywood's Forgotten Master
Gwenda Young